Klaus Wo

Walks on Corsica

85 selected walks on the coasts and in the mountains of the »Island of Beauty«

With 287 colour photographs,
85 walking maps to a scale of 1:25,000 / 1:50,000 / 1:75,000,
88 height profiles and 4 overview maps to a scale of 1:650,000

ROTHER • MUNICH

ROTHER Walking Guides

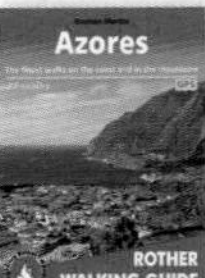

Preface

The island of Corsica is a holiday destination that could hardly be more perfect. Picturesque bays, miles of sandy beach, relaxing resorts, extensive forests, crystal-clear lakes and streams, sunny Mediterranean days and pristine natural landscapes – these are the blessings offered by very few tourist areas. Most importantly, however, it is the magnificent mountain scenery found in Corsica – the island is also called »Mountains in the Sea« – that provides its strongest attraction. Not only are the grand peaks of the Corsican coastal range impressive – snow-capped even until early summer, hugging the coast and reaching heights of up to 2706 metres above sea level – so too are the uniquely diverse natural landscapes and the wild, virtually unspoilt beauty of numerous mountain regions on the island.
For these reasons, the »Island of Beauty« has long been a closely guarded secret among hikers and mountain climbers – especially the famous long-distance alpine hiking trail *GR 20*, sections of which are included in this guide. The *GR 20* enjoys a far-reaching repute – and the same applies to the less-strenuous long-distance trails *Mare e Monti* and *Mare a Mare*.
This guide also includes some lesser known hiking trails far removed from the main tourist routes. The reader will find a wide choice of easy and varied routes, from beach walks to adventurous excursions passing numerous waterfalls, as well as easy hikes leading to mountain peaks offering panoramic views. Many hikes can be easily undertaken in the company of children and by older people. However, the indisputable climax of this guide concerns the magnificent 2000 metre peaks which presents you with a breath-taking panorama of all the other »Mountains in the Sea« below. These walks, however, should only be attempted by walkers with a good background in alpine hiking.
We found it extremely important when selecting the walks that all of the island's regions should be included and reasonably represented. Because of this, walkers following the described routes will surely be treated to an impressive overall view of Corsica's marvellous scenery.
This latest edition has been brought thoroughly up-to-date and five walks have been added. Forest fires, road construction and, last but not least, the constant forces of nature, can all lead to changes along the routes. For this reason I would invite all readers and lovers of Corsica's mountains to send any corrections to the publisher.
I would like to wish all readers many lovely and adventurous days while on holiday in the wonderful mountains of Corsica.

Summer 2019 Klaus Wolfsperger

Contents

Tourist Information

Grade

Most of the walks follow distinct paths and tracks. However, this should not detract from the fact that some walks demand a good level of fitness, surefootedness, a head for heights and above all, good route finding skills. Please take note that the routes might become more difficult after periods of bad weather. To help you judge more easily the level of difficulty of the suggested walks, the route numbers are colour-coded as follows:

Easy These walks follow paths which are generally well-marked, wide and only moderately steep – thus relatively harmless, even in poor weather. They can also be undertaken in the company of inexperienced walkers without any great danger.

Moderate These mostly waymarked routes are often narrow, and short stretches can be somewhat exposed. For these reasons, these walks should only be undertaken by the surefooted, experienced mountain hiker.

Difficult These routes are frequently narrow and very steep. Some stretches can be very exposed and sometimes the use of your hands may be necessary (I = easy scrambling, II = scramble demanding rock-climbing skills). This means that these paths should only be undertaken by the surefooted, experienced and physically fit mountain hiker who has a good head for heights.

Dangers

Most of the walks follow good, well-marked paths; extremely exposed or demanding stretches will be indicated in the route description. In alpine re-

Symbols

	accessible by bus/train		pass, col/turn-off
	places to eat on the way		church, chapel, monastery/tower
	suitable for children		watchtower/lighthouse
	village with bar/restaurant		picnic spot/viewpoint
	staffed hut, restaurant		bridge/gate
	mountain hut, shelter		cave/rock archway
	bus-stop		prominent tree
	train station		spring/water tank
† †	summit/oratorium, wayside-cross		bathing/waterfall

The best walks on Corsica

Monte San Petrone, 1767m
Marvellous panoramic peak in the Castagniccia (Walk 5; 4.45 hrs.).

Monte Astu, 1535m
One of the most beautiful hiking paths on the island (Walk 9; 6.00 hrs.).

Gorges de Spelunca
Popular gorge walk with bathing pools (Walk 22; 2.30 hrs.).

Calanche
Sightseeing at its very best (Walk 24; 4.25 hrs.).

Capu d'Orto, 1294m
Fantastic circuit above the Gulf of Porto (Walk 25; 6.20 hrs.).

From Tizzano to the Cala di Conca
Fabulous coastal walk to idyllic beaches (Walk 38; 5.10 hrs.).

Uomo di Cagna, 1217m
A celebrated balanced rock marks the summit (Walk 41; 5.15 hrs.).

Cascades du Polischellu
A superlative cascade walk (Walk 53; 4.30 hrs.).

Monte d'Oro, 2389m
Spectacular circuit above the Vizzavona pass (Walk 65; 9.00 hrs.).

Lac de Melo and Lac de Capitello
Walk to Corsica's most beautiful mountain lakes (Walk 68; 3.30 hrs.).

Monte Rotondo, 2622m
Second highest peak with all the scenic extras (Walk 70; 8.30 hrs.).

Lac de Nino
Mountain paradise with pigs, cows and horses (Walk 74; 4.45 hrs.).

Monte Cinto, 2706m
The »King« of the Corsican mountains (Walk 77; 8.30 hrs.).

Paglia Orba, 2525m
Challenging mountain walk on the »Corsican Matterhorn« (Walk 79; 8.30 hrs.).

gions, even in mid-summer, walkers should be prepared to encounter snow-filled gullies, sudden thunderstorms, thick fog and even snowfall. Therefore, before undertaking alpine routes, be sure to ask about weather forecasts and path conditions.

Best times of year

The most favourable conditions for alpine routes usually occur between the months of June and October (after an especially snowy winter, maybe even as late as the middle of July). All of the remaining routes, particularly those near the coast, can be walked at any time of the year – with the exception of those in regions under 1000m above sea level, where the heat of summer can often be excruciating. In spring and after heavy rainfall, flooded and raging streams must be expected, which makes them frequently impassable.

Equipment

Sturdy shoes with non-slip soles, durable trousers, protective gear against wind, rain, cold and sun are required for most routes as well as provisions for underway (especially sufficient beverage).

Maps

The walking maps to a scale of 1:25,000 – 1:75,000 with the routes highlighted in red, are an essential part of this guide. For those who wish to obtain additional maps, we can recommend the excellent IGN walking maps to a scale of 1:25,000 which are listed under the heading »Map«.

Walking times

The times represent only the actual walking time and do not include rests and photo stops.

Height difference

The figures are calculated from the cumulative height differences.

Refreshment and accommodation

In Corsica, there are hardly any staffed huts as would be expected in other alpine areas. From time to time, cheese can be purchased in a *bergerie* (shepherd's hut). The *refuges* (shelters) are self-service huts that are open all year round as a rule and only offer the »luxury« of a bed, a gas stove and a well or spring nearby – during tourist season, many of the *refuges* (especially those along the *GR 20*) offer simple refreshment. In summer, many of the *refuges* are overcrowded. When planning an overnight stop at a moun-

One of the best walks on Corsica – the hiking path to Nino lake.

Cairn on the highest point of Capu d'Orto.

tain hut, therefore, the absolutely essential equipment is a sleeping bag and at least a tarpaulin, or better still, a tent. The so-called *gîtes d'étape*, offering simple overnight accommodation, usually provide half-board as well.

Access

Many of the walks included in this guide can be reached by public transport. If the starting point is accessible by the Corsican narrow-gauge railway line, this will be indicated under the heading »Location« or »Starting point«. Public busses provide a connection once or twice daily to almost all of the larger towns. Some of the starting points can also be reached by bicycle from resort areas without any great problem.

Nature and the environment

Corsica is one of the few places in Europe that can boast a natural paradise. For this reason an environmentally friendly conduct is of paramount importance. Therefore, please show the utmost respect for the flora and fauna, take your litter away with you (toilet paper is more biodegradable so please refrain from using paper tissues), do not carelessly throw away cigarette stubs and do not make open fires (risk of forest fire).

GPS tracks

GPS data for the routes in this walking guide is available at www.rother.de for free downloading. To download, you need to use the following password: **WFCorGB05bw19x** (user name: **gast**).

Walking on Corsica

Mountains in the Sea

After Sicily, Sardinia and Cyprus, Corsica is the fourth largest Mediterranean island, covering an area of 8680km² and, with an average elevation of 568m, the most mountainous. From north to south, an S-shaped chain of mountains crosses the island's centre; the highest peak is Monte Cinto at 2706m. So it is not astonishing that Corsica is one of the least populated islands in the Mediterranean with approximately 325,000 inhabitants, whereby more than 100,000 of these live in the cities of Bastia and Ajaccio.
All major rivers find their source on the Corsican central ridge – the longest one is the Golo river with a length of 84km. Especially attractive scenery is found in the wild and rugged gorges cut into the mountain landscape by river waters – the Asco, the Santa Regina, the Spelunca and the Restonica gorges for example. The island also boasts many almost pristine mountain lakes, most of which nestle in shallow hollows fed by glacial water and surrounded by marshland (*pozzines*). Some of the most beautiful lakes are the Melo, Capitello, Nino, Creno and Oriente.

Flora and fauna

In the coastal regions and at elevations reaching approximately 1500m, *macchia* vegetation predominates: a scrub undergrowth made up of rock roses, broom, tree heather, dwarf mastic and strawberry trees, lavender, rosemary and many other scrub species treating walkers to a bewitching fragrance during the flowering seasons of spring and autumn, as well as plaguing them with thorns and spikes. At higher elevations you often encounter extensive beech and chestnut forests. Taking the prize, however, are

Mouflon in the Spasimata valley.

Yellow and green Western Whip snake.

the magnificent pine forests which can climb to altitudes of up to 1800m.
In contrast, the fauna lacks variety. It's rare to catch a glimpse of a golden eagle (only found in the Cinto massif) or mouflon (wild sheep, only found in the Bavella and Asco regions). But we can hardly avoid close encounters with feral pigs that are just about everywhere. In some regions, the porkers have created some serious problems – causing slope erosion through their rooting and foraging.

Tafoni rocks in the Calanche.

Nature reserve (Parc Naturel Régional de Corse)

Corsica's nature reserve, established in 1972, contains an area of about 3500km² and stretches from Calenzana in the north, embraces the Corsican main ridge and almost reaches Porto-Vecchio in the south. The purpose of the park is to preserve the environment and to improve the economic and tourist infrastructures of the central island region.

GR 20 (Sentier de Grande Randonnée de la Corse)

The famous alpine long-distance route, crossing almost the entire length of the island from north to south, is often underestimated. The *GR 20*, 168km long, waymarked in red and white, demands physical fitness, absolute surefootedness, an excellent head for heights and, above all, plenty of mountain-hiking experience. The route should never be attempted earlier than the middle of June, whereby the best time is from July until the middle of September. At least two weeks are needed to complete the route. Overnight accommodation is available in basic mountain huts (*refuges*; for booking see www.parc-corse.org). Skiing the *GR 20* in winter (Haute route à ski) is a very special adventure that should only be undertaken by the most experienced ski mountaineer.

The GR 20 in stages: Calenzana – Refuge d'Ortu di u Piobbu (6½ hrs.) – Refuge de Carrozzu (6½ hrs.) – Haut-Asco (5½ hrs.) – Refuge de Tighiettu (8 hrs.) – Refuge de Ciottulu di i Mori (4 hrs.) or Le Fer à Cheval (6½ hrs.) – Refuge de Manganu (8½ or 6 hrs.) – Refuge de Petra Piana (5 hrs.) – Refuge de l'Onda (4½ hrs.) – Vizzavona (5½ hrs.) – Refuge de Capannelle (4½ hrs.) – Refuge de Prati (6 hrs.) – Refuge d'Usciolu (5 hrs.) – Refuge Matalza (4¾ hrs.), Refuge d'Asinao (4 hrs.) – Refuge de Paliri (6 hrs.) – Conca (4 hrs.).
Recommended guides: »Topo-guide GR 20« and »Haute Route à Ski« (both published by the Parc Naturel Régional de Corse), »GR 20: Corsica – The High Level Route« (Cicerone Guide).

Other long distance paths

Mare e Monti: pleasant walking routes leading mostly near the coast in lower elevations. The stretch Calenzana – Cargèse is the loveliest and most popular (10 days / 50 hrs.). There are also the routes Porticcio – Burgo / Propriano (5 days / 26 hrs.) and Solenzara – Ghisoni. A long-distance route on Cap Corse is also planned for the future.
Mare a Mare: easy walking routes crossing the island from the east to the west. The walking route Moriani – Cargèse passes through the Niolu or the Venachese regions respectively (5–12 days / 38 or 52 hrs.). The walking route Ghisonaccia – Ajaccio leads through Fium'Orbu and Taravu (6–7 days / 34 hrs.). The walking route Porto Vecchio – Burgo / Propriano mostly crosses through the Alta Rocca and Sartenais regions (6–7 days / 26 hrs.).

Multi-day walks

Under the heading »Alternatives« which prefaces the individual route descriptions you will frequently find tips for combining routes or extending them into multi-day trips. We can highly recommend the following multi-day walks: Bonifatu – Haut-Asco (2 days) and Col de Verghio – Lac de Nino – Restonica valley – Monte Rotondo – Monte d'Oro – Vizzavona (4–5 days).

Information and addresses

Getting there

By ferry: there is regular ferry service to Corsica from the cities of Marseilles, Toulon, Nice, Savona, Geneva*, Livorno, Naples* and Sardinia by the following companies: Corsica Ferries, Moby Lines*, Corsica Linea / La Méridionale and Saremar (* no service available off-season).
By air: during the tourist season, charter flights from many European countries, otherwise scheduled flights via the French mainland.

Information

Tourist offices: Agence du Tourisme de la Corse – 17, boulevard du Roi Jérôme, BP 19, F–20181 Ajaccio Cedex 01, ✆ (0)4 95 51-00 00, Fax -14 40, www.visit-corsica.com, https://uk.france.fr/en
Information for the nature reserve: Parc Naturel Régional de Corse – 2, rue Major Lambroschini, F–20184 Ajaccio, ✆ 04 95 51 79 10, Fax 04 95 21 88 17, www.parc-corse.org
Branch offices (only open during tourist season) are located in, amongst others, Corte, Porto-Vecchio, Zonza and in the Asco valley.

Camping

Wild camping is not permitted. Officials turn a blind eye only at certain starting points for walks and near huts if it's only for a single night. In any case, the island offers more than enough official campsites.

Theft

Unfortunately, even in the mountain areas, parked cars are often broken into and valuables stolen. For this reason, never leave any valuables – even if you think they are well-hidden – in a parked car.

Public holidays

January 1, Easter Monday, May 1, May 8, Ascension, Whit Monday, July 14, August 15, November 1, November 11, and December 25.

Climate

The coastal regions are favoured by a Mediterranean climate, with mild winters and warm summers, while the island's central regions – especially the alpine areas – undergo extremely changeable weather with winters that are relatively colder with more rain and snow.

Climate table for Ajaccio

	Month	1	2	3	4	5	6	7	8	9	10	11	12	Year
Air (Ø max.)	°C	13	14	16	18	21	25	27	28	26	22	18	15	20
Air (Ø min.)	°C	3	4	5	7	10	14	16	16	15	11	7	4	9
Water	°C	13	13	13	14	16	20	22	23	22	20	17	15	17
Days of rain		10	9	10	8	5	3	1	2	5	8	11	10	82

Emergency telephone numbers

In the event of an accident in the mountains, it is best to call the police / gendarmerie ✆ 17, who deploy a special task force; fire brigade ✆ 18, emergency medical care ✆ 19, international emergency assistance ✆ 112.

Sport

The most interesting sports that Corsica has to offer are horseback riding, cycling, mountain biking, kayaking and canyoning. Sport fishing in the streams and mountain lakes is a popular pastime. The required fishing permit can be obtained through local fishing clubs as well as in shops selling fishing equipment. Corsica offers four small ski resorts open from January until March, depending on the snow conditions: Haut-Asco, Col de Verghio, Plateau d'Ese and Capanelle.

Telephone

The dialling code to France is 0033, from Corsica to Great Britain. 0044.

Transport in Corsica

Trains: the SNCF maintains two railway lines: Bastia – Ponte Leccia – Corte – Ajaccio (3 hrs.) and Bastia – Ponte Leccia – Calvi (2¾ hrs.). Time-tables are available from train stations, ✆ 04 95-32 80 61, www.train-corse.com.
Busses: there are services to almost all of the larger towns at least once a day. Bus station in Ajaccio ✆ 04 95-51 55 45.
Taxis: you should agree on a fixed price in advance for a longer taxi journey.
Hire cars: rental cars are on offer in many holiday resorts as well as in all larger towns.

Weather forecasts for the mountains

✆ 08 36 68-02 20 and -08 08, www.meteofrance.com.

Northern Corsica

Cap Corse – Nebbio – Balagne – Casinca – Castagniccia

At Punta Mortella with Cap Corse in the background.

Steeped in tradition, the regions lying in the north of the island once counted as the richest agricultural areas in Corsica. Fruit and vegetable gardens, lovely villages, magnificent churches and family mausoleums bear witness to a glorious past. Nonetheless, many young families continue to immigrate to the French mainland or move to the island's tourist centres on the coast so that, today, many communities have to fight for survival.

Cap Corse is an especially strong example, particularly at the northernmost tip. Garden terraces overgrown with *macchia* vegetation, dilapidated churches and houses, and last but not least, mountain slopes scarred by forest fires often characterise the countryside. Despite all of this, a visit to the northern tip of Corsica is worthwhile because, aside from offering a palette of picturesque villages like *Erbalunga, Sisco, Centuri-Port, Pino* and *Nonza*, there are a number of lovely, isolated sandy beaches between *Macinaggio* and *Barcaggio* to be enjoyed. One of Corsica's most beautiful vistas can be reached by road: *Serra di Pigno*, 961m (4km from Col de Teghime), where a view below embraces Bastia, the Étang de Biguglia and the Gulf of St-Florent. Similarly lovely viewpoints are at the *Moulin Mattei* near Centuri and the *Tower of Seneca* at Col de Santa Lucia.

Cap Corse
Barcaggio
Centuri-Port
Macinaggio
Rogliano
Morsiglia
Tomino
Marine-de-Meria
Pino
Luri
Minerviu
Barretali
Sta.Severa
Marine-de-Giottani
Marine-de-Porticciolo
Pietracorbara
Marine-de-Pietracorbara
Olcani
Balba
Albo
Marine-de-Sisco
Nonza
Mt. Stello
Castello
Brando
Erbalunga
P. di Mignola
Punta Mortella
Farinole
S.Martino-di-Lota
Miomo
P.di Malfacu
Golfe de St. Florent
Ville-di-Pietrabugno
Pietranera
P.di l'Acciolu
Patrimonio
Poggio
Bastia
St.Florent
Casta
Ogliastro
C. de Teghime
Furiani
Lozari
L'Île-Rousse
Oletta
Monticello
Revelata
Algajola
Sta.Reparata-di-B.
Belgodere
Novella
Urtaca
Sto.Pietro-di-Tenda
Rapale
Pigna
Occhiatana
Lama
Mt. Astu
Calvi
G. de Calvi
Lumio
Muro
Feliceto
Speloncato
Sorio
Murato
Zilia
Pietralba
Borgo
la Marane
Pinetu
la Canonica
Calenzana
Olmi-Cappela
Vallica
Castifao
Lento
Campitello
Casamozza
Barchetta
Vescovato
Pte. Novu
Campile
Bonifatu
Mt. Padru
Asco
Piedigriggio
Ponte-Leccia
Silvareccio
Popolasca
Morosaglia
Folelli
San Pellegrino
Haut-Asco
la Porta
Pero-Casevecchie
Tuarelli
Mt. Cinto
Monte S. Pietrone
Talasani
Francardo
Piazzole
Ponte-Castirla
San Lorenzo
Omessa
Piedicroce
Rusio
Carcheto-Brustico
S.Nicolao
Moriani-Plage
Carticasi
Lozzi
Calasima
Tralonca
Felce
Albertacce
Calacuccia
Port-de-Campoloro
Corte
Bustanico
Cervione
Sermano
Valle-d'Alesani
C. de Vergio
Favalello
Pietra-di-Verde
Ota
Evisa
Erbajolo
Zuani
Moita
Cristinacce
Marignana
Linguizzetta
Sto.Pietro-di-Venaco
Altiani
Piedicorte-di-Gaggio
Tox
Mt. Rotondo
Tallone
Pancheraccia
Letia
Soccia
Noceta
Balogna
Orto
Vico
Vivario
Marine-de-Bravone
Murzo
Guagno-les-Bains
Guagno
Vezzani
Arbori
Mt. Cervellu
Antisanti
Coggia
Rosazia
Salice
Pastricciola
Mt. d'Oro
C. de Sorba
Casevecchie
Campu-au-Quarciu
Lopigna
C. de Vizzavona
Vizzavona
Etang de Diane
Ambiegna
Ghisoni
Caterragio
Pinzalone
Aléria
Casaglione
Sari-d'Orcino
Vero
Bocognano
St.Antoine

The old town of Bastia, as viewed from the harbour.

The **Nebbio** region follows to the south-west, stretching from the Gulf of St-Florent into the hinterland in a shape resembling a seashell. The enchanting little harbour city of *St-Florent* sparkles here like sunlight on a lazy river, back-dropped by the somewhat dreary chain of hills surrounding the Aliso basin. While taking an excursion through the villages of the Nebbio, be sure to include a detour to the Pisan church of San Michele (12th century) in *Murato* and also to enjoy a *dégustation de vins* (wine-tasting) at one of the many wine cellars in *Patrimonio*. At the neighbouring **Désert des Agriates** – a nearly uninhabited hilly countryside covered in *macchia* vegetation – we can highly recommend a climb to *Cima di u Pesu*, 429m (from Bocca di Vezzu, 311m, ½ hr. there). However, the real attraction of the Agriates region is the sand dune beaches of *Loto, Saleccia* and *Malfalco*.

The delightful little harbour town of St-Florent.

The »Skyline« from Calvi – just on the other side of the gulf, the main ridge with the Cinto.

The *Ostriconi River*, which empties into the sea at the beach of Peraiola, forms the natural border to the neighbouring **Balagne** region. Vast sandy beaches, gentle chains of hills, picturesque and panoramically-situated mountain villages, and last but not least, and only a few kilometres inland – the mighty peaks huddled around Monte Grosso that are often snow-capped even into the month of May – all these elements support Corsica's nickname of the »Mountains in the Sea«.

The Balgane region claims some of the most beautiful, but also hectic seaside resorts on the island: *Calvi, Algajola* and *Île-Rousse*. Along the walks in the Balagne, we will get acquainted with several striking spots situated in this lush landscape. However, walkers will find other interesting trips, too. One is to the *Tartagine Forest*, a starting point for climbs to the northern bulwark of the Corsican main ridge, *Monte Padru*, 2390m (4½ hrs. there from the forestry house at Tartagine, some easy scrambling). Also appealing are the ascents onto *Monte Grosso*, 1937m (5 hrs. there) or to *Capu di Ruia*, 1194m (3 hrs. there), from Calenzana. Finally, a very special tip: the *Fango River* with numerous tributaries offers pleasant walking trails (Barghiana – Bocca di Capronale – Refuge de Puscaghia, 3 hrs. one way).

South of *Bastia* – the beautiful old town around the old fishing harbour is well worth a stroll where you are greeted by the hilly landscapes of the **Casinca** and the **Castagniccia** (chestnut wood). In the lush green chestnut and beech forests, picturesque villages are hidden away. Pigs, goats, cows and donkeys await you almost everywhere. Towering above is *Monte San Petrone*, whose peak sticks out like a turtle's head from its shell, keeping watch over his realm.

Be sure to visit the lovely, pristine mountain villages with names ending in *»di-Casinca«* as well as *Vescovato, Morosaglia, La Porta, Piedicroce* and *Cervione*.

1 Monte Stello, 1307m

6.00 hrs.

Popular panoramic peak on Cap Corse

Monte Stello offers a fabulous view of wide areas of Northern Corsica and Cap Corse. The ascent follows the well-marked path from Pozzo and the hiking path to Silgaggia is an alternative for the descent.

Starting point: at the car park 100m from the main square of Pozzo, 277m, a friendly village located above Erbalunga, on the east coast of Cap Corse.

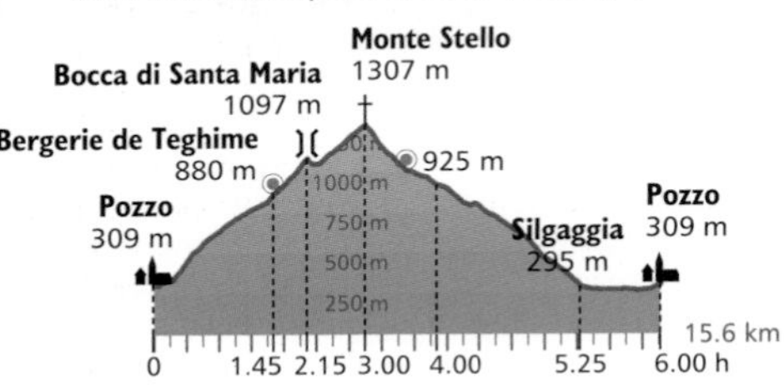

Height difference: 1100m.
Grade: moderately difficult route that demands physical fitness. The ascent trail is well-marked but the descent trail, on the other hand, is often very difficult to follow.
Refreshment/accommodation: a bar in Pozzo, hotels and campsites on the coast.
Map: ign 4347 OT (1:25,000).

At the church on the road through **Pozzo**, a narrow street turns off to the square (signpost for Monte Stellu, car park on the right after 200m). From the village square, go straight on up the steps following the orange waymarkers through the village. Past the last houses, the trail merges onto a roadway; turn left to follow this for 3 minutes until a distinct path turns off to the right up some steps to Monte Stello (sign). Usually the ascent is gentle as it passes through *macchia* vegetation and keeps high up on the right-hand side of the valley. After just under 1¾ hrs., pass a spring and then immediately after, the stone hut of the **Bergerie de Teghime**. Another half an hour later, the top of the **Bocca di Santa Maria** pass, 1097m, is reached. The orange-marked path leads downhill on the other side of the ridge for a few minutes and then traverses the slope to the right (to the left, the turn-off to Chapelle St-Jean, shortly after, one to Olmeta/Nonza). The trail leads directly towards the summit of **Monte Stello** and eventually climbs up to the top of the peak over the north ridge (on a flat section about 20m below the summit, the trail is joined from the left by the yellow/red-marked trail from Silgaggia).

For the return, take the trail to Silgaggia (only when visibility is good): the initially yellow/

Panoramic view southwards from the peak. – Below: the descent to Silgaggia.

red- (later also orange-) marked trail leads in a north-easterly, then easterly direction descending the ridge. (Be careful: some minutes later do not turn left onto the red-marked trail!). After about 20 minutes, the ridge levels out noticeably and you pass a rocky knoll. 50m after that, the trail, waymarked with posts, turns right away from the ridge, leads 100 vertical metres downhill and then turns left back to the ridge along a lovely traverse passing a spring and crossing over a rocky plateau, to join a **roadway** which ends at this point (925m; 1 hr. from the summit). The roadway (100m on, turn right) runs half an hour later between two pylons and shortly afterwards, turns off to the right, following the yellow waymarkers, onto another roadway where you continue downhill to **Silgaggia**, 300m (¾ hr.). From here walk back along the road to **Pozzo** (½ hr./2.3km; keep right at all junctions).

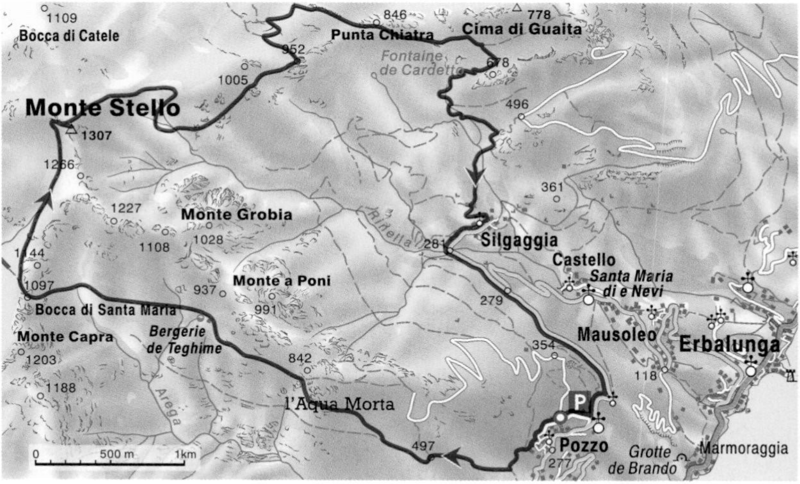

2 Sentier des Douaniers – from Macinaggio to Barcaggio

6.40 hrs.

Popular coastal walk to the northern tip of Cap Corse

The Sentier des Douaniers (tax collector's path) is one of the most popular coastal paths on Corsica – it connects the villages of Macinaggio and Centuri at the northern tip of Cap Corse. Since this is a significantly longer walk of 7 to 8 hours and there's no suitable bus service from Centuri to Macinaggio, we have limited ourselves to the especially interesting, but also much visited section as far as Barcaggio, which offers spectacular views of the neighbouring islands of Capraia and Elba. You can return by boat from Barcaggio (after making a reservation), but most walkers like to stop at one of the inviting beaches along the way…

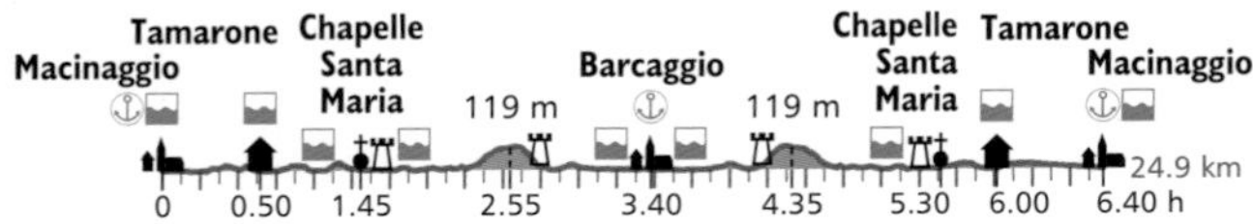

Starting point: Macinaggio harbour, at the north-eastern tip of Cap Corse.
Height difference: just under 650m in total.
Grade: easy walk on well-marked trails.
Refreshment and accommodation: bar-restaurant in Tamarone, in Macinaggio and Barcaggio bar-restaurants and hotels, campsite in Macinaggio.
Alternative: from Barcaggio you can continue along the *Sentier des Douaniers* via Tollare (¾ hr.; very pretty) as far as Centuri-Port (4¾ hrs. from Barcaggio).
Tip: the »U San Paulu« boat operates a service during the tourist season from Macinaggio to Barcaggio, and you can buy a single ticket (daily 11.00/15.30) or a return (daily 12.00/16.30) by boat (reservation needed: tel. +33 495350709/ +33 614781416, www.sanpaulu.com). If you prefer a shorter round walk, turn back at Chapelle Santa Maria to return to Macinaggio (3 hrs. in total).
Map: ign 4347 OT (1:25,000).

Start the walk at the harbour of **Macinaggio** near the mooring for the »U San Paulu« pleasure boat which operates between Macinaggio and Barcaggio in the tourist season (→Tip). At first, follow the main road in the directon of Rogliano, and when you come to a left-hand bend go straight ahead on the little road along beside the harbour. The trail then runs directly across the sandy beach. At the end of the beach follow a lovely footpath which forks immediately – go right here up to **Punta di a Coscia** (boat mast and canons; with a beautiful view across the bay of Macinaggio) and continue across the slope along the main trail, waymarked in yellow, to a track which brings you down to the marvellous **Plage de Tamarone** – at the end of the track there are two beach bars to welcome day-trippers. The tax collector's path continues along the beach. Just before the end of the beach, a path branches off left inland to the Chapelle Santa Maria, but stay on the nicer coastal path. At the end of the bay it passes through a gate and a quarter of an hour later reaches the **Plage des Îles**, a narrow strip of sandy beach directly opposite the Finocchiarola islands. It's now only another quarter of an hour to reach the **Chapelle Santa Maria della Chiappella** (left finally at the fork). At the Romanesque chapel you come to a broad path which you follow to the right, past the beach, to the nearby **Tour Santa Maria**.

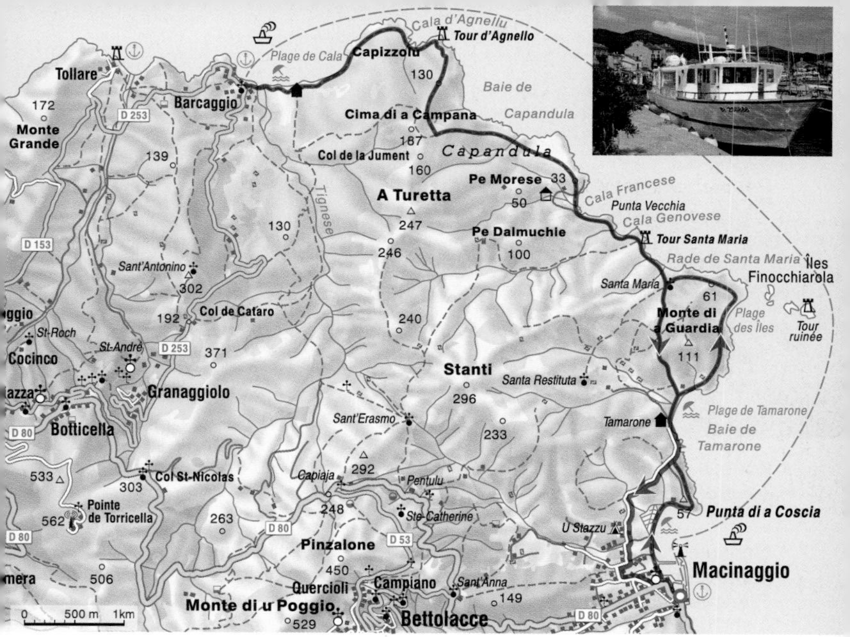

The marvellous beach at Tamarone.

Watchtower on the northern tip of Corsica – the Tour d'Agnello. In the background, the island of Giraglia

5 minutes past the tower the trail crosses a beautiful sandy beach (**Cala Genovese**) and a good 5 minutes later a path turns off right to the **Cala Francese** with a small lagoon (straight on along the broad trail brings you to a shelter). About 20 minutes after that you pass the impressive **Capandula** cliffs. Eventually the coastal trail climbs steeply up 100 vertical metres to lead over to a mountain ridge from which you have your first view of Barcaggio and the offshore island of Giraglia. The trail now runs on the right along the ridge above the steep coastline down to the **Tour d'Agnello**. Shortly afterwards you come past the **Cala d'Agnellu** (beautiful rocky and sandy bays). The trail ascends again for a short way to Capizzolu, then leads past gnarled juniper trees across to the delightful sand dunes of Barcaggio (Plage de Cala). Here, a comfy café awaits at the beach and, further along, pass a snack bar; then continue on to reach **Barcaggio**.

At first, the return route follows the approach. At the Chapelle Santa Maria, however, stay on the broad trail that leads directly inland and across to the Tamarone beach (after just under 20 minutes go straight on through a gate). Just beyond Tamarone, again keep on the track; this leads leisurely through the countryside past the U Stazzu campsite back to **Macinaggio**.

3.40 hrs.

From St-Florent to the Punta Mortella

3

Along the coast to the unspoilt sandy inlets of the Désert des Agriates

Numerous remote sandy bays, accessible only along well-trodden footpaths or by boat, make this coastal walk especially attractive. Without a doubt, the most beautiful of these is Plage de Loto which can also be reached by boat during the tourist season (→Alternative).

Starting point: the car park above Fornali Beach. The approach is from St-Florent: from the village centre, head south along the main road. At the roundabout, 1km on, turn right over the Aliso bridge and then diagonally right along the coastal road (Route de la Roya) for not quite 4km until reaching the car park, somewhat above the beach (1.5km along a gravel track).
Height difference: 100m in total.
Grade: easy walking on clear paths.
Refreshment and accommodation: in St-Florent.
Alternative: boat service from May to Sept. between St-Florent and Plage de Loto which then offers you an extension of the walk to Plage de Loto (just under 1 hr. from Punta Mortella) with a return to St-Florent by boat – or start the walk at Plage de Loto (book your ticket early, or even better, the night before). From Loto beach, you can continue on to Saleccia beach (¾ hr. along a track through the interior, 1¼ hrs. along the coastal path).
Map: ign 4348 OT (1:25,000).

A pretty sandy bay awaits you at the mouth of the Buggiu.

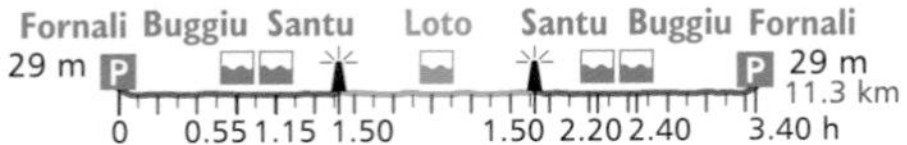

Above **Fornali Beach**, leave the track behind by turning right onto the second gravel trail forking off to the right (sign »*Chemin du Littoral*«; parking places). This trail becomes a path before reaching the cove and continues to the left following the seaside. After a few minutes pass through a gate. The path now crosses private property for a good 15 minutes (do not leave the coastal path) and then exits through another gate. Shortly afterwards turn right along the coastal path to reach the small beach with its delightful dunes at the mouth of the **Buggiu** (1 hr.).

This is certainly the prettiest beach on this route – but such a statement is only a matter of opinion so continue your walk. 20 minutes later, after passing numerous stretches of charming sandy beach, reach the wide sandy bay

Landing manoeuvres on the delightful Loto beach. In the meantime, a boat mooring has been built so that you can now disembark without getting your feet wet.

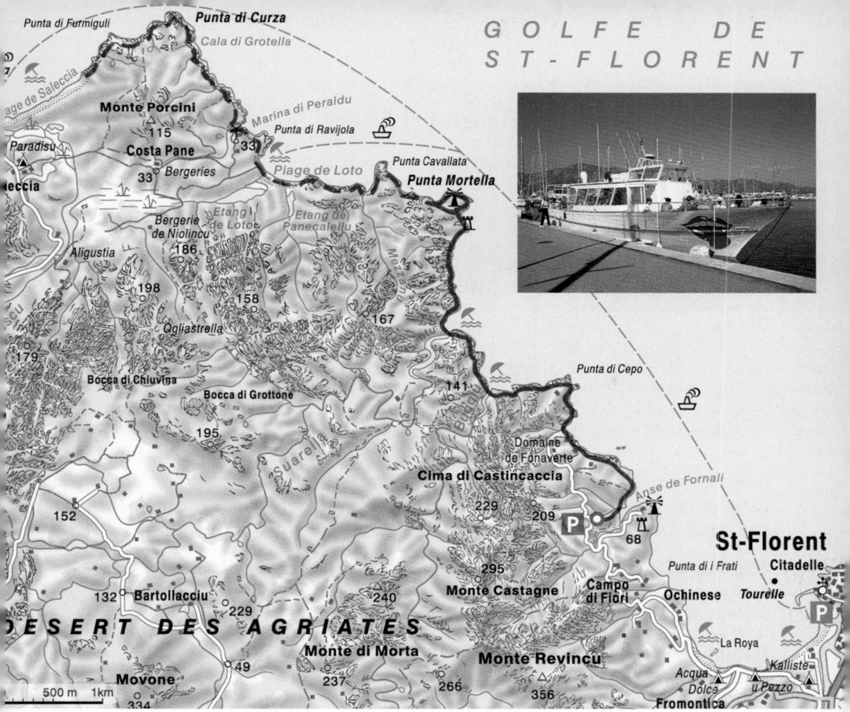

at the mouth of the **Santu**. To visit the lighthouse at **Punta Mortella** you need to continue (a good ½ hr.). If the water at the Santu delta is very deep, you have to plod along the river bank for a good ways toward the interior until you can cross over to the other bank by fording the river at a narrow point).

Loto beach is not only a favourite place for day-trippers – it's also very popular with cows.

4 Monte Sant'Angelu, 1218m

3.10 hrs.

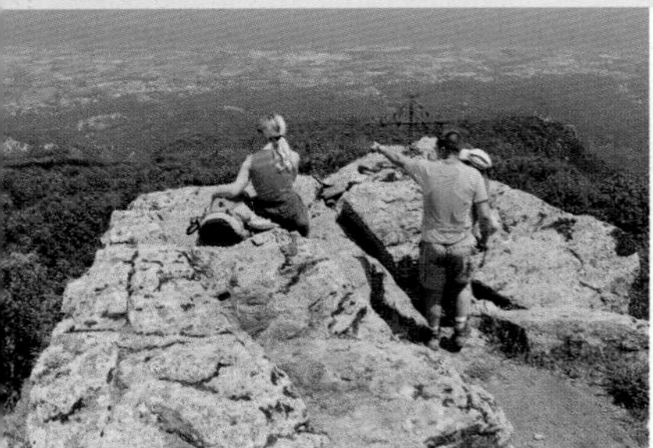

Dramatic peak with views overlooking the east coast

The summit of Monte Sant'Angelu offers a marvellous view, not unlike that from the more famous neighbouring peak of Monte San Petrone (→Walk 5). When weather permits, the view stretches from Cap Corse via Bastia to the east coast and the villages of the Casinca region, and to the highest peaks in the island's north. You can ascend from two sides – from Loreto-di-Casinca or from Silvareccio. We prefer the path from Silvareccio – from the point of view of route finding, it is less problematic and the huge rocky summit is displayed from its best side.

Starting point: bar in Silvareccio, 661m, typical village in the Casinca region (access via Venzolasca – Loreto or Castellare – Penta).
Height difference: just under 600m.
Grade: easy walk, but sometimes a rather indistinct path.
Refreshment and accommodation: bar in Silvareccio, hotels and campsites on the coast.
Map: ign 4349 OT (1:25,000).

50m before the bar in **Silvareccio** the path, waymarked in red and orange, turns off to the right (signpost for San Anghjulu). After 10m it leads up right between stone walls and bends to the left after a gate. A few minutes later the path veers

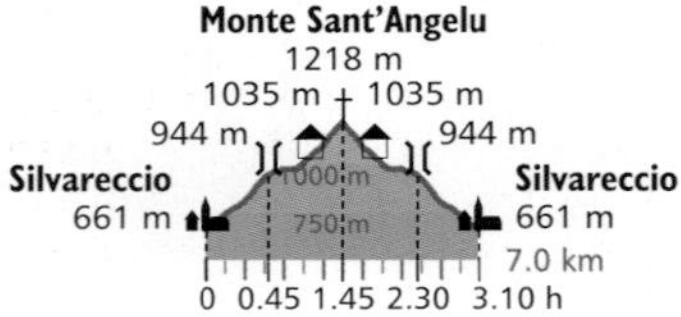

The path leads through a fairytale forest of holm oak just before the summit.

right (keep a good lookout for the orange waymarkers, sometimes arrows as well) and continues uphill through the deciduous forest. After a good quarter of an hour, before the Acqua Freddola stream, a path joins from the left. The path now ascends beside the stream and forks after 5 minutes – continue uphill to the right here (not left over the stream) through a beautiful chestnut forest overrun with ferns. At the top edge of the forest your path now turns left (another path turns off to the right) and soon afterwards reaches a wide **col**, 944m (cross), with a superb view of the broad summit wall of Monte Sant'Angelu.

The path now runs to the right up a gentle incline heading for the summit wall and then goes left below the wall in a sustained traverse through the forest (after 5 minutes do not turn off sharp right). After a good 10 minutes the path bends up to the right at a ravine and, after another 10 minutes, reaches a **col**, 1035m, next to a shelter (a hiking path joins from Loreto). Continue right (then 10m on, left) uphill along the beautiful path with orange/ yellow/red waymarkers that leads beside a fence over the ridge to the foot of **Monte Sant'Angelu's** summit (10 mins.). Then, after a short stretch of scrambling over rock, the high wooded ridge brings you to the small plateau at the very top (20 mins.).

TOP

5 Monte San Petrone, 1767m

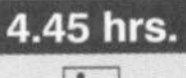

Marvellous panoramic peak in the green landscape of Castagniccia

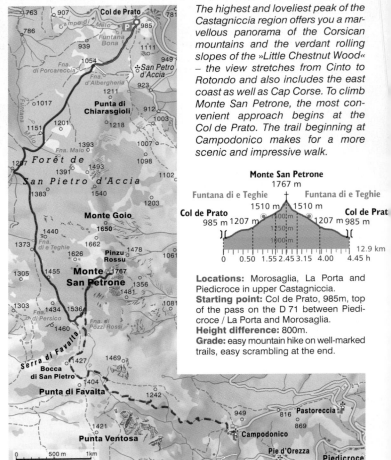

The highest and loveliest peak of the Castagniccia region offers you a marvellous panorama of the Corsican mountains and the verdant rolling slopes of the »Little Chestnut Wood« – the view stretches from Cinto to Rotondo and also includes the east coast as well as Cap Corse. To climb Monte San Petrone, the most convenient approach begins at the Col de Prato. The trail beginning at Campodonico makes for a more scenic and impressive walk.

Locations: Morosaglia, La Porta and Piedicroce in upper Castagniccia.
Starting point: Col de Prato, 985m, top of the pass on the D 71 between Piedicroce / La Porta and Morosaglia.
Height difference: 800m.
Grade: easy mountain hike on well-marked trails, easy scrambling at the end.

Monte San Petrone as viewed from the Piedicroce – Col de Prato road. The rocky summit looks like a turtle's head peaking out from its shell.

Refreshment and accommodation: snack bar at the starting point, restaurants and hotels in the valley settlements.
Alternative: ascent from Campodonico (4¾ hrs.): from the car park, 100m before reaching the village, follow the road into the village and turn right before the church along the orange-marked trail. The ancient trail, often cobbled, leads continuously straight ahead, traversing the slope (a few minutes later, a trail forks off to the right, ascending to Campana) and soon enters a shady wood. 20 mins. later, the trail forks – keep straight on here as it noticeably narrows. A good ½ hr. later, pass a little meadowland plateau (rest break!). Shortly after, the trail levels out and then forks at a stream – turn right to follow the stream and, at a *bergerie* (beneath marvellously gnarled beech trees) cross to the other side of the stream and pass to the right of a tumbledown *bergerie* (spring) to continue, ascending along the left-hand edge of the meadow depression (be sure to take good note of the following stretch for the return route!). Before the trail begins to gently descend (Bocca di San Pietro) turn right onto the trail that ascends along the broad ridge to a little beech wood – before reaching it, turn right to continue through a untamed and romantic rocky landscape, passing a *bergerie* (spring). The trail keeps its distance from the beech wood and does not cross through it until some minutes later on, then crosses over to the next ridgeline and picks up the trail from Col de Prato. Turn right onto this trail to continue to Monte San Petrone (see text).
Maps: ign 4349 OT, 4351 OT (1:25,000).

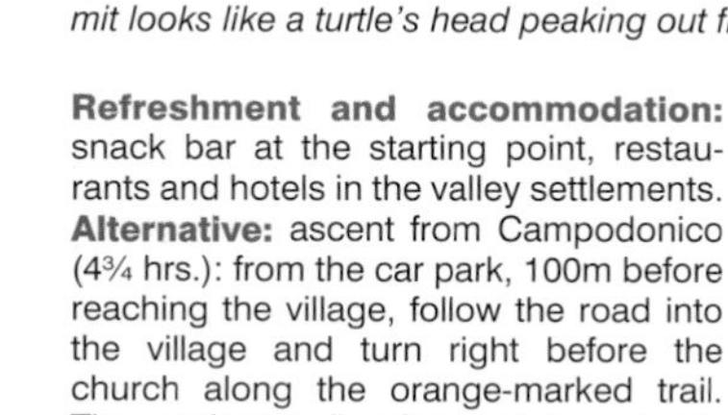

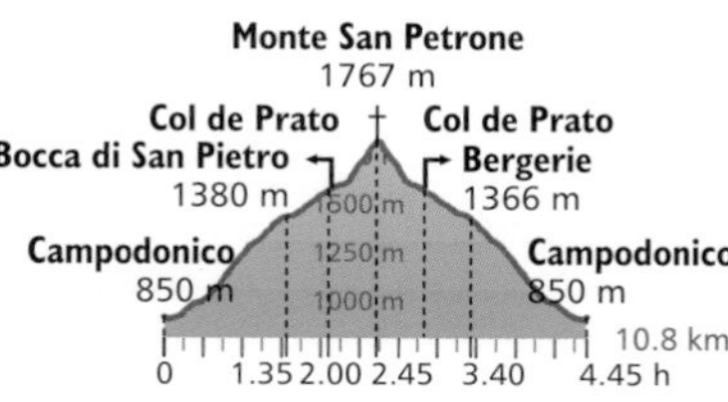

On the summit of Monte San Petrone – as the day progresses, often shrouded in clouds.

The signposted orange-marked hiking path begins between the houses at the top of the **pass**, following a forestry road that gently climbs straight ahead in a southerly direction. After 15 minutes the road enters a sparse pine wood (at the junction here, keep straight on / diagonally left to continue ascending). Shortly after, the pines give way to a majestic beech forest.
After a good 45 minutes of walking, reach the crest of an ill-defined **hilltop**, 1207m, where you turn left onto the orange-marked path (dogs must be leashed). The ascent is gentle for the most part, leading at first through pines then soon afterwards through a beech forest. Half an hour later, the path passes directly above a mountain spring and, not quite a quarter of an hour after that, passes above a rocky viewpoint. After another 15 minutes, reach a sunny clearing on the **crest of the ridge**, 1510m – a pleasant relief after lurking so long in the shadows of the beech wood. Straight ahead (right) a path forks off to Compodonico (→Alternative), but keep left instead, heading in a northerly direction on the orange-marked path. Soon afterwards this path turns to the left again towards the beech forest. Following a level section, the path becomes rapidly steeper, finally bearing to the right and heading for the summit. Reaching the highest point of **Monte San Petrone** involves a bit of easy scrambling. Not quite at the summit, a wrought-iron cross has been erected with an inlaid statue of San Petru.

Belvédère de Cervione, 632m

6

Panoramic view of the endless sandy beaches on the east coast

The Belvédère de Cervione is an easily-reached panoramic overlook commanding a wonderful view of the east coast and revealing the boundless sweep of beaches lying between the lagoons of Biguglia and Diane. Twilight time leaves a singularly lasting impression as the rays of the sun, setting behind you, reflect in the deep blue sea and the horizon slowly disappears in the haze.

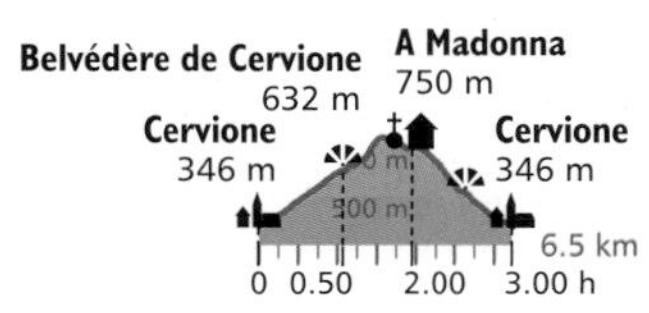

Starting point: main road in Cervione, 320m, main village of the Castagniccia.
Height difference: a good 450m.
Grade: easy walk but demands sure-footedness and some route-finding skills (Belvédère de Cervione – Chapelle a Madonna sometimes without a path).
Refreshment and accommodation: Restaurant a Scupiccia by the chapel (open June 20 to Aug 25). Bars, restaurants and hotels in Cervione.
Alternative: circuit route via Santa-Maria-Poggio (a total of 5 hrs.): 200m past the chapel, a path turns off to the right (signpost for Castellu, orange way-markers). After 50 mins., it reaches a wide, fern and gorse covered col, 1003m, between the huge Castellu (on the left) and the rather rocky Monte Negrine (on the right). From here, keep straight ahead (now along the *Mare a Mare*), and at the fork 5 mins. later, turn right towards Funtana di Felicio (sign, the *Mare a Mare* turns off to the left) The orange-marked trail crosses over the ridgeline ¼ hr. later and then forks 5 mins. after that (Col de Felicione). Here, straight on (right) towards Santa-Maria-Poggio (sign). 5 mins. later, the trail leads past a stone house to your left, and 15 mins. after that, turns right at a saddle in front of a little rocky peak. Not quite ½ hr. later, pass a little vantage point with a view of Poggio, and shortly afterward, a mighty boulder (turn right here). 20 mins. later, keep above the settlement and along the trail towards Cervione (sign), with steady up-and-down walking through the shady cork oak forest and heading back to Cervione (½ hr. on, keep straight ahead on a street leading to the main street).
Map: ign 4351 OT (1:25,000).

Col de Felicione
945 m
Chapelle A Madonna
750 m 1003 m
Belvédère de Cervione
632 m
Santa-Maria-Poggio
339 m
Cervione
346 m
750 m
500 m
Cervione
346 m
11.2 km
0 0.50 2.00 2.50 3.15 4.20 5.00 h

Belvédère de Cervione.

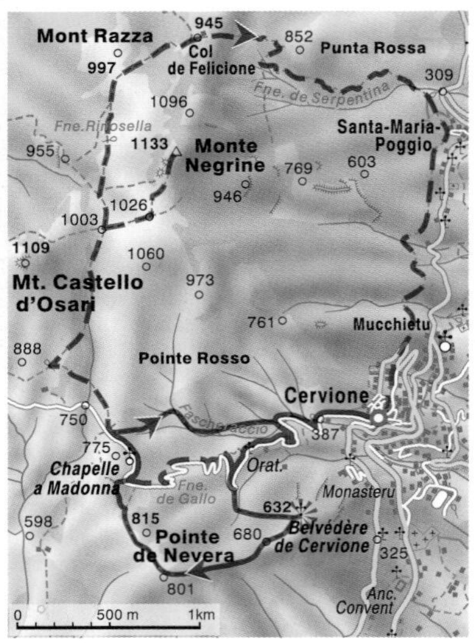

Park on the main road in **Cervione** and enjoy a lovely view of the coast. Walking towards Piedicroce, at the end of the promenade, quite a steep little road (*Traversa François Giacobbi*) branches off sharp right just before a left-hand bend (the village limits) from which you turn off onto the first narrow road to the left, the *Strada MSG T. Struzzieri* to the Eglise Scupiccia (orange waymarkers). After half an hour, a good 5 minutes after passing a shrine, reach the turn-off of a clearly marked path at a sharp right-hand bend. The path bears to the left at the fork, climbing through a shady primeval forest to the open crest of the ridge (¼ hr.). To the left from here, it's only a stone's throw to the little **viewing platform** protected by railings and sporting a cross.

There are two possible routes to reach the Chapelle a Madonna: you can either go back to the track and ascend this to the chapel (40 mins., the easier choice) or you can walk along the path that climbs directly over the ridge (rather overgrown and requiring a bit of easy scrambling; keep a close eye on the red waymarkers!) and ¾ hr. later – after passing the take-off spot for paragliders – reach the highest point on the ridge, 801m (to the north is the somewhat higher **Pointe de Nevera**, 815m). Shortly after, at the fork, keep diagonally left and then, some minutes later, ascend along a fence. Turn left onto a track, and descend to the **Chapelle a Madonna**, 750m (20 mins.; refreshments available in the Restaurant a Scupiccia during

View of Cercione from the hiking path.

the season). From the chapel, it is an easy walk to return along the track to Cervione (1 hr.). However, follow the track for 200m until reaching a col (turn-off, →Alternative).

Turn right here onto a broad, descending trail. The trail soon narrows and climbs down along the left flank of the valley. Half an hour from the chapel, the path merges with the track which leads back to **Cervione**.

7 Punta di Caldane, 1724m

6.00 hrs.

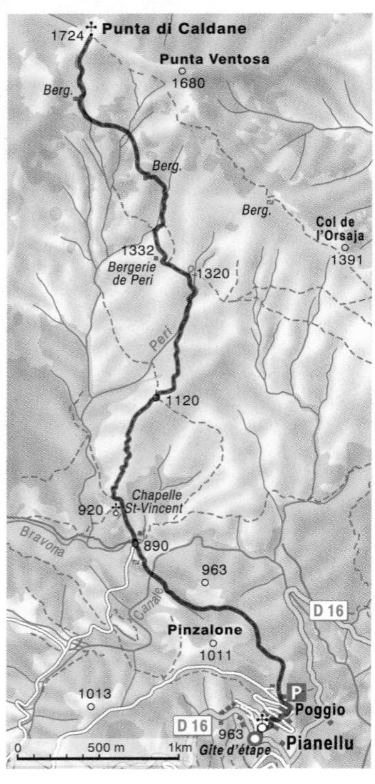

Secluded summit walk

On Castagniccia's third highest summit, a breath-taking view awaits us, taking in the east coast on the one side and the 2000 metre peaks perched on the main ridge on the other side – but above all, we can expect a very pristine and often secluded alpine experience along paths that are sometimes barely discernible and lacking in waymarking. Adding to the experience are the remote mountain villages of Pianellu and Poggio with their offbeat charm.

Starting point: *Gîte d'étape* at the church square in Pianellu, 807m. The village is situated on the southern flank of Castagniccia on the D 16, Moïta – Col de Casardo, 30km from the east coast (San-Giuliano) or from Corte (mostly a narrow, twisting road).
Height difference: 1050m.
Grade: uncomplicated alpine tour, however, good physical fitness and especially good route-finding skills are demanded (with low-lying cloud or fog, it is best to turn back!). Do not attempt after heavy rainfall (muddy stretches of trail, streams lacking bridges).
Accommodation: *Gîte d'étape* at the starting point.
Map: ign 4351 OT (1:25,000).

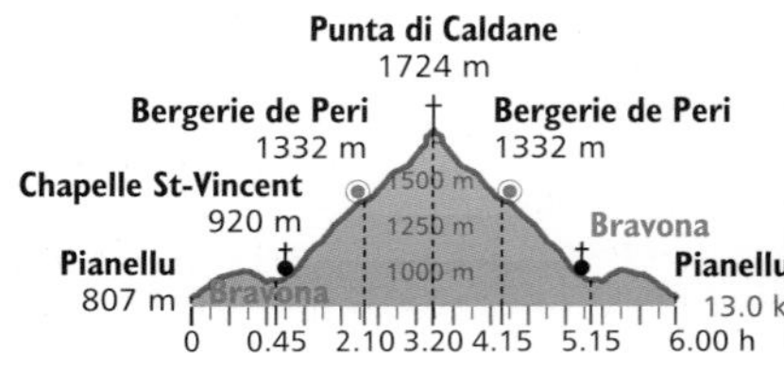

The Bergerie de Peri, surrounded by fields of asphodel

From the *Gîte d'étape* in **Pianellu**, skirt around the church to the left. At the information board, ascend the orange-waymarked *Mare a Mare Nord* to **Poggio**. Follow the waymarkers to ascend along the steps to the road above the village (parking possible), but leave this promptly behind (sign »I Pirelli«). The trail continues in easy up-and-down whilst traversing the slope and taking in a view of the east coast as well as the peak which is our destination. 25 mins. later, cross over a stream (channel) and just after that, yet another one, the **Bravona**. Now leave the *Mare* trail behind and, after crossing a stream, ascend to the left along the yellow-waymarked trail. A few minutes later, pass by the **Chapelle St-Vincent** (on a meadow to the left) and then continue, ascending steadily over a ridge covered in heather trees whilst enjoying a lovely view of the east coast and some 2000-metre peaks. After a somewhat rocky section, the path leads along the Peri stream, soon changing over to the opposite bank (a path forks away to the right) – this is an unspoiled and idyllic stretch, especially when in flower during the months of May / June (myrtle, asphodel). At an enclosed spring, the trail leaves the stream behind and veers left to cross over to the **Bergerie de Peri**, which we skirt around to the right.

The continued course is not always clear – therefore, keep an eye out for the yellow waymarkers (somewhat few and far between). The path veers slightly to the left as it ascends, climbing to a point about 50m left of a solitary beech tree standing in a field of ferns and then, shortly after (keep left!) passes yet another little *bergerie*. Traversing a broad meadowland slope, flanked by beech trees on both sides, continue bearing left, passing somewhat above a little stone-built hut. Now the path bears left, crossing over to an open beech wood and, from there, ascends further whilst continuing left and passing yet another *bergerie* with two huts. Ascending over a broad meadowland ridge, finally reach the apex of the **Punta di Caldane**, graced with a wooden cross. Walkers with good route-finding skills can continue over the ridge (to the Col de l'Orsaja) to return to the spring (scantily marked, frequently indistinct).

8 Punta Liatoghju, 223m, and Plage d'Ostriconi

A little rocky peak and two grand beaches with dunes

This little circuit route captivates the walker as it leads along lovely, easy trails in the admittedly desolate, but indeed, charming landscape of the Agriates Desert, and includes a joyful summit and wonderful beaches.

Starting point: restaurant l'Agriate Café on the main road, Ponte Leccia – Île-Rousse (N 1197), 500m east of the Camping Village d'Ostriconi.
Height difference: 400m.
Grade: easy, except for the rocky ascent route to the summit. Not during hot weather!
Refreshment and accommodation: restaurant at the starting point, Camping Village de l'Ostriconi at the Ostriconi estuary.
Alternative: a long circuit route (a total of 3½ hrs.): at the junction of the trail to Punta Liatoghju (see below), continue along the track. After a total walking time of 1 hr. reach the Bocca di Mercuriu. At this point, a broad stone wall intersects the track – 20m to the left, a path forks off, passing through a breach in the wall. 25 mins. later, cross over a stream bed (afterwards, pass the wall for the *bergerie* to your right, and then turn right again; sign). 20 mins. more, at the Bocca Affacatoghju, the path merges with the coastal trail (sign); turn left to follow this. 10 mins. later, cross over a saddle and, shortly thereafter, past another breach in the wall, the trail becomes a path. 5 minutes later, ignore a path branching off to the right, pass through an abandoned shepherd's settlement, and then cross a stream bed. 20 mins. later, reach Vana beach (see below).
Map: ign 4249 OT (1:25,000).

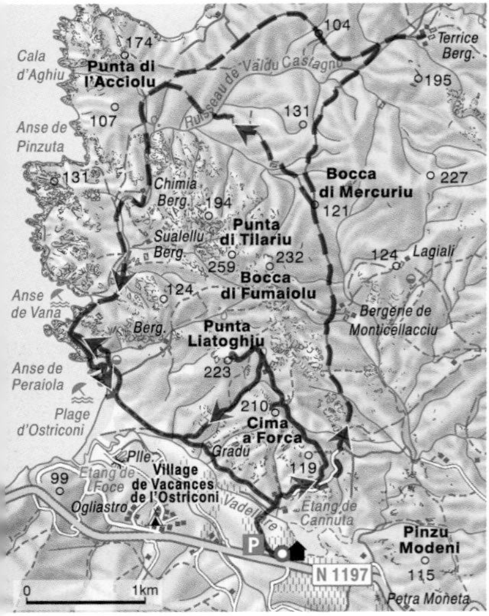

From the **car park** near the restaurant, follow the main road a few paces toward Ostriconi and then turn right at the road resembling a hollow way (Agriate trail board; parking possible under eucalyptus trees). Some minutes later, the road crosses the Vadellare stream; in the bend that follows, ignore the path to the left that leads to Ostriconi Beach. Just afterwards, pass a stone house. A few minutes later, pass a house built into the rock face – turn diagonally left here onto the trail to Punta Liatoghju (posts; straight ahead

The walk leads to two dune beaches – Plage d'Ostriconi (above) and Anse de Vana (below).

→Alternative). At the outset, the path runs parallel to the track, and 20 minutes later, reaches a valley basin. It then ascends through a broad gully, shaded with trees, to reach the **saddle** (170m) near the Cima a Forca (a blocked-off path forks off to the left and leads to the summit – ¼ hr there and back).

The trail descends straight down on the other side, and a few minutes later, passes two stone houses and an old threshing yard. Shortly after, the trail forks: to the left, a path branches off towards Gradu (our continued route later on); we keep straight on towards the Punta Liatoghju. The path soon ascends through a shady gully, up to the rocky ridge, and then follows this (now slightly more challenging) to the summit of **Punta Liatoghju**, 223m. Here, Peraiola bay with the Ostriconi beach lie at your feet. The view of Monte Padru and Monte Astu is also marvellous.

Unfortunately, taking the trail that continues along the ridge towards the coast is officially prohibited, for this reason, we must return to the last trail junction and then turn right to follow the trail towards Gradu. 10 minutes later, the trail touches on a stream bed and then merges, another 10 minutes further on at a barrier, into the trail leading to the beach. Turning left, you head back to the road and to the starting point (just under ½ hr); a right turn leads, in a good 10 minutes, to the northern end of **Ostriconi Beach**, the beach is about 750m in length. If you follow the coast trail (*Sentier littoral*) from here, you will reach the equally beautiful **Vana Beach** in 20 minutes.

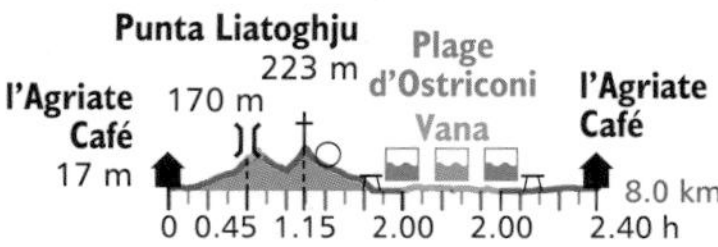

9 Monte Astu, 1535m

6.00 hrs.

A treat for walking afficionados

The hiking path onto Monte Astu is described, without exaggeration, as one of the most beautiful on Corsica. The old path that starts in the delightful village of Lama, follows an extremely panoramic route lined with white and pink rock roses, up to the spectacularly located Refuge du Prunincu. The remaining ascent to the summit is not quite as attractive as the first part but, in compensation, you are rewarded with a fabulous view from the top.

Starting point: church in Lama, 502m, a pretty village in a scenic location above the Ponte Leccia – Île-Rousse road (N 1197).
Height difference: just under 1100m.
Grade: easy as far as the *refuge*, then sometimes more overgrown and more demanding, especially in poor visibility. Very little shade, so an early start is recommended (avoid this walk when it's hot).

Refreshment/accommodation: bars, restaurants and *Gîtes* in Lama; Camping Village de l'Ostriconi (Ostriconi estuary).
Important tip: due to the danger of burning your skin on the fennel type plants at the side of the path (Peucedanum paniculatum), you are advised to wear long trousers on this walk (info at the tourist office).
Map: ign 4348 OT (1:25,000).

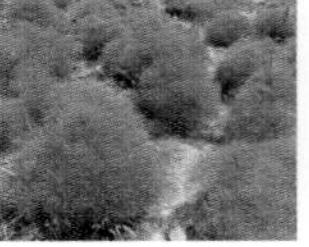

From the church in **Lama** continue along the street and after 100m, turn right to the steps which you keep following uphill through the village. After a few minutes at the top end of the village, meet a road. Follow the road to the left for 20m to then turn off onto the hiking path up to Monte Astu (signpost, yellow waymarkers). After a few minutes it passes a cistern and ascends the ridge with a beautiful view of Lama as well as of Monte Padru and Cinto (a ¼ hr. later, at the fork on the ridge, turn right). After a good half an hour pass by a small spring and immediately afterwards on the right-hand side of the path, a viewing platform. A good 20 minutes later reach a hilltop (910m, a nice place to stop for a rest) – and now the view reaches as far as the Rotondo. The path from then onwards keeps to the right and leisurely crosses the hillside of Pinzalone and after

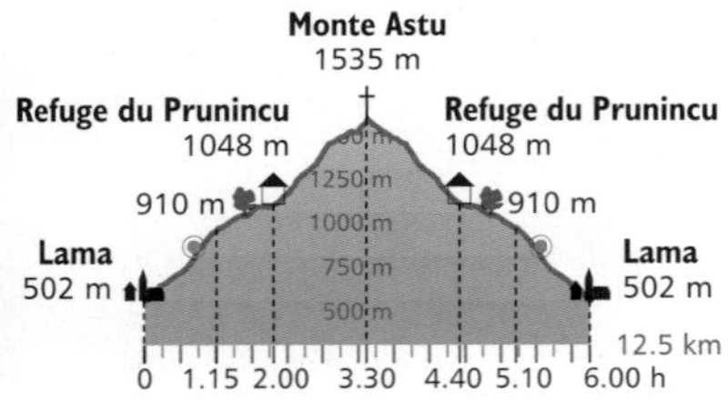

The superbly located Refuge du Pruníncu.

20 minutes leads between four chestnut trees (soon afterwards go straight on at the fork; below a *bergerie*). 10 minutes later, you come to a dramatic ridge with wonderful views. The path continues ascending along the ridge to the **Refuge du Prunincu**, 1048m (10 minutes; a simple hut, open) sitting in a picturesque location next to a group of rocks. Many hikers turn round here. However, continue further up the ridge, soon keeping slightly left, and after half an hour you reach **Bocca Tiobuli**, 1238m, on the main ridge. Walk up along this ridge to the right. After a few minutes you come past a small stone hut and you continue to climb up the ridge to a fern-covered gully (take care: do not continue straight on toward another stone house nestled among rocks, instead turn right onto the path marked by cairns!). The gully runs steeply upwards next to the rocky ridge to a small flat meadow on the far side of a rocky spur (½ hr.). The path bends here towards the right-hand side of the ridge, now with views of **Monte Astu**, and continues to lead across the hillside to the flat col at the foot of the summit (20 mins.). From there follow a well-marked path over the rocky ridge up to the summit cross (¼ hr.; some easy scrambling at the top). The panoramic view is fantastic and stretches from Île-Rousse across the Agriates, St-Florent, Cap Corse and Monte San Petrone as far as the two-thousanders.

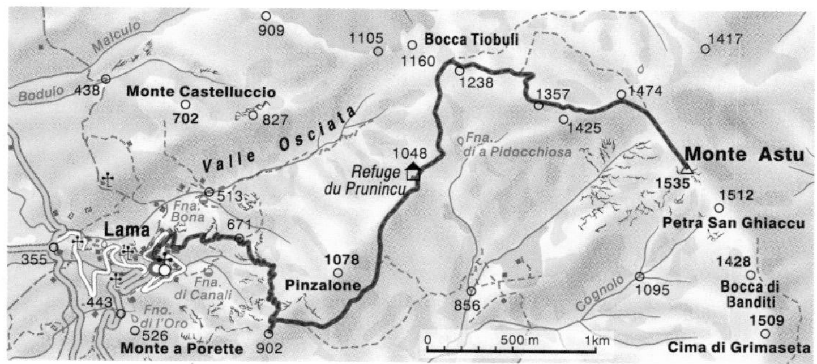

10 Lumio / Algajola – Monte Sant'Angelo – Algajola

On hiking paths through the villages of the Balagne region

The Balagne is one of Corsica's oldest and most fertile agricultural regions. The route through this blessed landscape touches on numerous churches and monasteries as well as some lovely villages offering fine views which, despite the hurly-burly of the nearby coast, have managed to preserve a traditional character. A special treat is enjoyed by taking advantage of the approach using the local trains serving the »Tramways de Balagne« railway line connecting the coastal villages of Calvi, Lumio, Algajola and Île-Rousse.

Starting point: Lumio, 185m, village in a superb location between Calvi and Algajola offering wonderful views. Train station Ondari-Arinella on the »Tramways de Balagne« railway line, 40 mins. on foot below the village (several trains a day).

Destination: Algajola, seaside resort with a long, sandy beach. Train station on the »Tramways de Balagne« railway line (during the season, several trains a day).

Height difference: 1000m.

Grade: for the most part, an easy walk, but stamina is required.

Refreshment: numerous bars and restaurants along the way.

Alternatives: the route can also be started in Algajola: from the train station, walk to the main road in the direction of Île-Rousse; shortly afterwards, turn right along the minor road (D 551) leading to

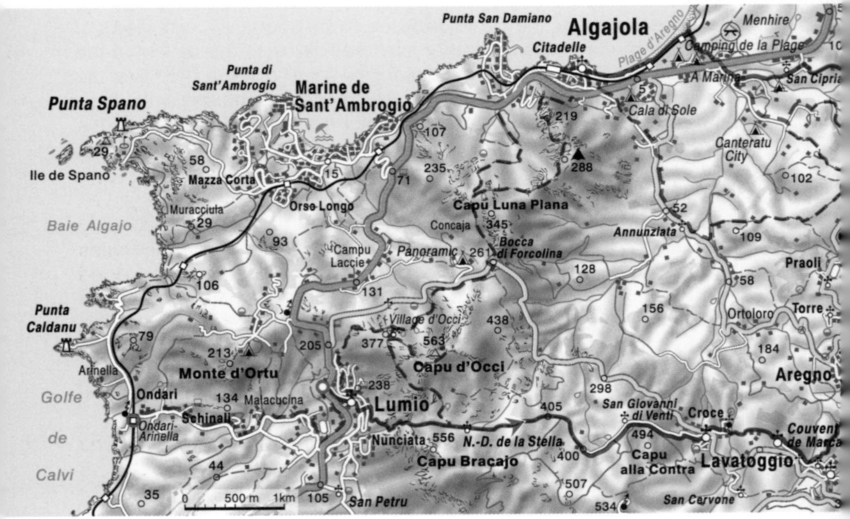

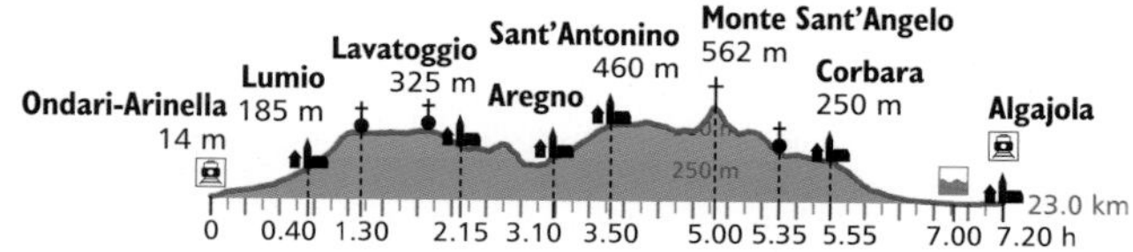

Aregno (1¼ hrs.). – From Corbara Monastery, a detour can be made via the artists' village of Pigna (½ hr.) and from there along a country lane (on the right of the car park at the entrance of the village, then immediately turning off left) to Algajola (1¼ hrs.). – From the foot of Monte Sant'Angelo (1½ hrs.) or from Corbara (1¼ hrs.) descents possible to Île-Rousse. **Maps:** ign 4149 OT, 4249 OT (1:25,000).

Starting at the church in **Lumio**, climb up the stepped trail that passes the memorial and ascends to the upper village street. Turn right and, a good 100m on, pick up the trail that begins to the left (sign »*Chemin de Randonnée*«, yellow waymarked. The lovely trail, sometimes cobblestone, climbs up to a broad col (402m, a good ½ hr.) situated between Capu d'Occi, 563m (left), and Capu Bracajo, 556m (right). From here, enjoy a final view of the Bay of Calvi. 5 mins. after leaving the col, reach the **Chapelle Notre-Dame-de-la-Stella** (just before that, the yellow waymarkings turn away to the left towards Occi). A roadway leads over the alpine pastureland for a good half an hour and then meets up with the little Chapelle San Giovanni di Venti. Then, the narrow road descends down to **Lavatoggio** (¼ hr.), opening marvellous views towards Aregno and Sant'Antonio as well as of Monte Sant'Angelo.
Below the church, you meet up with the main road which you follow for 25m to the left to then turn off sharp right onto the little road leading downhill. After a

few minutes at a narrowing in the road, a broad trail turns off right, bordered by stone walls. Shortly afterwards, at a narrow course for a stream, the trail forks (to the left, a water tap) – turn right here to cross the stream and continue towards Cateri (sign; turning left leads to Aregno). The trail traverses the slope, ascending, and 5 mins. later, crosses over a roadway (do not turn left or right!) and, not quite 10 mins. after that, meet up with the Couvent de Marcasso. Continue walking along the access road (if you don't want to visit Cateri, you can keep going along the walking trail) and walk along the D 71 straight on to **Cateri**. At the road junction above the hotel »U San Dume« (restaurant »Chez Léon«) descend to the left. 30m afterwards a lovely stone-paved trail turns off left where you continue downhill. After a few minutes keep right at the fork (straight on is the trail to Marcasso) – after an ascent of a few metres, the narrow trail descends in steep bends onto a little valley floor and, on the other side of the valley, traverses the slope, heading directly towards Aregno. At the fork, some minutes later, bear diagonally right, heading gently uphill and, at the rocky plateau, 10m on, keep straight on through the small valley notch (well) over to **Aregno**. Now stay on the ascending narrow road or via steps up through the picturesque village to the main square with the church (bar) and straight on along the narrow road uphill, passing to the right of the memorial, to reach the Eglise de la Trinité (12th century) on the main road. To the left of the cemetery wall, continue along a roadway for about 50m and then take the path branching off to the right that climbs up to Sant'Antonino. Shortly before reaching the mountain village, meet up with the road and, bearing left, reach the car park by the church (a good ½ hr.). **Sant'Antonino** is one of the most beautiful villages on the island due to its pretty passageways and its panoramic location.

The delightful Eglise de la Trinité in Aregno – the Romanesque-Pisan church was built from coloured stone.

At the car park, a roadway passes to the left of the church, and after a few minutes reaches a fork: left goes to some burial chapels and then continues via a footpath towards the Corbara Monastery (100m before reaching the monastery, a right fork serves as the approach to Monte Sant'Angelo). However, take the roadway branching off to the right that leads over the ridgeline, heading towards Monte Sant'Angelo. At a trail junction with a gate (a good ½ hr.), leave the roadway behind to the left by passing through the gate. A trail, flanked by stone walls, de-

View from the hiking path of Monte Sant'Angelo and Corbara Monastery.

scends to the Corbara Monastery (later on, our continued trail) but turn right instead, crossing over the pastureland to reach the foot of the Monte Sant'Angelo. Here, follow the distinct and waymarked path that, past a low stone wall close to the ridgeline, leads uphill. After half an hour, reach the highest point of the triple-peaked **Monte Sant'Angelo**, 562m. Now you can enjoy a marvellous 360° panorama: a sweeping view from the coast of Algajola via Île-Rousse as far as the Agriates, on the other side, Monte Grosso.
The descent to the Corbara Monastery follows the same route as the approach. After crossing the pastureland and before the gate, turn right along the trail flanked by low walls. Descend along this trail to reach the Franciscan **Couvent de Corbara**, 298m, founded in 1456 (a good 30 mins.; at the end turn right at the fork). Past the monastery continue to the main road where you turn right (left leads to Pigna) and reach **Corbara** (20 mins.).
Near the A Cantina bar/restaurant (on the right-hand bend just after passing the square on the main road), turn left into a narrow street that leads through two arches, then left down to a roofed well. Here, turn right following the old connecting footpath (with yellow waymarking along the way) downhill and finally turn left along a roadway that leads to the main road between Île-Rousse and Calvi. A good 100m before reaching the main road turn left, past a campsite on the left, along a marked path bordered by little stone walls. Keep straight on and finally along a road towards the main road (a good 10 mins.) which you pass underneath through a tunnel. A lovely meadow path brings you parallel to the stream and along beside the campsite, and finally under the railway line, to the marvellous sandy beach of **Algajola** – go left along the track/road to the station (a good ¼ hr.; you could also abort the walk beforehand at the Aregno Plage railway station).

11 *Monte Tolu, 1332m*

3.20 hrs.

Short walk with marvellous views of the Balagne region

On the route, you can already enjoy a wonderful view of Monte Padru and Monte Grosso. But the panorama from Monte Tolu, embracing the Balagne region and wide stretches of the north-west coast, provides a climax and certainly counts as one of the island's most beautiful views.

Location: Speloncato, 553m, idyllic picture-book village in a panoramic location above the Balagne region.
Starting point: Bocca di a Battaglia, 1099m, mountain pass on the D 63 between Speloncato and Olmi-Cappella, lovely view of the Balagne region.
Height difference: a good 350m.
Grade: mostly an easy walk with a short scramble at the summit that requires a little head-for-heights.
Refreshment and accommodation: during tourist season, a bar/restaurant on the Bocca di a Battaglia. Restaurants/hotels in Speloncato.
Alternative: from Monte Tolu you can climb in 1 hr. onto San Parteo, 1680m – the next prominent peak continuing along the ridge (cairns).
Map: ign 4249 OT (1:25,000).

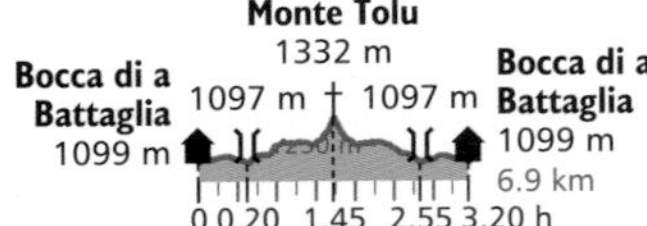

A country lane starts off from the crest of the pass **Bocca di a Battaglia** (gate, orange waymarkers) and turns in a south-westerly direction towards the radio masts above the

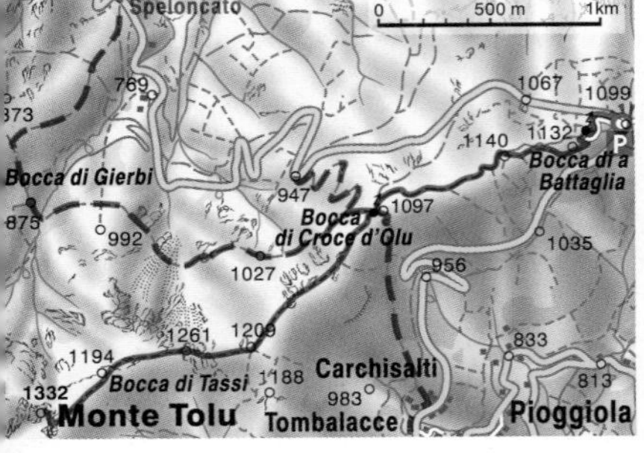

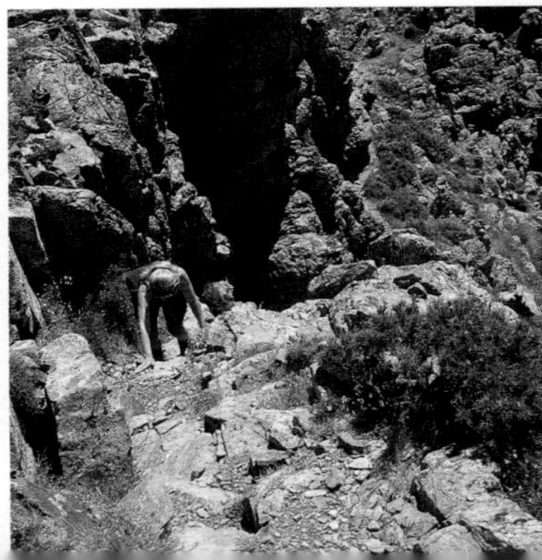

On the way to Monte Tolu (centre, San Parteo on the left).

road. The pleasant ridge walk leads to **Bocca di Croce d'Olu**, 1097m (20 mins.) where you meet an intersecting trail near a radio mast (the trail to the left descends to Pioggola, 20 mins.). Not quite 10 minutes from the saddle, the ridgeline trail reaches a gate (access prohibited). Now continue plodding along whilst traversing the slope and following a fence. About 25 minutes later, the path crosses over the ridge and, next to a gate, merges back again with the ridgeline trail. The trail now keeps steadily to the left-hand side of the ridge, passing beneath a little rocky peak, then crossing pleasantly over to a saddle in front of the craggy summit region of the Monte Tolu. The trail ascends through the slope to the saddle on the other side of the ridge – 20m before this point, the orange-marked summit route forks to the right: climb up through a gully (easy scramble, I) to a faintly defined gap. After a short traverse you reach the **summit**.

View of San Parteo from the summit – left, Monte Padru, right, at the edge, Monte Grosso.

12 Capu di a Veta, 703m

4.30 hrs.

A walk onto Calvi's local mountain

Starting this climb early in the morning, you can enjoy a marvellous view embracing the Gulf of Calvi and also have enough time to pass a few idle hours on the sandy beach at Calvi's lovely bay.

Starting point: holiday village »Zum störrischen Esel« in Calvi on the main road from Calvi to Île-Rousse, 1.5km from the centre (20 mins. on foot).
Height difference: 700m.
Grade: quite laborious, especially in the heat, but easy apart from short stretches of scrambling.
Refreshment/accommodation: in Calvi.
Map: ign 4149 OT (1:25,000).

In front of the **holiday village »Zum störrischen Esel«** on the main road between Calvi and Île-Rousse, a road branches off in a southerly direction (sign »Pietramaggiore«) which you follow straight ahead to reach **Hotel Corsica** (a good ¼ hr.). Here, bear to the right until the street reaches a fork after 5 mins. at a *gate*. Now you have to make a decision: to the left is the regular route to Capu di a Veta; to the right, awaits an ascent trail of about the same length (100m along the road until a red-marked

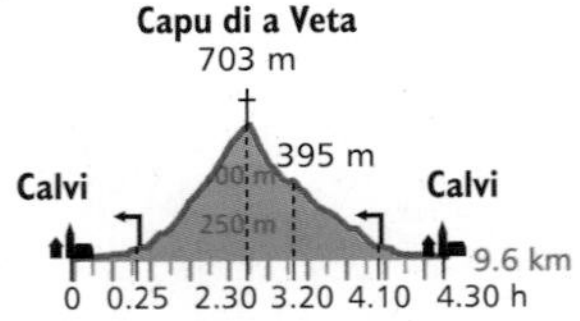

Backwards view of the summit from the boulder field along the descent trail.

trail turns left to cross through the rock rose undergrowth). We choose the regular route, thus turning left along the road until, not quite 5 mins. later, a red-marked path forks left, leading over squat boulders (do not follow the roadway). This path is somewhat overgrown and, some minutes later, forks in front of a fence – turn right to continue along the fence in a steady traverse, crossing over to a large level area of bare rock. Continue over this to reach the neighbouring mountain ridge, then through *macchia* and over bare rock to ascend some more. After a total of 2¼ hours (at the end, bearing somewhat to the right), reach the ridgeline. Bear right here and climb up towards the north-west to reach the nearby summit of the **Capu di a Veta** (cross) – a marvellous stretch, passing tafoni rock formations.

The descent begins with some simple scrambling: at the cross, marking the summit, a red-marked, stony path descends. After the initial steep downwards climb through a gully, this keeps mostly snug to the ridge and traverses a field of boulders along with gigantic slabs of bare rock (a **high tension power pylon** simplifies orientation). At the power pylon, reach a roadway to follow this steeply downwards (a short-cut can be made along a waymarked path). About 20 mins. later, another roadway forks sharply away to the right (keeping straight ahead, you could continue on to the Chapelle Notre-Dame-de-la-Serra, 243m, and from there, descend directly to Calvi). Down below, at the first houses, the roadway meets up with a road (bear right at the end). Turn right, cross over to a gate (see approach) and, passing the hotel »Corsica«, return to the **holiday village**.

13 Revellata peninsula

2.35 hrs.

Panoramic walk with a constant view of the deep blue sea

The circular walk to the lighthouse on the Revellata peninsula, visible from quite a distance away, is a panoramic route par excellence – the charming harbour town of Calvi with its fortress is, naturally, an eye-catcher. On top of that, we can enjoy a marvellous view taking in the coastal cliffs and the deep blue sea as well as the 2000-metre peaks along the main ridge.

Starting point: the car park at the turn-off of the Revellata track, 3.5km from Calvi's village centre, on the coast road D 818, Calvi – Galéria.

Height difference: 250m.
Grade: an easy but, when it's hot, a somewhat strenuous walk along a track and coastal path.
Refreshment / accommodation: bar/restaurant Mar a Beach on the Plage de l'Alga. Hotels and campsites in Calvi.
Map: ign 4149 OT (1:25,000).

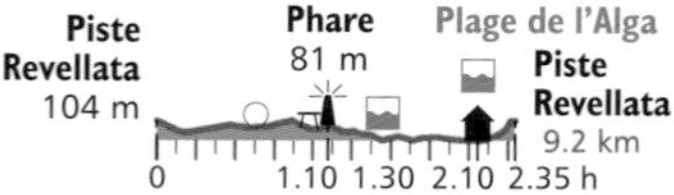

Piste Revellata 104 m — Phare 81 m — Plage de l'Alga — Piste Revellata 9.2 km
0 — 1.10 — 1.30 — 2.10 — 2.35 h

During the walk, we pass some inviting bathing coves – in the background, Calvi.

Take the **track**, sometimes concrete-paved, to descend whilst enjoying a marvellous view of the peninsula and the lighthouse. 10 mins. later, a roadway forks off to the right towards a sandy cove surrounded by palm trees (our return route) – but keep to the track which now heads out towards the peninsula in an up-and-down course. Subsequently, keep steadily along the straight main track. 25 mins. later, pass a cistern (to the right, a roadway descends to Anse de l'Oscelluccia, in case you want to shorten the walk). 15 mins. later, at a fork in the track, bear right (cul-de-sac). Below the lighthouse, a ramp forks off sharp to the left to descend to the **Phare de la Revellata**, from where you can enjoy a spectacular view over the Golfe de la Revellata all the way to Calvi and also of Corsica's main ridge with Monte Cinto and Paglia Orba; towards the north-west, a view of Cap Corse.
Turn back for 5 mins. to reach the point where a path forks off (sign, at the next intersecting trail, turn right; yellow slash waymarkers). Down below, you can spot a small harbour with the installation for the oceanographic research station STARESO. The trail continues above the coast like a walk over a panoramic viewing platform. 15 mins. on, it passes the **Anse de l'Oscelluccia**. Just afterwards, it is worthwhile to take a path for an excursion to the promontory with the same name. Pass some more idyllic, little bathing coves. Then the trail becomes a roadway to the **Plage de l'Alga** with the Mar a Beach bar/restaurant. Here, keep following the roadway inland. After 100m, this becomes a trail and meets up with the track already met during the approach. Take the track, or the path running next to it, to return to the **car park**.

14 Bocca di Bonassa, 1153m

Circular route through the deciduous and coniferous forests of Bonifatu along varied footpaths

This route presents a real alternative to the often over-crowded path leading to the Carrozzu mountain hut (→Walk 16). In addition, the route offers a number of lovely viewpoints from which you can see the main ridge around Capu Ladroncellu as well as the Gulf of Calvi.

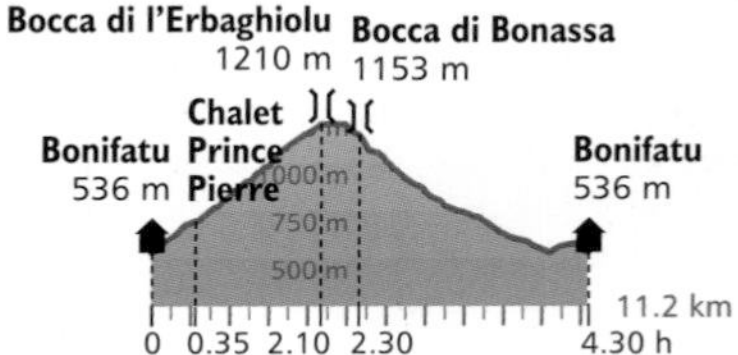

Starting point: Auberge de la Forêt de Bonifatu, 536m, 21km south of Calvi (pay and display car park).
Height difference: 650m.
Grade: mostly an easy circuit along well-marked footpaths.
Refreshment and accommodation: in the Auberge de la Fôret de Bonifatu.

Alternative: descent from Bocca di Bonassa along the *Mare e Monti* into the Fango valley. An excursion starting at Bocca di l'Erbaghiolu to Capu Formiculaghiu as well as Capu a u Ceppu is only recommended for experienced mountain walkers (easy scrambling).
Map: ign 4149 OT (1:25,000).

Starting at the **Auberge**, return along the road for about 50m until reaching the bridge where, just beforehand, you turn left onto the *Mare e Monti* long-distance path with orange waymarkers. At first, the path is somewhat steep and stony, leading along the left bank of the Nocaghia stream (do not go left after a few minutes in the direction of Candia) and finally crossing over the

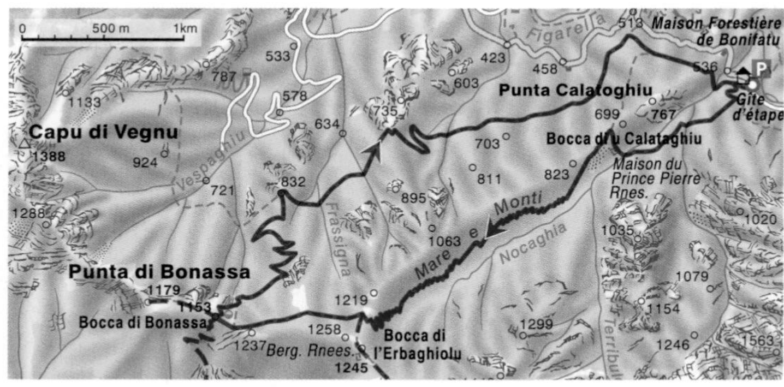

stream after just under half an hour. Soon afterwards you come past the Chalet Prince Pierre (ruin). A few minutes after that ignore a path branching off to the right (Boucle de Calatoghiu). 50m on, enjoy a marvellous view to the right, taking in the Figarella valley and on to Clavi. The lovely mixed forest begins to thin out and here and there you are afforded a view of the jaunty Punta Pittinaghia as the path narrows. Afterwards, it ascends round bends through the pine forest to the ill-defined **Bocca di l'Erbaghiolu**, 1210m, with a view of the Gulf of Calvi in the distance. Now the *Mare e Monti* crosses over to the **Bocca di Bonassa** (20 mins., nice spots to take a break, especially past the crest of the pass near the little hut). At the top of the pass, a red-marked hiking path forks to the right leading downhill through marvellous pine forests, in places covered in moss, and *macchia*. Just before the road (a good 1½ hrs.) a path turns off right to Bonifatu (sign). It ascends a short way to a ridge and a few minutes later joins with the Calatoghiu circular path (left downhill). Shortly after crossing over the Nocaghia stream it meets your ascent path which brings you back left to the nearby **Auberge**.

From the Bocca di Bonassa there's a detour to the Punta di Bonassa.

15 Refuge d'Ortu di u Piobbu, 1588m

Long, but pleasant climb to the mountain hut at the foot of Capu a u Dente

The Refuge d'Ortu di u Piobbu, easily accessible, is one of Northern Corsica's most beautiful mountain hut excursions. It offers walkers numerous possibilities for extending the walk and an ascent of the panoramic Monte Corona is highly recommended.

Starting point: Auberge de la Forêt de Bonifatu, 536m, 21km south of Calvi (pay and display car park).
Height difference: 1170m.
Grade: mostly pleasant route on a well-marked path, strenuous final ascent.
Refreshment and accommodation: Auberge de la Forêt (rooms and restaurant); Ortu mountain hut (bunks, basic facilities).
Alternatives: ascent to Monte Corona, 2144m (a good 1¼ hrs. one way, great view): behind the Ortu mountain hut, take the yellow-marked path to ascend to Bocca di Tartagine, 1852m, go right at the fork after ¼ hr., (40 mins., from here, a descent is possible into the Tartagine valley), then turn right for an easy ridge walk to the summit (40 mins.). Circular walk (2–3 days): Ortu mountain hut – Refuge de Carrozzu (*GR 20*, 6½ hrs., sometimes very steep) and then via →Walk 16, return to the Auberge de la Forêt de Bonifatu.
Map: ign 4250 OT (1:25,000).

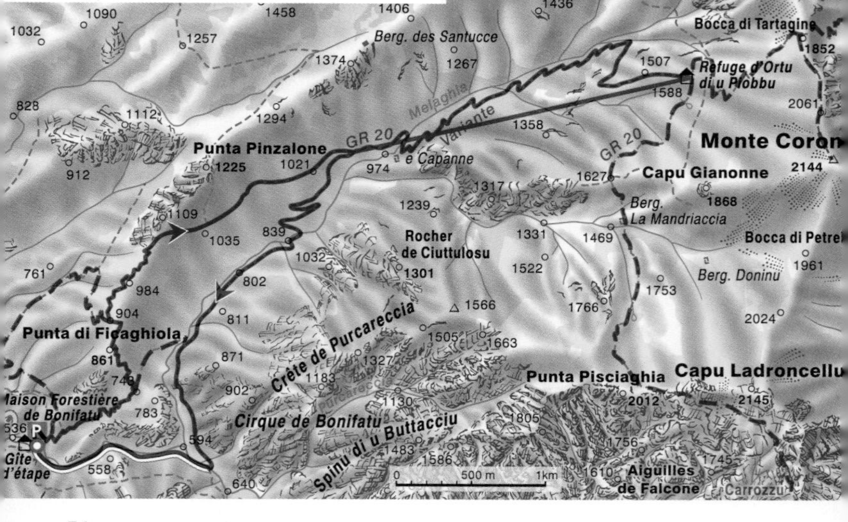

Crossing Figarella stream on a suspension bridge just after the car park.

After the **Auberge** turn left onto the gravel road waymarked in blue/red down to the lower end of the terraced car park. A hiking path starts here (signpost »Boucle des Finocchi«) that crosses the Figarella stream after 5 minutes on a suspension bridge. A minute later keep right at the fork (blue/red). The path goes uphill through a shady forest and after 45 minutes reaches a flat **col**, 743m. Go left here at the fork in the direction of Ortu di u Piobbu (yellow/red; if you follow signs to the right to Boucle de Ficaghiola you can return to Bonifato; total time for the round walk 1½ hrs.). The path continues gently up the ridge in zigzags – with a marvellous view of the Cirque de Bonifato – and forks ½ hr. later (if you go left following signs to Boucle des Finocchi you can return to Bonifato; total time for the round walk, 3 hrs.). Keep following the yellow waymarkers on the right uphill. After a good quarter of an hour your path leaves the panoramic ridge with its bizarre

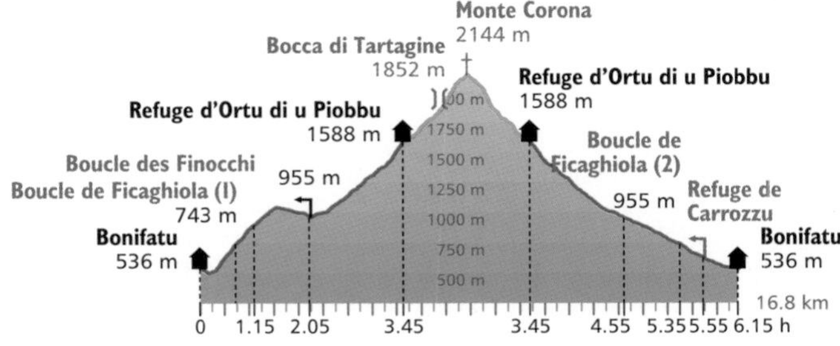

The Refuge d'Ortu di u Piobbu is situated in a panoramic location. The hut burned to the ground in May 2019 but a rebuild is planned; at the moment, the walker must make do with a temporary refuge.

rock formations and bends right towards the hillside to then lead into the **Melaghia valley**, keeping more or less on the level. After ½ hr. the path joins a broad path which you follow to the left uphill (your later return path on the right). Shortly afterwards the yellow waymarkers take you to the left along a narrower path but you can also continue along the broad path. Both paths meet up again after 10 mins., 50m before crossing the Melaghia stream.

After reaching the other bank turn left onto the yellow-marked path to the Refuge d'Ortu di u Piobbu (signpost). The path leads along the right-hand side of the valley, climbing through a lovely pine forest with towering trees. An hour later, just before reaching the valley head at the foot of the pinnacles of Capu a u Dente, the path breaks out of the pine forest, bearing to the right, to cross over to a treeless mountain ridge covered in juniper and alder scrub. Along this ridge, the path ascends quite steeply in a fairly straight line. Another half an hour's climb it leads to the **Refuge d'Ortu di u Piobbu**, beautifully-situated in a high valley. The area surrounding the mountain hut is a perfect place for a lengthy break. On the path towards the Carrozzu hut there's a spring (after 200m).

The descent at first follows the ascent path, but after crossing the Melaghia stream keep on the broad hiking path which leads down through the valley. This path, like a track, is concreted in places and changes twice over onto the other side of the valley. After an hour it crosses the Figarella stream at a ford (after heavy rainfall this can be a problem, in which case it's best to turn back and return down your ascent path; junction with the hiking path from the Carrozzu hut). The **Auberge** is reached a good quarter of an hour later.

Refuge de Carrozzu, 1270m, and Spasimata bridge

16

Popular hike to a mountain hut with an optional ascent of Muvrella

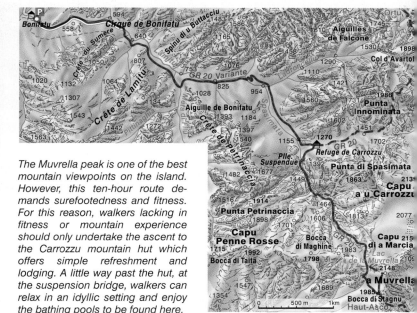

The Muvrella peak is one of the best mountain viewpoints on the island. However, this ten-hour route demands surefootedness and fitness. For this reason, walkers lacking in fitness or mountain experience should only undertake the ascent to the Carrozzu mountain hut which offers simple refreshment and lodging. A little way past the hut, at the suspension bridge, walkers can relax in an idyllic setting and enjoy the bathing pools to be found here.

Starting point: Auberge de la Forêt de Bonifatu, 536m, 21km south of Calvi (pay and display car park).
Height difference: 750m to the Carrozzu mountain hut, a good 1800m to Muvrella.
Grade: well-marked paths, an easy hike to Carrozzu hut; the extended route to Muvrella is difficult – stamina and surefootedness are required (sections of scrambling, I; best to make an overnight stay at the Carrozzu hut). Beware: by heavy rainfall, the stream fording can be tricky, so only by stable weather!
Refreshment and accommodation: at the Auberge de la Forêt (rooms/restaurant; beds in the staffed Carrozzu mountain hut (drinks, cakes, simple food).
Maps: ign 4149 OT, 4250 OT (1:25,000).

Starting at the **Auberge**, follow the forestry path leading along the right bank of the Figarella stream right to the end (20 mins., lovely bathing pools below the path). It joins here with a variant of the *GR 20*. The path to the left crosses

The suspension bridge across Spasimata stream – a chain-secured stretch of the route.

the stream and continues on to Calenzana (→Walk 15) – however, turn to the right following the yellow-marked path (sign). The path ascends more steeply after the second stream crossing (suspension bridge) through the pine wood. After a total of 2¼ hours reach the **Refuge de Carrozzu**.

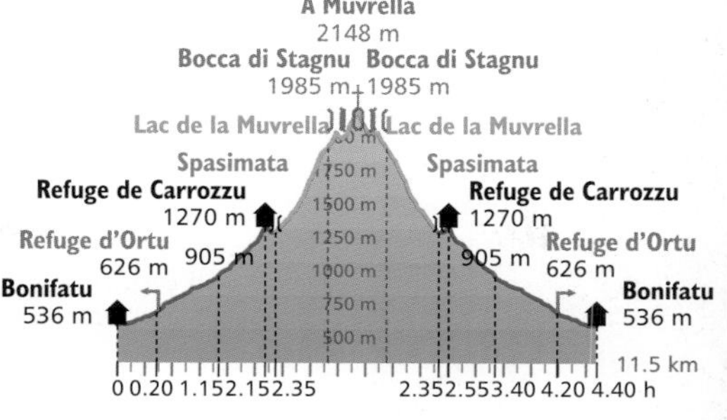

To the suspension bridge spanning the Spasimata stream: go a short way at first back along the ascent path as far as the signposted junction. Here, take the footpath towards Asco with the white/red waymarkers branching off to the left which brings you, in places protected by chains while crossing plates of rock, to the **suspension bridge**. Crossing the suspension bridge is somewhat of a challenge and can be bypassed upstream when the waters are shallow.

To the Muvrella (only for fit mountain walkers with stamina): the *GR 20* ascends steeply at first and soon leads across some slightly exposed and sloping rock slabs (I), usually following the crest of a rocky ledge, until reaching the tiny **Lac de la Muvrella**. The *GR 20* now leads to a gap between two pinnacles resembling rabbit ears (Bocca Muvrella, 1980m) and then onwards to the **Bocca di Stagnu**, 1985m (from here, in 1 hr. to Haut-Asco). A path marked with cairns and faint turquoise waymarkers turns off left and scrambles over rock (I) to reach **Muvrella**, 2148m (→Walk 83, 5½ hrs. from Bonifatu). The summit can also be reached by ascending to the left from the path between Lake Muvrella and »Rabbit-ear Gap« (waymarked, ½ hr. shorter).

View from the Muvrella direct ascent to the Muvrella lake; in the background, Calvi.

17

Fango valley: Pont de Tuarelli – Ponte Vecchiu

Pleasant river walk – along the banks or through the river bed

The Fango River is widely known for crystal-clear waters and beautiful, spacious rock pools and basins. The river banks are easy to access by a road running parallel on one side and by the trail, »Tra Mare e Monti«, on the other. Especially during the high season, you will search in vain for a »private« pool. Nevertheless, during hot weather, the stream is an excellent option for avid river bed walkers!

Starting point: Pont de Tuarelli, 93m, the bridge next to the D 351 between Galéria and Barghiana, 4.5km from the turn-off on the D 81. You can park your car at the bridge or along the D 351. (parking prohibited June 15 – Sept 15; in this time, better to set off from the Ponte Vecchiu, boasting a large car park).
Height difference: insignificant.
Grade: the trail along the bank is easy and only requires sturdy footwear. The river bed walk, however, demands some physical fitness in both swimming and fording as well as sure-footedness (balance needed for negotiating rocks); water sandals with straps and a slip-proof sole are required; be sure to bring along sun protection!
Refreshment and accommodation: bar/restaurant/pizzeria Ponte Vecchiu, *Gîte*/campsite in Tuarelli.
Tip: a kayak excursion in the Fango delta near Galéria is worthwhile: www.delta-du-fangu.com.
Important notice: the river walk should only be undertaken during stable weather and never after heavy rainfall, despite the fact that you can abort the route any time by returning to the road or the walking trail.
Maps: ign 4149 OT, 4150 OT (1:25,000).

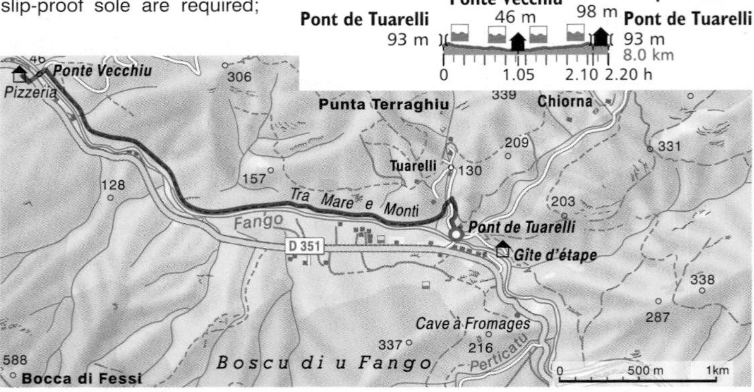

At the **Pont de Tuarelli**, you have to make your decision: if you wish to walk the river bed (swimming and wading), you must descend at the bridge into the long pool surrounded by rock faces, which is also one of the most beautiful rock pools of the entire tour (→photos above/ left). Heading downstream, you must either swim or belly crawl through other pretty pools varying in depth. Mostly, however, expect long stretches of wading, especially in the middle section. Towards the end, just before the Ponte Vecchiu, meet a small cascade which is a bit tricky; it's better to scramble around it. Otherwise, this is an easy bathing route; just be careful not to slip on any of the slippery stones and rocks. (For the river bed walk from the Pont de Tuarelli to the Ponte Vecchiu, you can reckon on 2–3 hours but you can leave off any time by picking up the walking trail.)

If you opt for the traditional walk along the banks of the Fango, follow the road over the bridge and then bear left at the fork. 3 minutes later, the orange-marked trail, *Tra Mare e Monti*, forks as a path to the left (sign »Galéria/Girolata«) and soon leads along the banks of the Fango, constantly passing lovely bathing pools. Perhaps the most beautiful is the rock pool which appears a good half an hour later (→photo, right); after that, the trail leaves the river behind for some minutes. 10 minutes later, reach the **Ponte Vecchiu** and the pizzeria of the same name on the D 351 which runs along the opposite bank of the river.

Returning to the Pont de Tuarelli, an excursion to the **Gîte d'étape L'Alzelli** (bar-restaurant, camping) is worthwhile; continuing upriver, there are even more lovely pools and rock pools.

18 Capu Tondu, 839m

3.45 hrs.

Adventurous hike on Galéria's native mountain

Right from the beginning, the ascent to Capu Tondu is a real pleasure – at least for nature-loving walkers who prefer to walk along unspoilt paths and do not mind a bit of easy scrambling. As a reward for the strenuous climb to the summit you are afforded a superlative 360° view sweeping across the Golfe de Galéria, over the Scandola Peninsula, on to the Gulf of Porto flanked by the pillars of Monte Senino and Capu Rossu, and finally ending at Corsica's main ridge that includes Paglia Orba.

Starting point: the square in front of the church in the village of Galéria, 35m (car park above the church).
Height difference: a good 800m.
Grade: aside from a few easy scrambles, an easy walk.
Refreshment and accommodation: in Galéria – bars, restaurants, a *Gîte d'étape* and campsites.
Maps: ign 4149 OT, 4150 OT (1:25,000).

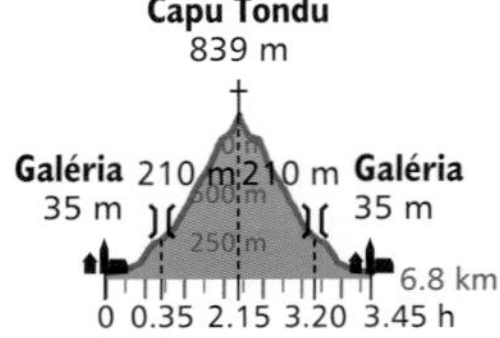

Starting from the church in **Galéria** walk along the street past the post office and the *mairie* (town hall), and then turn right 50m later into the first street which you follow uphill to the left, then to the right again. 5 minutes later (at one of the last houses on the left-hand side) the street becomes a roadway and another roadway forks off, ascending to the left. Shortly afterwards, it swings to the right and then to the left 100m further on. 30m on, turn right onto the distinct, red-marked footpath (cairns). The path ascends fairly easily through a scrub forest. After a quarter of an hour it climbs to a small col (210m; to the right, a small rocky peak with a view of Galéria). Your route now bears to the left and climbs along the almost imperceptible north-west ridge of Capu Tondu.

View of Galéria bay from Capu Tondu.

After a good quarter of an hour you reach the first easy scramble, then the route continues through alternating stretches of scrub wood and rocky scrambling.

A good hour after leaving the col, the red-marked path leads over a longish sloping rock slab. Eventually you can see the summit ahead. Now the path leads for a short time to the right away from the rocky ridge (col) and bearing slightly to the right at first, then to the left beneath an eroded rock face, finally climbs to the highest point of **Capu Tondu**.

The West Coast between Porto and Ajaccio

Golfe de Porto – Golfe de Sagone – Cinarca – Golfe d'Ajaccio

The »Island of Contrasts« presents you with an entire spectrum of scenic highlights on the west coast. The savage and gentle aspects of Corsica lie together here in happy wedlock.

The **Gulf of Porto** represents the savage side; here nature presents its most uncompromising face. The bay, cutting deep into the interior and surrounded by bizarre, shimmering red crags, combines with the hinterland to offer a paradise to adventurous and nature-loving walkers. The nature reserve on *La Scandola* peninsula establishes the northern border to the gulf, as does the grandiose panoramic peak of *Capu Rosso* the southern border. Above all, the *Calanche* region charms you with its rough, surreal craggy landscape between the azure sea and Capu d'Orto. Leaving the coast behind, inland visits are worthwhile to the villages of *Piana*, *Ota* and *Evisa*.

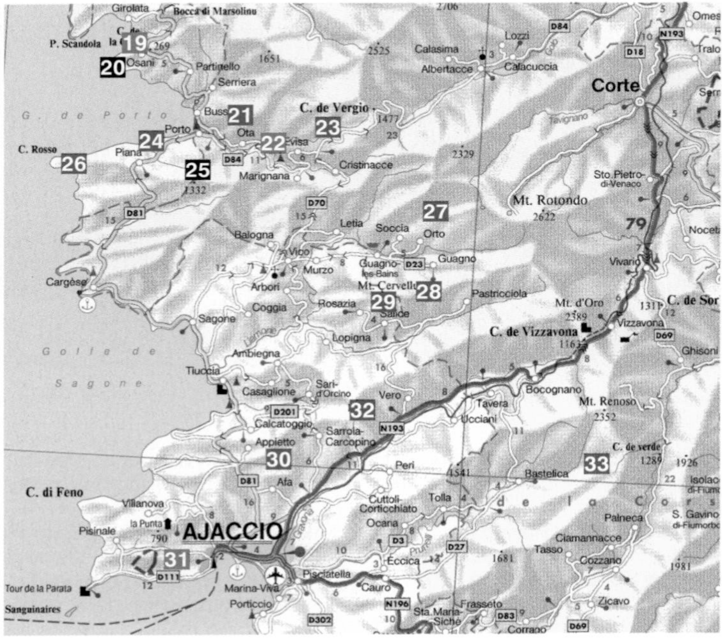

View from the Calanche of the Gulf of Porto and Monte Senino.

The **Gulf of Sagone** beguiles you with vast sandy beaches; in the hinterland between *Vico* and *Guagno*, numerous secluded mountain villages provide starting points for peaceful and pensive walks. Starting at Guagno, a lovely two-day trek can be made: via the *Bergerie de Belle e Buone* to the *Refuge de Manganu*, then return via *Creno lake* and *Orto*.

The gentle side of the region is revealed on the pleasant **Gulf of Ajaccio** with its famous, but unfortunately often over-developed, sandy beaches. The cultural treasures offered by the island's capital, *Ajaccio*, are an interesting prelude for excursions to the tower of *La Parata*, to the *Punta Pozzo di Borgo*, 779m (½ hr. from Château de la Punta), as well as for a walk along the *Sentier des Crêtes* on *Monte Salario*. In the hinterland, many other walking excursions can be undertaken, especially in the areas surrounding the *Gravona valley*, *Bastelica* and *Tolla lake*. At least two peaks with wonderful views must be mentioned here: *Punta di l'Alcudina*, 1313m (3 hrs. starting at Peri) and *Punta d'Isa*, 1630m (1 hr. starting at Col de Scalella).

19 From the Col de la Croix to Girolata

Leisurely coastal walk along the Tra Mare e Monti

Girolata is famous for its unique location on the Gulf of Girolata in the immediate neighbourhood of the nature reserve on Scandola peninsula. The fishing village, a Natural World Heritage Site, is only accessible by sea or on hiking paths – nevertheless there's a lot of hustle and bustle here at midday in particular when the excursion boats from Porto, Calvi and other ports on the western coast unload the tourists for two hours in the beach bars and restaurants. The hiking path from Col de la Croix is also popular – and justly so on account of its scenic delights and leisurely path.

Starting point: Bocca a Croce (Col de la Croix), 269m, on the Galéria – Porto road (22km north of Porto), above the village of Osani.
Height difference: 600m.
Grade: easy walk on a good path. Since there is no shade on the second half of the walk, an early start is recommended (best to avoid when hot). The alternative return requires sure-footedness and a lack of vertigo.
Refreshment: bar-restaurants in Girolata, snack bar at the Bocca a Croce.
Map: ign 4150 OT (1:25,000).

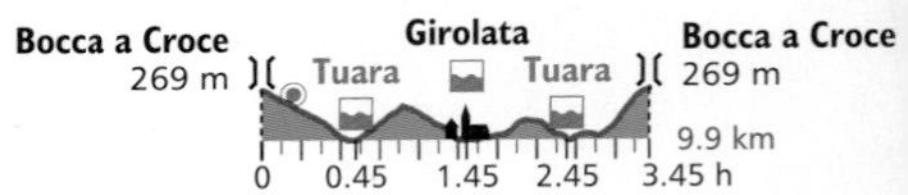

From the top of the **Bocca a Croce** pass, walk in a northerly direction along the signposted hiking path with orange waymarkers down to Girolata, at first parallel to the road to Galéria. Two minutes later, ignore a trail forking off to the left (this descends to the coastal trail Vignola – Plage de Tuara, a very pretty alternative to our route and only slightly longer). The lovely gentle path is frequently shaded by the *macchia*, now and then with views of the splendid Gulf of Girolata which is bounded on the north side by the

A breathtaking view of Girolata and the Scandola peninsula.

reddish shimmering Scandola peninsula and on the south side by Monte Senino. After a quarter of an hour you pass by the Fontaine de Spana and a half an hour later, reach the **Plage de Tuara**. There are usually boats anchored at the pretty sandy beach. On the other side of the beach you will find a broad trail from which a hiking path branches off 50m further on the left. It climbs steadily uphill with a beautiful view back along the beach and is exposed to full sun. After 20 minutes keep straight on at the crossroads and just under 10 minutes later arrive at a hill, 180m, with a spectacular view of Girolata (shady resting place, an orange-marked trail forks off to the right). The path now runs more or less on the level, then gently descending across the hillside. After 25 minutes you come past a tiny cemetery and some minutes later **Girolata** is reached – there are a number of inviting bars and restaurants to be found beyond the shingle beach.

Return the same way. Sure-footed walkers with a good head for heights, however, should take the more attractive coastal path; the narrow path turns off from the beach to the right after a 10m ascent, (sign »*Chemin du Facteur*«) and runs gently up and down above the coast (after a few minutes ignore the descent to the right to the tiny beach). The path soon steepens up as you head for a ridge (about 80m, lovely view of Girolata), across which the path still ascends for a short way to then turn right again towards the hillside. The sometimes airy, but wonderful traverse across the steep hillside above the coast takes about 10 minutes, then the terrain becomes less precipitous again. After 40 minutes a small strip of sand is passed and 5 minutes after that you find yourself at the **Plage de Tuara** from where you follow the now recognisable path back to the **Bocca a Croce**.

20 Punta Castellacciu, 585m, and Monte Senino, 618m

Splendid walk along the northern »pillar« of the Gulf of Porto

Despite its lack of height, Monte Senino is one of the most adventurous and beautiful of the Corsican peaks, and without a doubt, one of the most photographed. Along with Punta Castellacciu, it creates the pillars between the Gulf of Porto and the Gulf of Girolata while affording a unique view of both bays and the central ridge (see photo).

Starting point: Bocca a Croce (Col de la Croix), 269m, on the Galéria – Porto road (22km north of Porto) above the village of Osani.
Height difference: 350m (Monte Senino an additional 300m).
Grade: extremely steep footpath (with some easy sections of scrambling) that requires a certain amount of route finding.
Refreshment: *buvette* (snack bar) at Bocca a Croce.
Alternative: continued route to the summit of Monte Senino (1 hr. one way; some stretches of easy scrambling): to the right

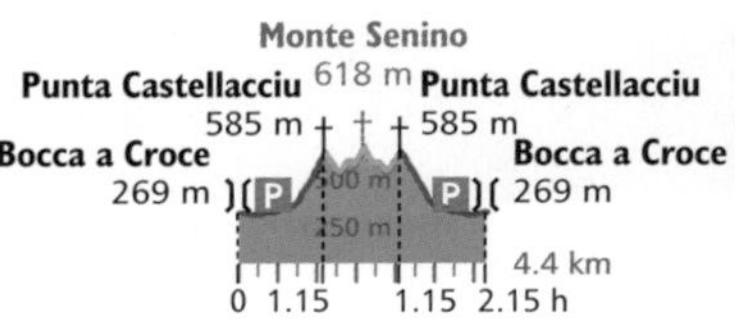

(north-west), a distinct path marked with cairns continues beneath the crags of Punta Castellacciu. The path follows the ridge, more or less, towards Monte Senino, and after a few minutes, drops steeply diagonally left only to soon traverse the slope to the right and return to the ridge-

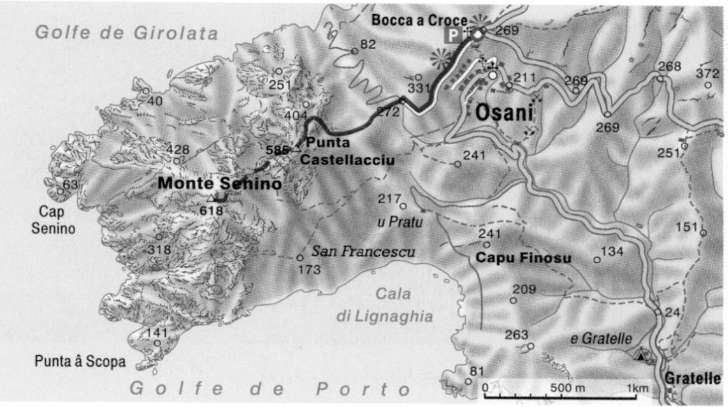

line. Shortly after, reach a saddle in front of a pillar-shaped crag. Do not ascend directly to this crag but instead, pass to the left along its foot and immediately ascend along a steep, narrow gully (chimney; climbing Grade I). Afterwards, climb over a saddle to the right side of the ridge to continue on to the next saddle in front of a mighty rock face. Here, descend a short way to the left and then go right along the foot of the rock face to reach the next steep gully. Ascend along this then bear somewhat to the left, through the crag-dotted slope, along the left-hand side of the ridge all the way to the peak.

Map: ign 4150 OT (1:25,000).

The summit of Monte Senino as seen from Punta Castellacciu.

From the top of the **Bocca a Croce** pass, a track forks off in a westerly direction and after 800m (10 mins.) crosses a mountain col (272m, parking places). Leave the track here (which descends toward the boat mooring Vignola) to follow a distinct path turning off in a westerly direction. The path is rather precipitous in places and leads on the right of the ridge through scrub wood finally arriving at the foot of Punta Castellacciu (10 mins.). Here, bear right continuing your ascent along the path. Reaching a fork in the path after 3 minutes, take the right-hand path which now ascends very steeply and with some very precipitous sections in places – fortunately, trees and rocks usually provide good handholds for the exposed climb. After about 10 minutes – you have now reached the north flank of Punta Castellacciu – a short traverse leads you over to the north ridge. The ridge approach continues uphill very steeply, opening up marvellous views of the Scandola peninsula and towards Girolata. After a quarter of an hour's climb, you reach the foot of a high rock face where you keep to the left and continue the ascent through a wide gully flanked by boulders. You gradually come back to the east side of the summit where a short traverse to the left follows after 10 minutes (make a note of this spot for your return). The final ascent along the eastern ridge is not quite so steep as it leads past gigantic crevices in the rocks to your left, and at last you reach the highest point of **Punta Castellacciu**, 585m (a good 10 mins.).

7.30 hrs.

Capu San Petru, 914m 21

Along the Mare e Monti to one of the most beautiful viewpoints above the Gulf of Porto

Capu San Petru rises directly above Porto and presents walkers with a marvellous panoramic view sweeping over the entire Gulf of Porto – from Capu Rosso to Monte Senino.

Starting point: village centre of Ota, 340m.
Height difference: a good 1100m.
Grade: long, strenuous round walk.
Refreshment: bars/restaurants in Ota.
Alternatives: descent possible from Capu San Petru to Porto (2 hrs.), or from Bocca San Petru to Serriera (2¾ hrs.).

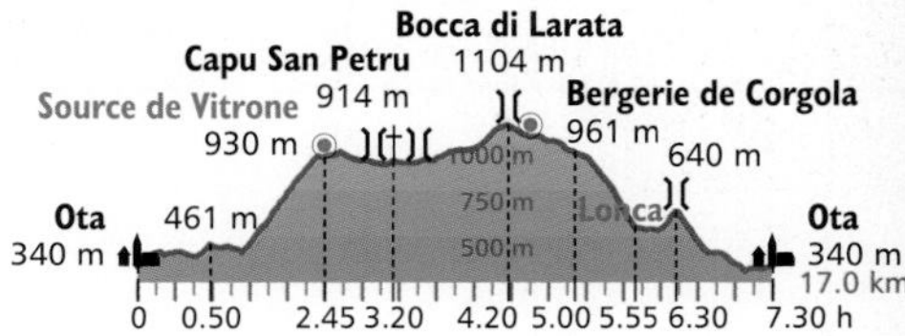

Tip: if you return back down the ascent path your walking time is reduced to 6 hrs.
Map: ign 4150 OT (1:25,000).

At the crossroads in the centre of **Ota** turn onto the ascending village road (signpost »*Mare e Monti*«), then at the first sharp right-hand bend turn off left onto the orange-marked path, climbing up steps and leaving the last houses

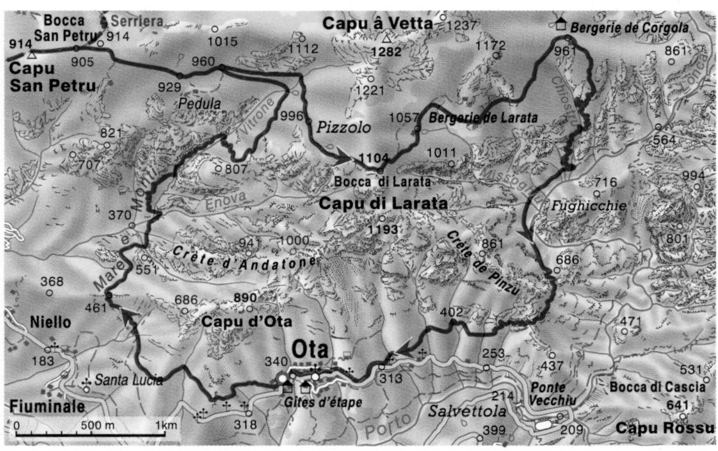

View from Capu San Petru of Porto beach, the Calanche and Capu Rosso.

of the village behind you. Now, the route crosses over the hillside high above the road which leads to Porto. During the pleasant high walk you can enjoy a wonderful view of Capu d'Orto and, a good half hour later, an equally beautiful view of Porto. After 50 minutes in total (from Ota) – at the end, a steady ascent – you reach a mountain ridge with a pretty place to picnic in the shade (461m). Now the path descends gently (do not follow an ascending path up to the right) and, shortly afterwards, ascends to a craggy plateau with a viewpoint. 10 minutes after leaving the plateau, change over to the left-hand side of the valley. The absolutely lovely path now ascends through a small pine forest until reaching a mighty, bizarrely-eroded rock face and then soon crosses again over the **Vitrone valley**, immediately returning, however, to the left-hand side of the valley. 25 minutes later, cross over once more to the other side of the valley, ascending to a mountain ridge (20 mins.) which provides a superlative view stretching from the Gulf of Porto to Capu Rosso. The ascent continues through lovely pine forest until the path swings again to the left towards the valley and then crosses over the valley (Vitrone Spring, 20 mins.) in a traverse that leads over to a chestnut wood (sign, 960m; just under 10 mins.). At this point, a footpath forks off sharply to the right towards the Bergerie de Larata (your return path). The route continues

Descent into the wild and idyllic Lonca valley.

straight ahead, descending slightly, and reaches a fork at the **Bocca San Petru**, 905m, after another 15 minutes. Here, you leave the *Mare e Monte* route, which descends to the right towards Serriera, and turn to the left along the distinct trail over the ridge to the nearby summit of **Capu San Petru** (10 mins.). The most beautiful viewpoints are to be found on the left-hand side of the ridge from where you can enjoy views of the entire Gulf of Porto.

Now return to the turn-off to the Bergerie de Larata (25 mins). If this circular route is too long for you, turn back along your ascent path to return to Ota (2¼ hrs.), but otherwise go straight on (left) onto the path marked with blue dots. It runs leisurely, mostly up a gentle incline across the hillside, and after a good half an hour reaches the **Bocca di Larata**, 1104m, where the view opens out of Capu d'Orto, Porto and Capu Rosso (possible ascent route on the right to the Capu di Larata, 1193m, ¼ hr.). The waymarked hiking path now descends through chestnut forests to the **Bergerie de Larata**, 1057m (10 mins.), passes a spring 5 minutes later (at the fork afterwards, turn right to keep on the blue-marked path) and after another 5 minutes a rocky plateau with a lovely view towards Evisa as well as of Paglia Orba and Capu Tafunatu. 20 minutes later you arrive at the **Bergerie de Corgola**, 961m, situated in a chestnut wood, where there's a fork in the path – follow the yellow/blue waymarkers downhill to the right, past a stone house. Next you walk through a pine forest and then the path descends delightfully between rocks, but with increasing steepness, into the **Lonca valley**. About an hour from Corgola, just above the Lonca stream, you meet a now yellow/orange-marked, intersecting path which you follow to the right. It runs in a gentle up-and-down above the stream and now and then you can catch a glimpse of marvellous pools and waterfalls. After 20 minutes the last laborious incline begins – a fabulous stretch of the path: past a viewing platform (lovely view of the wild rocky basin of the Lonca Gorge) and through an impressive cirque with boulders the path now ascends to a **notch**, about 640m (¼ hr.). Just as beautiful is the zigzag descent on the other side with a view of the Spelunca Gorge. The path levels out somewhat later on and after 50 minutes joins the road to **Ota** which brings you to the right in 10 minutes back into the centre of the village.

TOP 22

Spelunca Gorge

2.30 hrs.

A popular hike with lovely swimming places in the Porto river

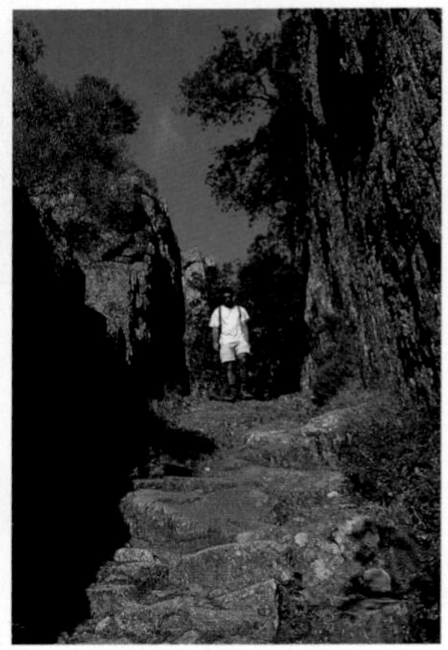

Since the Spelunca Gorge is one of the most popular tourist attractions on the island it is frequently visited by busloads of tourists. Most of the visitors, however, walk only a short distance into the gorge from the bridge on the road between Ota and Evisa – or content themselves with a cool dip in the pools near the road bridge or the Genoese bridge. Unfortunately, there is no bus service between Ota and Evisa so you will either need to arrange a second car at Ota, take a taxi or hitchhike back. If all else fails, you can, of course, retrace your steps and walk back to Evisa (2½–3 hrs).

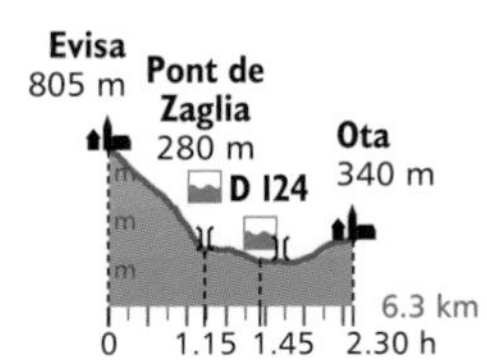

Starting point: Evisa, 829m. The path begins at the cemetery near the exit from the village towards Porto (signpost). There is no bus service to Porto/Ota.
Destination: Ota, 340m, alternatively at the bridge spanning the Porto on the D 124 road from Ota to Evisa, 210m. There is no bus service to Evisa (only to Porto); you have to have a second car, take a taxi (Evisa taxi: tel. 0614154627) or hitch-hike.
Height difference: a good 600m in descent and 140m in ascent.
Grade: easy valley walk on well-marked path.
Refreshment and accommodation: restaurants/hotels in Evisa and Ota, *Gîte d'étape* in Ota, campsites in Evisa and Porto.
Map: ign 4150 OT (1:25,000).

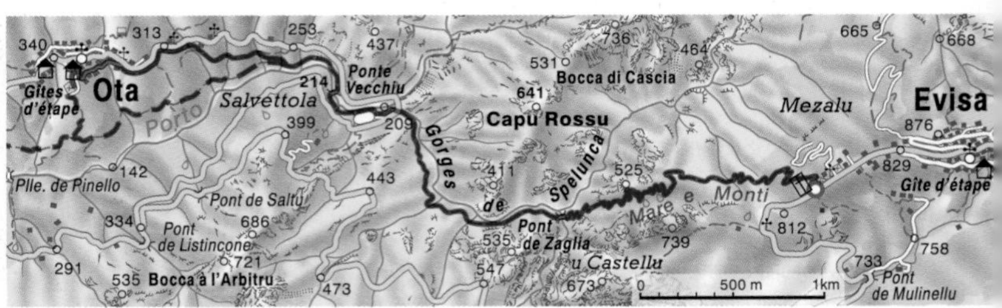

Beautiful bathing pools await you at the Pont de Zaglia.

The orange-marked path begins at the **cemetery** on the main road (signpost); this is a section of the *Mare e Monti* long-distance hiking path. The walk immediately enters a lovely, shady scrub wood that allows only fleeting views into the gorge. After a good half an hour, the mule path, sometimes flanked by little stone walls, becomes steeper. Now some sections of the path are stepped for easier going. As you descend to the valley floor, the sound of a rushing stream grows louder. The first bathing pools await you at the arched Genoese bridge **Pont de Zaglia** – a pleasant place to take a dip and enjoy a break (1¼ hrs.). Cross over the bridge and walk through the **Spelunca Gorge**. Rock faces tower above on both sides of the path. Enclosed by *macchia* vegetation, the path finally leaves the banks of the stream behind and does not return to the stream until almost reaching the **road bridge** (a good ½ hr. after leaving the Pont de Zaglia). Lovely spots for a swim can be found under the bridge – just as lovely is the pool under the old Genoese bridge **Ponte Vecchiu** only another ten-minute walk away (follow the street for 50m then pass the sports ground). The orange-marked path crosses over the stream by the Ponte Vecchiu, leads for a short way along the right-hand bank and then ascends to **Ota** (40 mins. from the road bridge).

23 Col de Cuccavera, 1475m

4.15 hrs.

Peaceful and panoramic high route above the Aitone valley

The Aitone forest is one of the most beautiful pine forests on the island. The route leads mostly through the partial shade provided by towering laricio and black pine trees, making it a good choice for a hot summer day.

Location: Evisa, 829m.
Starting point: from the crossroads above Evisa drive 4.7km along the D 84 towards the Col de Vergio as far as the left-hand turning of the *Piste du Salto* (barrier, signpost »*Sentier de la Sittelle*«, 1160m), just between the *Village de vacances d'Aitone* and the Catagnone forestry house. Car park on the left.
Height difference: about 550m.
Grade: easy, although rather laborious mountain walk along a forestry road and footpath. Ascent to Capu â Scalella is cross-country and requires sure-footedness.
Refreshment and accommodation: in Evisa restaurants, hotels and campsite.
Alternatives: 1) begin the walk at the Piscines d'Aitone (an additional 1 hr. one way): about 1.5km past the crossroads above Evisa, a track forks away to the left from the D 84 (P 74, *Mare a Mare*). 10 mins. later, the trail (orange) descends to the left. 20m further on, it veers again to the right towards the slope (straight ahead,

via the steps, reach a natural swimming hole). Just afterwards, the trail crosses over the suspension bridge spanning the Aitone stream and then continues for 1¼ hrs. (at the outset and the end, a steeper ascent) to the *Piste du Salto* next to the Pont de Casterica. 2) A descent is possible from Col de Cuccavera via the Refuge de Puscaghia into the Fango valley.
Map: ign 4150 OT (1:25,000).

At first, descend the forestry road (straight on after 100m) to reach the Aitone stream, cross over via the **Pompeani bridge**, 1130m (¼ hr.), then continue straight ahead, climbing the steep gravel road. Shortly afterwards, cross over another bridge – **Pont de Casterica**. The alpine wood is made up of mighty *laricio* pines interspersed with gigantic boulders. After a good hour, you reach the mountain hut at **Bocca a u Saltu**, 1391m. It's well worthwhile making a detour to a neighbouring peak of the **Capu â Scalella**, 1460m, ½ hr.: the unmarked footpath (some scrambling, I) leads from behind the hut onto the rocky plateau near the cross marking the summit. From here, enjoy a view of Evisa and Marignana – however, for a view taking in the Gulf of Porto, you must climb the rocky main peak, 1480m.

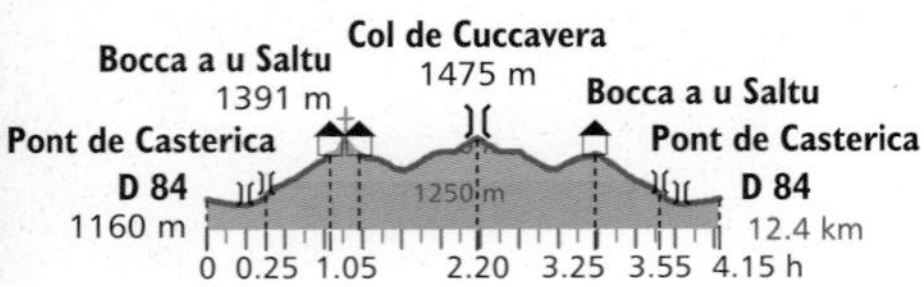

At the summit of Capu â Scalella. In the background the 20m higher main summit.

Continue straight ahead along the slightly descending forestry road. Immediately before the first hairpin bend in the road (just under 10 mins.), a signposted forest path branches off, continuing straight ahead to Col de Cuccavera (yellow waymarkers, cairns). It descends along the foot of rock faces, then slightly ascends into the Cuccavera valley. From time to time, the route crosses over rather precipitous stretches of bare rock. (If you prefer, continue along the forest road instead, keeping right at all junctions). After 1 hr. traversing the hillside, cross a small stream. Immediately afterwards, you find yourself back at the forestry road. About ¼ hr. of walking brings you to the top of the pass at the **Col de Cuccavera**. The little craggy peak to the left of the pass provides a lovely view of Paglia Orba and Capu Tafunatu as well as the nearby summit of Capu â Cuccala. You can also just make out Monte Senino on the coast.

TOP 24 Calanche

4.25 hrs.

The very best in sightseeing – fantastic rock formations and an azure sea

As if hewn by ancient ancestors, the bizarre rock formations of the Calanche silhouette the sky in a shimmering reddish light, rising out of the green macchia and firing the imagination. No one should miss the challenge of beating a path through this jungle of thicket and castellated rock. The trail (1) is not quite as rewarding – but the trail to Château fort (2) and the mule path (3) are all the more so.

Locations: Piana, 440m, and Porto, 80m, on the enchanting Gulf of Porto.
Starting point: Chalet des Roches Bleues (kiosk), 428m, on the D 81 from Piana to Porto (4km north of Piana).
Height difference: not quite 800m in total.
Grade: easy, at times somewhat steep, but well-marked paths.
Refreshment and accommodation: restaurants and hotels in Piana, campsites in Porto and on Plage d'Arone.
Map: ign 4150 OT (1:25,000).

(1) Path to the chestnut wood (la Châtaigneraie; 2¼ hrs.): a good 10m above **Chalet des Roches Bleues**, a yellow-marked footpath ascends steeply from the road (sign »Capu di u Vitullu«). Clearings in the pine forest allow you a view of the bizarre rock formations of the area. It takes ½ hr. until the footpath broadens out into an easier forest track. After ¼ hr., reach a distinct crossroads and bear left to follow the yellow-marked path (the path to the right leads to Piana). Soon you enter a small chestnut wood (lovely

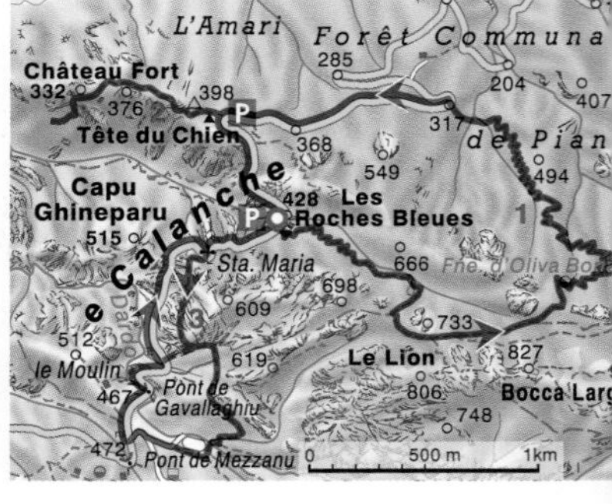

Calanche – new surprises await you at every bend in the path.

picnic spots). The path forks here once more. Continue straight ahead on the yellow-marked path in the direction of Ruines de Dispensa. After a short climb, the path descends steeply in seemingly never-ending zigzags – after 5 mins. passing by the Fontaine d'Oliva Bona (do not fork left to go there!) – and meets the road (1¼ hrs. from Châtaigneraie). Turn left and in 15 mins. reach **»The Dog's Head«** (Tête du Chien).

(2) Path to the Château fort (¾ hr.): to the right of **»The Dog's Head«** a yellow-marked path with a signpost for »Château fort« descends for 20 minutes through a gallery of incredible rock formations to a **rocky plateau** and a view of Château fort – a massive castle-like crag towering over the deep blue sea. Return the same way back to the road.

In the next right-hand bend in the road, past the parking lay-by (5 mins. further up from the »Dog's Head«), the Corniche Path forks off to the left (at the end, extremely overgrown, apparently no longer maintained). Therefore, continue along the road to the **Chalet des Roches Bleues** (a good 5 mins.).

(3) Mule Path (Chemin des Muletiers; 1¼ hr.): starting at the **Chalet** and walking uphill for 5 minutes, you come to the shrine of *O Marie Immaculée* set into the cliff face. Left of the shrine, a yellow-marked path (signpost »Capu d'Ortu«) turns off. This is a very beautiful trail, only steep at the outset, that leads us high above the road through a bizarre world of rock formations with spires and natural sculptures. Just after entering a forest, you could descend back to the main road (this stretch, however, is very overgrown), at the fork after leaving the forest, continue straight ahead (yellow; left leads to Châtaigneraie) climbing down to the football pitch at Piana (at the end, turn right to cross the bridge over the stream). Via the access track, further on to reach the main road, then turn right and return to the **Chalet** in 20 minutes.

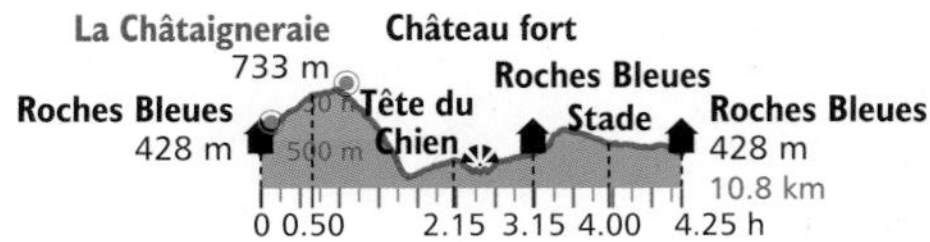

TOP 25 Capu d'Orto, 1294m

6.20 hrs.

Adventurous circular route offering fantastic views

The ascent of Capu d'Orto is one of Corsica's most adventurous walks and is crowned by an absolutely fantastic view of the Gulf of Porto below.

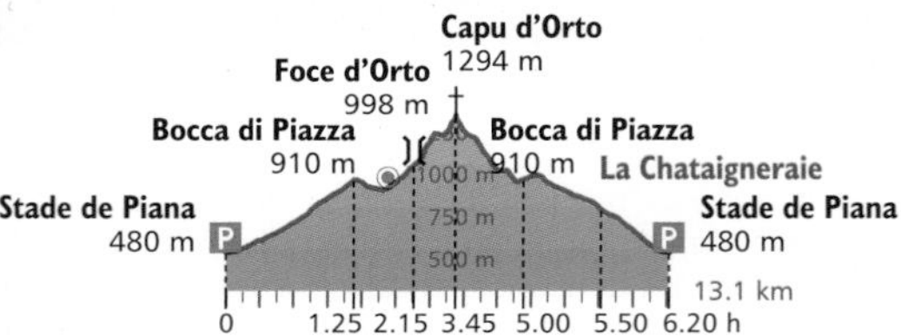

Location: Piana, 440m.
Starting point: football pitch (*stade*) of Piana, 480m, via a roadway starting at the D 81 road between Piana and Chalet des Roches Bleues (2km away from either point).
Height difference: 930m.
Grade: mostly easy route, however sometimes strenuous hiking via well-marked footpaths. Ascent to the summit from Foce d'Orto requires sure-footedness (I+).
Refreshment and accommodation: in Piana – restaurants / hotels; campsites in Porto and on Plage d'Arone.
Map: ign 4150 OT (1:25,000).

View from the summit of Capu d'Orto of Porto below.

On the descent trail – left, the Capu d'Orto; right the Capu di u Vitullu.

1.7km above Chalet des Roches Bleues, a roadway turns sharp left to the **football pitch** (signpost »Stade«). Cross the football pitch by bearing to the left, and follow the yellow-marked path that crosses a little bridge over a stream (then right at the fork). At first, the path follows the left bank of the stream and then soon ascends through a pine forest round zigzag bends. After not quite 1½ hrs. of walking, the path forks. Go right here and via the **Bocca di Piazza**, reach another fork not quite 5 minutes later – on the left the green-marked, shorter descent path (you should ascend this path if you are not confident about your footing), on the right the orange-marked ascent path. At first, this leads a little downhill to reach a stream bed; ascend left here following the orange waymarkers and 2 minutes later, pass the Fontaine de Piazza Mononca (signpost). Straight afterwards keep left at the fork towards Foce d'Orto (yellow-marked) and 10 minutes later ignore a path turning off right to the Capu di u Vitullu. Just under 10 minutes afterwards you are standing at **Foce d'Orto**, 998m, located at the foot of some bizarrely-

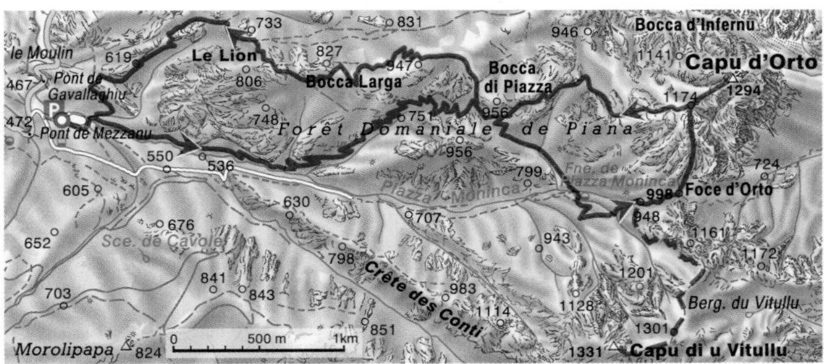

From the trail, stupendous views open up time and again over the Gulf of Porto. Below: a 360° panoramic view of the peaks.

formed crags, a minor peak of Capu d'Orto. Cairns now mark the continuing trail. Bearing to the left in a traverse towards the crags, reach an extremely steep and partially overgrown couloir. Negotiating the climb through the ravine requires scrambling, often using handholds (rough-surfaced plates of rock; I+). Further up, veer noticeably somewhat to the right, leaving the couloir behind at the end, and then reach a small saddle situated to the right of a crag (the summit appears in front of us). Now head left in a bend to ascend further, then descend slightly to the left across a small plateau (1174m; here, meet up with the »normal« route) to reach the final rise leading to the summit of **Capu d'Orto** where you have to climb over boulders to finally reach the peak. The loveliest spots to enjoy views are marked by cairns.

For the **descent**, first take the trail used for the ascent, but now, at the plateau at the foot of the final rise of the summit terrain, continue straight ahead along the waymarked main trail to reach a small, rocky plateau. Bizarre *tafoni* boulders flank the subsequent descent to an ill-defined col. At this point, turn right to descend, following the green waymarkers that lead through a broad rocky gully to yet another saddle facing a cluster of crags. Turn left here along the foot of a spacious rock face to cross over to a notch and, on the other side, go down to the junction with the ascent trail at the **Bocca di Piazza** (1 hr.). Here go right over the saddle and at the next trail junction turn right onto the green-marked footpath. Shortly afterwards go left at the fork towards Roches Bleues, via the ridge of mountains (helicopter pad) and, enjoying a wonderful view of the Calanche region below, reach a little chestnut wood (1 hr.). Here, take the yellow-marked path to the left towards Piana (soon after, head straight on) to return to the **football pitch**.

26 Capu Rossu, 331m

3.45 hrs.

Panoramic walk to the Genoese tower perched on the red craggy cliffs

The walk to the craggy cliff that falls 300 metres in a sheer drop near the Genoese Turghiu watch-tower is one of the most impressive adventures to be found on the island. Hear the crash of the waves on the cliffs far below while enjoying a lovely view sweeping over the Gulf of Porto.

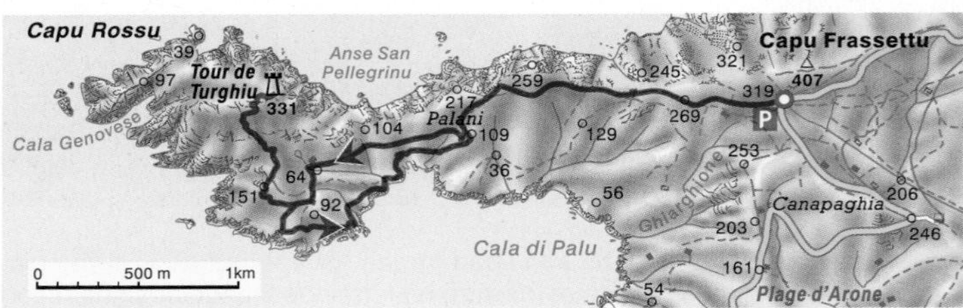

Starting point: starting from the centre of Piana, take the D 824 towards the Plage d'Arone; 6km later, at a left-hand bend in the road (snack bar), a large car park on the side of the road, at 319m.
Height difference: 570m.
Grade: the walk along a well-marked path is not difficult but somewhat steep at the end (and strenuous when hot).
Refreshment and accommodation: snack bar at the start; in Piana – restaurants/hotels; campsites on the Plage d'Arone and in Porto.
Tip: visit the beautiful Plage d'Arone by continuing on the D 824 southwards.
Map: ign 4150 OT (1:25,000).

At the **car park**, take the distinct path to cross over and join the walking trail (this sets off from the road 50m above the car park). The trail descends pleasantly, heading towards Capu Rossu and the Geno-

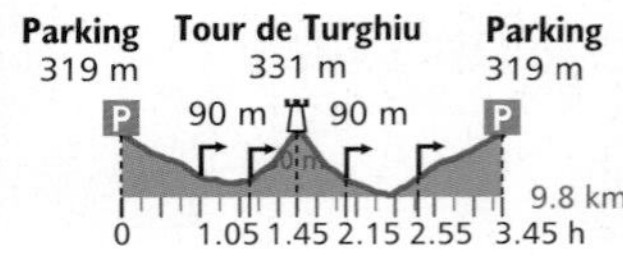

ese tower. After a 15-minute walk, pass a gate. Shortly afterwards near a prominent stone block, reach the ruins of a stone hut. In springtime, you are treated to a feast of flowers, and bushes of rock-roses catch the eye; far below, a sea stack towers up from the sea floor – images straight out of a tourist flyer. A good ½ hr. later, meet up with a threshing circle. 10 mins. on, the trail forks in front of a stone-built house – turn right here (to the left, a coastal trail forks away; refer to the return route). Another 10 mins. later, a path forks to the right over the rocky ridge (easy scrambling) – but we continue along the main trail (sign). Passing a spring, meet up with a house with a threshing circle (lovely spot for a break). 100m past this, the trail branches: the coastal path forks away to the left (our return route later on), to the right, ascend to the foot of the rock face and, in zigzags, continue climbing arduously up over the rock to reach the **Tour de Turghiu** (½ hr.). The viewing platform is open and accessible (be careful – the steps are steep and unprotected!).
For the return route, you really should choose the coastal trail that forks away 100m before the house with the threshing circle (sign »*Sentier littoral*«). This descends pleasantly to the seaside near the towering sea stack and then, before a little sandy cove, continues by ascending steeply, finally merging back again with the main trail at the stone-built house. A splendid stretch of trail, even though 20 minutes longer!

Near the Genoese watchtower the cliffs drop vertically down to the sea.

27 Lac de Creno, 1310m, and Monte Sant'Eliseo, 1511m

3.15 hrs.

Easy hike to an idyllic mountain lake in the woods

Surrounded by pine forests and flecked with grassy islets, the little Creno lake is easy to reach and attracts many visitors. The lake is swampy, not an inviting place for a swim; nevertheless, near the shore, lovely picnic spots await you where feral pigs scavenge for the hiker's left-over scraps. In any case, the route should be combined with a climb to the chapel on Monte Sant'Eliseo with lovely panoramic views.

Location: Soccia, 729m, pretty mountain village 31km east of Sagone. Just as lovely is the neighbouring village of Orto, which can also be chosen as a starting point for a hike to Creno lake.
Starting point: car park, 1000m, including a snack bar beneath a large metal cross – from Soccia in a north-westerly direction via a narrow asphalt road (3km, signposted).
Height difference: to Lake Creno about 350m, another 200m to Monte Sant'Eliseo.
Grade: easy, very well-marked route, strenuous climb to Monte Sant'Eliseo.
Refreshment and accommodation: snack bar at the car park, bar and hotel/restaurant in Soccia, campsite in Vico.
Alternative: possible descent to Orto via well-marked paths from Creno lake and also from Monte Sant'Eliseo (1½ hrs.; partially unmarked and overgrown path), and from there in 1 hr. to Soccia (add another ½ hr. to the car park).
Map: ign 4251 OT (1:25,000).

Starting at the **car park**, follow the concrete track for another 100m. Passing the cross, turn right onto the sign-posted, yellow-marked trail which leisurely ascends, traversing the flank on the right-hand side of the valley. A good half hour later, to the left and below, you can spot the tiny lake along with the

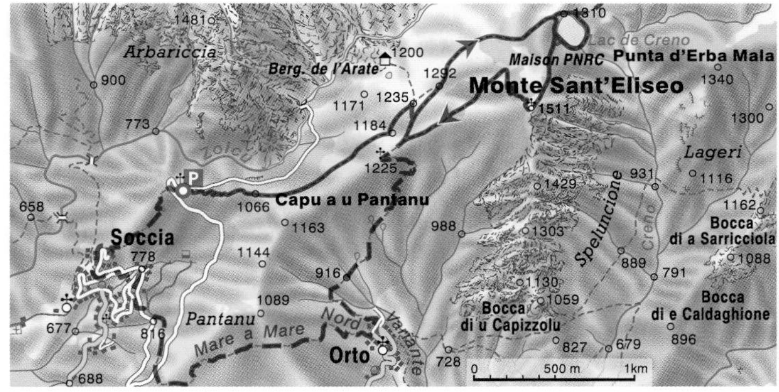

Bergerie de l'Arate – our trail forks off to the right from the broad gravel trail and, a few minutes later, forks left (the trail to the right heads towards Ortu, and will be our return trail from Monte Sant'Eliseo later on. After a fleeting view opens up revealing the 2000 metre peaks of the main ridge, the footpath plunges again into the pine forest and continues there all the way to **Creno lake** (nature reserve building).

If you are not fully stretched with the walk to the Creno lake you should certainly take the detour onto Monte Sant'Eliseo: from behind the nature reserve building go uphill for 50m to the ridge along which an obvious steep path ascends to the left (cairns) to the summit. Before reaching the chapel on the summit of **Monte Sant'Eliseo** the forest thins out. The views of Corsica's main ridge, towards Orto and into the Guagno valley, are phenomenal. From the summit, you can return to the walking trail straight ahead through the gate (not left to the white cross; 40 minutes later, at the fork 40m before meeting another white cross, turn right, then left).

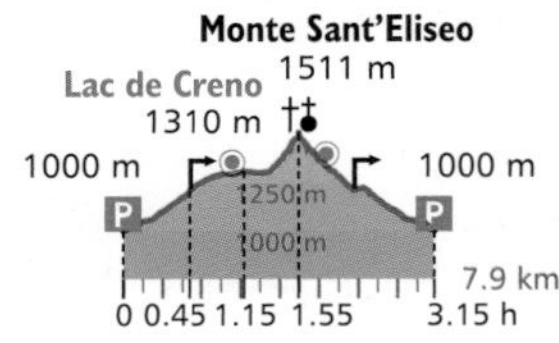

28 Mont Tretorre, 1509m

5.00 hrs.

Absolutely unique – the »Sugar Loaf« peak of Mont Tretorre

Mont Tretorre offers not only a first-class view, but it is also a unique geological rarity: the triple-peaked summit, towering over 100m in height, is formed from syenite, an igneous rock, that has been metamorphosed from quartz. This is an impressive walk, but the summit ascent should only be undertaken by walkers with climbing experience and a good head for heights.

Starting point: centre of Guagno, 760m, 33km east of Sagone.
Height difference: 800m (add another 150m for the climb to the summit).
Grade: easy mountain walk, the climb to the summit requires absolute sure-footedness and a lack of vertigo (some stretches of Grade II climbing).
Refreshment and accommodation: bar-restaurants in Guagno, hotels and campsite in Vico.
Alternative: from the foot of Mont Tretorre, bear to the left following along the cliff face and then climb over the ridge to Monte Cervellu, 1624m (1½ hr.).
Map: ign 4251 OT (1:25,000).

Starting just past the church in **Guagno**, descend along the flight of steps, turn left along the intersecting street for 10m and then turn diagonally right, climbing down towards Tretorre (sign). A good 100m further on, an old footpath descends to the left to the bridge over the Albelli stream (¼ hr.).
On the other side of the valley, the path climbs straight on, bearing right at the walled natural spring and following the slope (watch out for orange waymarkers).

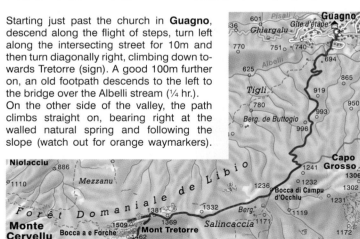

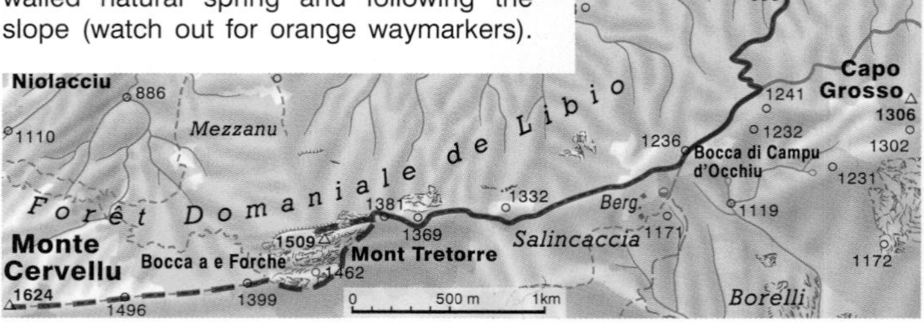

The ridge path leading to the foot of Mont Tretorre leads over impressive slabs of rock.

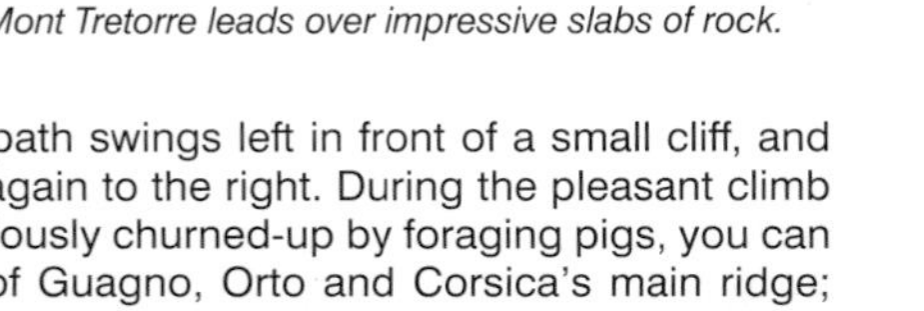

A quarter of an hour later, the path swings left in front of a small cliff, and then, a few minutes after that, again to the right. During the pleasant climb on the old path, sometimes seriously churned-up by foraging pigs, you can snatch some pretty glimpses of Guagno, Orto and Corsica's main ridge; chestnut trees provide some welcome shade. After another ¼ hr., the path breaks away to the left towards a small valley gap and leads past a dilapidated house, climbing to a gentle col. Now, continue by ascending to the right (keeping to the right and paying attention to the cairns and orange waymarkers). After 10 minutes, the path leads left again through a small ravine, passing another derelict house to the left. Now the path begins to steepen. Bearing slightly to the right, ascend across the slope and, a half an hour later, pass gigantic boulders. Pines dominate the landscape now. Just afterwards, the path veers to the left and ascends to a forest track; turn right here to reach **Bocca di Campu d'Occhiu**. The track ends here (turnaround), and the yellow-marked trail continues straight ahead. This leads at first along the other

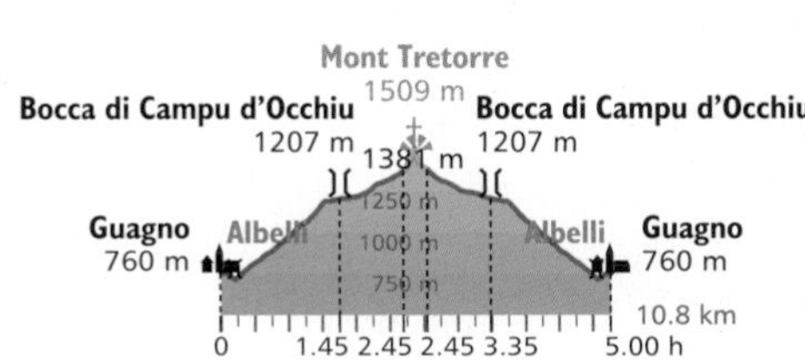

side of the ridge, bearing left whilst traversing the slope (ignore the trail forking off to the left towards Salice), and soon climbs directly to the high ridge through stretches of fern and broom undergrowth – while walking, enjoy a beautiful view of Mont Tretorre. Half an hour from the *bocca* go round a small rocky peak to the left; afterwards, the path continues directly along the ridge again, soon crossing over gigantic rock slabs, which slope down to the left towards the valley. After an hour, reach the foot of the rock face of Mont Tretorre at 1381m.

Experienced scramblers can climb from here through the steep, boulder-strewn gully (the best way is along the right rim, then the left) towards the summit (some places of Grade II;1 hr. there and back). You need about half an hour to scramble up this extremely steep, strenuous and sometimes precipitous section to reach the marvellous panoramic plateau at the top – a perfect place for a break. If you choose to attempt the last metres to reach the summit, walk from the gully for a good 10m out onto the plateau and then climb sharply to the left over an extremely narrow and precipitous ledge (exposed climbing, no handholds, bolts for a safety rope) which leads to the highest point on **Mont Tretorre**. The panoramic view is sublime: one side of the main ridge includes Paglia Orba, Cinto, Rotondo and Monte d'Oro – the other side, the Gulf of Sagore.

The climb to the summit through the steep, boulder-strewn gully is very strenuous and includes numerous stretches of scrambling. Guagno can be seen in the background.

4.30 hrs.

Monte Cervellu, 1624m

29

Remote summit – only a stone's throw away from the hustle and bustle on the coast

The isolated mountain village of Rosazia with Monte Cervellu.

The drive up along the narrow road is rather adventurous in places and can prove to be an experience in itself. Rosazia is one of the most isolated villages on the island – you will not find this place in any of the travel guides – and the walk onto Monte Cervellu correspondingly remote. The ascent is not very spectacular but from the summit you are rewarded with a fabulous view towards the Gulf of Sagone, the Gulf of Ajaccio and, above all, the view of the neighbouring Mont Tretorre and the central ridge.

Starting point: the entrance to the village of Rosazia, 673m, 31km east of Sagone (a narrow road from Murzo and rather airy in places).
Height difference: just under 1000m.
Grade: mostly good hiking path as far as the Bergerie de Manganu; the summit ascent itself is more or less over rough ground, but offers few difficulties (possible route-finding problems in periods of poor visibility).
Refreshment: bar/restaurant in Rosazia, hotels and campsite in Vico.
Map: ign 4151 OT (1:25,000).

On the hairpin bend just before the centre of **Rosazia** the road crosses the Mulinacciu stream (bridge, 100m before the bar Novala). A narrow concrete road (sign »Guagno«) turns off here that immediately crosses over a bridge. 15m afterwards a yellow-marked path branches off to the right that forks after 10 minutes – go left here (straight on) following the yellow waymarkers.

The lovely path, somewhat overgrown in a few places, now ascends steadily in zigzags through an open forest of pine and scrub. A good half an hour after the fork ignore a path with red waymarkers off to the right. Soon afterwards you come past a small rocky knoll to reach the **Bocca di u Capizzolu**, 1096m, an ill-defined col on an elongated mountain ridge.

Now walk along to the right over the ridge beside a stone wall. The path affords some great views with Rosazia lying at your feet – on the other side you can see some bizarre rock pinnacles. After 20 minutes your path meets a disused roadway (a possible return route to Rosazia, however, the roadway is very overgrown) which you then leave again after a few minutes along the path beside the wall. The waymarked trail continues on along the ridge. 10 minutes later the path crosses the wall leading down to the left, eventually goes round to the left of a small rocky peak with a white cross and con-

The last stretch from the Bergerie de Manganu (photo centre, left) to the summit sometimes lacks a distinct trail.

tinues uphill on the other side of it to the **Bergerie de Manganu**, 1390m (spring, it's worth making a detour to the white cross).

Now the yellow waymarkers disappear. The easiest way to continue is, past the first *bergerie*, turn right at the spring to cross over to the second *bergerie*, then pass this to the left whilst ascending to a scree field. Cross over this and then turn right over the ridgeline to climb up to the summit of **Monte Cervellu** (virtually pathless; cairns).

Return along the same way as the approach route. Hard-nosed walkers (but only of that ilk!) might want to take the descent, one hour further along, that turns left onto the extremely overgrown roadway. This loops along bends into the valley and forks after a good 45 mins. at a derelict house – go right at this point. Finally pass through a gate to reach the road in **Rosazia**, where you arrive directly by the bar Novala.

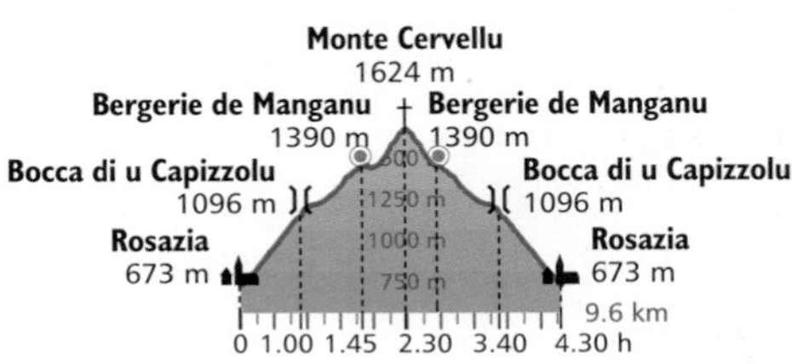

30 Rocher des Gozzi, 716m

3.15 hrs.

Through macchia vegetation to the rocky viewpoint above Ajaccio

This peak, a sheer rock face dropping down to the Gravona valley, provides a viewpoint par excellence. From here, you can calmly contemplate the hustle and bustle taking place in the fertile delta inland from the skyline and sandy beaches of Ajaccio.

Starting point: Chapelle San Chirgu, 417m. As you enter Appietto (before reaching the cemetery) a roadway forks off to the right to the chapel (car park).
Height difference: not quite 500m.
Grade: easy mountain walk; the climb to the summit is somewhat exposed. The return route via Punta Pastinaca follows a narrow path (not recommended when visibility is poor).
Refreshment/accommodation: Ajaccio.
Map: ign 4153 OT (1:25,000).

From the car park by the **Chapelle San Chirgu**, head for 30m towards the transmitter hut and turn right through the gate, then left along the trail (at the beginning, unpleasantly eroded) which ascends via the ridge. About 20 minutes later, pass a gate and, 10 minutes after that, pass a small rocky plateau on your right. Here the path turns away from the ridge to the right and brings you, at first ascending, then travers-

Summit view of the Gravona valley towards Monte Renoso.

ing the slope, to a stone hut perched on the col in front of the Gozzi crags (1½ hrs.). A distinct path leads from here to a rocky cirque, separating the towering rock face of the summit from the *macchia*-blanketed slope, and continues on from there onto the **Rocher des Gozzi**.

If you wish to prolong the walk, from the stone hut, you can ascend to the **Punta Pastinaca**, 814m – here, the view opens up fantastically, taking in Rotondo and the Cinto massif! Past the little cross on the summit, a path continues, as first somewhat indistinct, and leads in easy up-and-down walking steadily along the ridgeline (some stretches are red waymarked; sometimes somewhat overgrown). Afterwards, this drops steeper downward and then forks (½ hr.): to the right, you could descend to Appietto, but we choose the left-hand path and, 75m on, meet up with the approach route. Turn right to return to the starting point.

The summit of Punta Pastinaca.

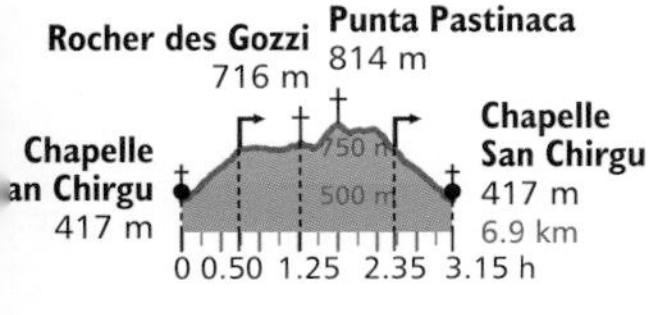

Rocher des Gozzi 716 m
Punta Pastinaca 814 m
Chapelle San Chirgu 417 m
750 m
500 m
Chapelle San Chirgu 417 m
6.9 km
0 0.50 1.25 2.35 3.15 h

31 Sentier des Crêtes: Ajaccio – Cinaraggia, 528m

4.30 hrs.

Panoramic walk above the Gulf of Ajaccio

The Sentier des Crêtes is not only the local landmark route for Ajaccians but also one the most famous walks in the entire region. This is rightly so, since the tour along the Salario ridge is not only enchanting due to the lovely, pleasant course of the trail, but especially because of the marvellous views of the city and the gulf, and thanks to its fantastic scenic landscapes.

Starting point: starting point for walkers »Bois des Anglais«, 75m (bus stop for line 7), in Ajaccio. Approach: take the N 193 (Cours Napoléon) into the city centre. At the Place de Gaulle, turn right and then keep straight ahead to reach the Place d'Austerlitz. In front of the square, turn right to follow the signs for »Bois des Anglais« (Av. Nicolas Pietri) and 650m on, reach a roundabout. Directly before the roundabout, a narrow street forks off sharp to the left – the walk begins here (large sign, small car park: you could also park at the Place d'Austerlitz or Av. Nicolas Pietri/Av. de Verdun).

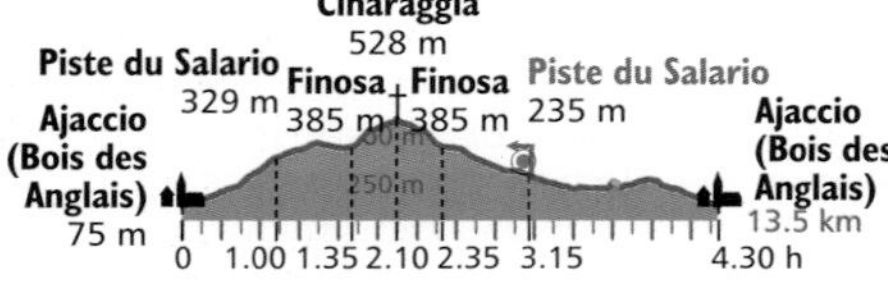

Height difference: 550m.

Grade: mostly a pleasant, well-marked walking path.

Refreshment and accommodation: in Ajaccio.

Map: ign 4153 OT (1:25,000).

At the walker's car park **Bois des Anglais** (large sign) turn left towards the narrow road that, 50m on (barrier) becomes a broad trail. Follow the yellow/blue-marked main trail which, 150m further on, begins to ascend in pleasant bends (sign »*Sentier des Crêtes*«). This leads through open brush wood whilst presenting views of the city and the gulf below. After the eighth bend, the trail veers left towards the slope and, after a few minutes, ascends steeply for a short stretch and then forks. Here, continue ascending straight ahead towards *Piste du Salario* (our return trail is to the left) – this is an absolutely beautiful piece of trail, opening

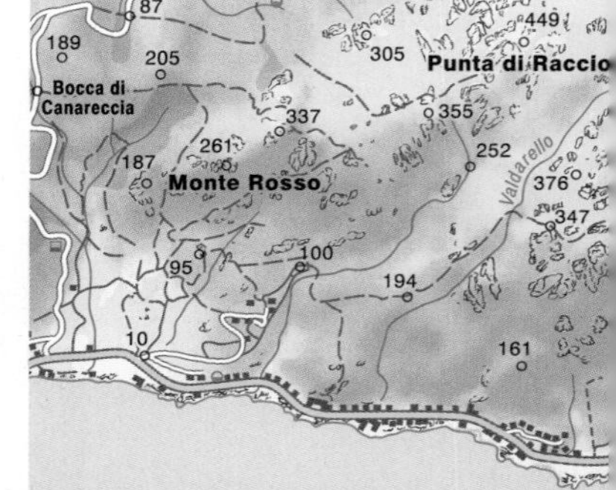

On the return, enjoy a splendid view of the city.

up marvellous views! Soon afterwards, the *macchia* becomes denser and the trail merges into a broad intersecting trail. Turn left onto this trail. 70m on, it merges into a broad track road (***Piste du Salario***). Turn right to follow this road. 100m on, a blue/orange- (later also yellow-) marked trail forks away, passing two water tanks (a breath-taking view towards the Gravona valley!). This leads more or less directly over the broad ridge with fantastic views of the gulf (later on, also the Îles Sanguinaires) and, to the right, the visually striking rocky crown of the Punta di Lisa. The trail now traverses through the slope to the right of the Salario ridge, sometimes enjoying the shade of a primeval forest. Then the trail returns to the ridgeline and forks – here, head

straight on towards »Vignola«. Soon afterwards, reach the one-time shepherd's hut of **Finosa**, behind which the trail forks (a lovely spot for a break; to the left, our return trail later on). Straight on, the excursion to the summit of Cinaraggia is worthwhile: the trail ascends more steeply for some minutes to reach a little ridgeline area and then leads through a depression to the next height where fantastic *tafoni* rock formations are awaiting, a »dinosaur« amongst others. About 5 minutes later, a narrow path forks to the right into the *macchia* (cairns), and ascends in a few minutes to the summit of the **Cinaraggia** (wooden cross; easy scrambling) – a splendid viewpoint with a view reaching the outskirts of Ajaccio, to the Îles Sanguinaires and Minaccia beach. After the excursion, at the **Finosa** intersection, fork left to continue. The trail traverses the slope, passing a huge crag some minutes later (a lovely viewpoint) and, at the end, opening a view to the attractive Ariadne beach. Shortly afterwards, meet up with an intersecting trail, the *Sentier des Crêtes*; turn sharp left onto it for the return to Ajaccio. The trail leads constantly on the level, traversing the slope, and passes an enclosed spring, 20 minutes later. Shortly afterwards, reach a major intersection with another spring and

The trail to the summit of Cinaraggia leads through a realm of legendary creatures.

benches – here, keep straight ahead (to the left, a trail forks off to the *Piste du Salario*). 20 minutes later, at a fork, you could bear diagonally right to reach the cemetery of Sanguinaires on the coastal road (½ hr.) – we, however, keep diagonally left along the *Sentier des Crêtes*, which ascends somewhat for a short stretch to reach a saddle and then continues on the level above the multistorey buildings of Ajaccio. Some minutes later, meet another saddle with a trail crossing (from the little peak to the right, a breath-taking view of the city!); here, bear left (and 70m on, keep straight ahead), ascending slightly. A good 10 minutes later, pass a tumbledown house and, just afterwards, meet up with approach route, to turn right onto it and head back to the **Bois des Anglais**.

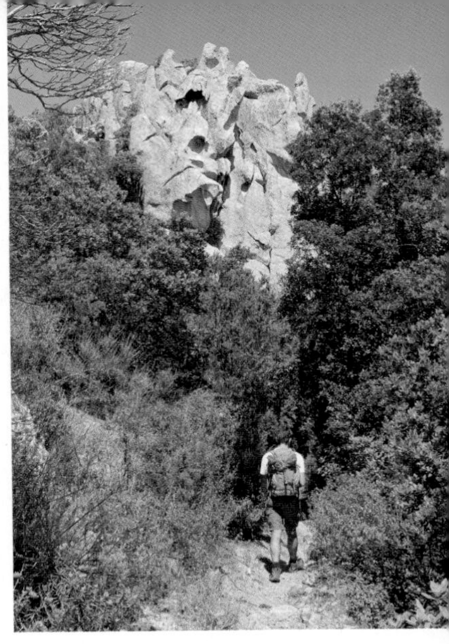

The return along the Sentier des Crêtes.

32 Punta Sant'Eliseo, 1271m

4.30 hrs.

Solitary ridge hike with a marvellous 360° panoramic view

On this isolated walk you will most likely encounter only cows. It seems that hikers, however, hardly ever stumble upon this spectacular panoramic peak which not only affords a lovely view of the bays at Ajaccio and Sagone but also of Monte d'Oro, Renoso, Rotondo and Paglia Orba.

Starting point: Tavaco, 481m. Parking in the centre, at the outset of the path or at the church on the eastern village limits.
Height difference: 800m.
Grade: mostly well-marked, sometimes strenuous footpath. Some physical fitness and a sense of direction is required (especially during the descent!). Very little shade.
Refreshment/accommodation: Ajaccio.
Tip: visit the tortoise park A Cupulatta on the N 193 at Km 21 (www.acupulatta.com).
Alternative: a descent is possible to

Sari-d'Orcino from the peak in a westerly direction along the ridge.
Map: ign 4151 OT (1:25,000).

At the first right-hand bend in **Tavaco**, bypass a house to the left via a narrow side alley and continue (keeping left) between fenced pastures and past a tiny cemetery in a westerly direction until reaching the end of the asphalt road. Here by a **walnut tree** (signpost), a path branches off to the right. The footpath, somewhat overgrown at the outset, ascends gently through a valley blanketed in *macchia* keeping to the left of the little brook. Soon you reach a water tank, where the distinct path crosses over to the right side of the valley.

Punta Sant'Eliseo's summit as seen from a neighbouring peak.

After half an hour, you find yourself on the **ridge** which sets the direction of your continued ascent (just before this point, keep on the marked main trail by bearing right at the fork). Accordingly, when you reach a path forking off to the right, continue straight ahead. The path remains distinct and the *macchia* not overly troublesome.

After 1½ hours in all, the first minor karst peaks appear ahead. Soon afterwards, the waymarked trail turns left to make a traverse (sign »Tavaco«). 150m past the sign, fork away to the right onto a steep path (cairns) that ascends over the fern-covered ridge with a small peak-like rise (with low stone walls). Take good note of this point and the continued trail for the return. Now keep following the ridgeline in a northerly direction, avoiding the rocky outcrops by bearing left. At the ridge that follows, turn right (sign) and then. finally complete the steep climb to the summit of **Punta Sant'Eliseo** (radio tower).

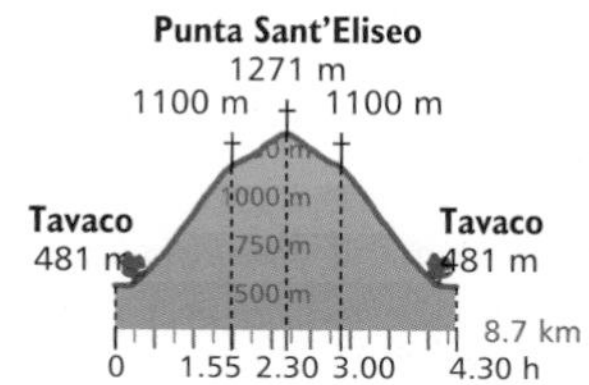

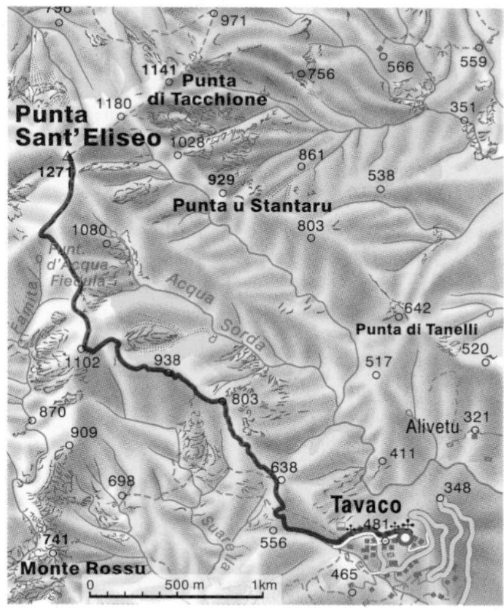

33 Bergeries des Pozzi, 1746m

Ridgeline hike to the pozzines at the foot of the Renoso massif

The Plateau d'Ese would be a wonderful destination if it wasn't for the ski station with its numerous lifts. In complete contrast the heavenly pozzi above the Bergeries des Pozzi, which are easily approached via a short but popular panoramic walk starting at the Plateau d'Ese. Cows graze on the swampy meadows, criss-crossed with many streams; sometimes you will find pigs and horses there too.

Location: Bastelica, 780m, south-west of Monte Renoso.
Starting point: ski station in Val d'Ese, 1610m, approach via a good mountain road from Bastelica (12km).
Height difference: 600m.
Grade: easy hike along well-marked footpaths.
Refreshment / accommodation: perhaps, a snack bar at the ski station; restaurants, hotels, campsites in Bastelica.
Alternatives: detour to the remote Lac de Vitalaca, 1777m (1 hr., one way): at the fork just behind the waterfall follow the scanty red waymarkers along the sometimes somewhat indistinct and overgrown trail to the left up the valley to the Bocca della Calle, 1946m (a good half an hour). From here the path descends steeply keeping left. A good 20 mins. later, before a final ascent, climb down to the left and then turn right at the fork along an obvious path (cairns), finally over boulders, to the western shore of the lake (outflow; ½ hr.). – From the Bergeries des Pozzi there's an interesting hiking path to the Col de Verde.
Map: ign 4252 OT (1:25,000).

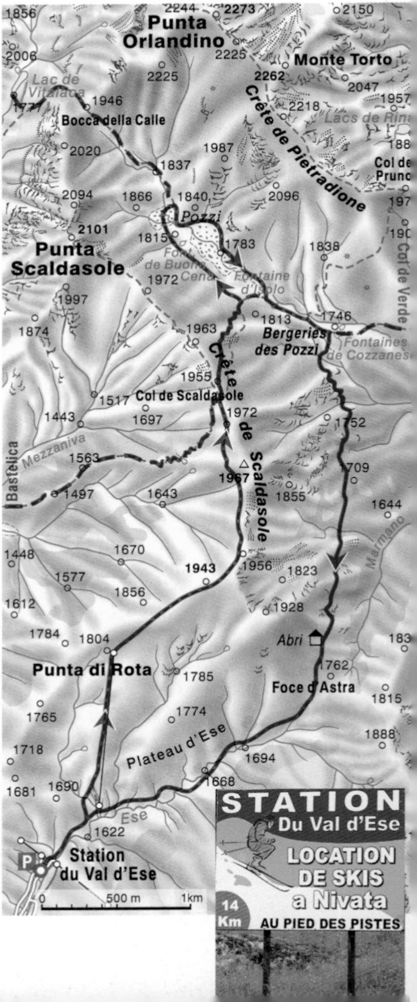

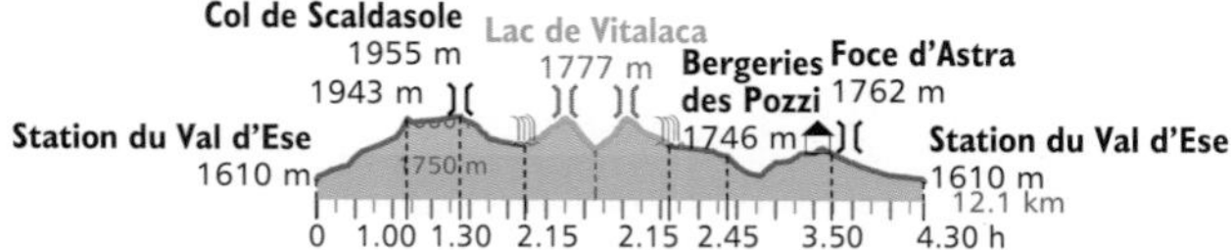

At the car park, take the gravel track and head past the **ski station** towards the valley, then keep diagonally left uphill at the fork after 5 minutes and cross over a stream. After this, the trail ascends along the cableway for the last and longest of the tow lifts. Not quite 45 mins. later, pass the hut at the terminus of the tow lift and, a quarter of an hour after that, reach the **Punta di Rota**, 1943m. Here you can enjoy a wonderful view of Bastelica, the Renoso massif and over to the Arrête des Statues. Your footpath swings over to the **Scaldasole ridge** and leads almost on the level along or to the left of the broad ridge, with only a steep drop eastwards. After half an hour, you find yourself on the **Col de Scaldasole**, 1955m. At this point, another path intersects, coming from Bastelica. Turn right onto it towards Pozzi

The marvellous stretch of the path on the Scaldasole ridge (in the centre, Punta Orlandino).

A small paradise – the upper end of the pozzines with the waterfall.

(yellow-marked). The path descends along the right-hand side of the ridge to the *pozzines*. Just above the bottom of the valley with the lush green marshland and streams ignore a path branching off right to the Bergeries des Pozzi. A few minutes later the path forks again – turn left here (signpost »Vitalaca«). The path runs for a few minutes on the level across the hillside and then heads for a waterfall at the upper end of the *pozzines*. Just before the waterfall follow the path across the stream to the right and on the other side of the valley, about 100m on the right from the waterfall, meet an indistinct path that joins a scantily red-marked path on the left after a short incline. If you fancy making a detour to Vitalaca lake follow this path left up the valley (→Alternative). Otherwise walk down the valley along the path to the right – at first across the hillside, then directly across the valley bottom parallel to the stream. There are

The remote Vitalaca lake.

some inviting crystal-clear streams and pools in the lush-green wetlands where you can take a dip. Where the stream disappears into the scrub alder, a footpath leads along to the right of the stream to the nearby **Bergeries des Pozzi**, 1746m. Cheese can be purchased from the quaint stone huts during the tourist season. If you prefer to walk the shortest way back to the ski station choose the same way back over the *pozzines* and then go left over the Col de Scaldasole (1½ hrs.). Otherwise make your return through the idyllic Marmano valley covered in marvellous beech woods: on the right below the huts a path continues (signpost »Eze« after 50m). The clear path, waymarked yellow and with cairns, descends past wind-bowed trees and after a good 10 mins. crosses the stream to the right. Immediately after, turn right at a fork (not left towards Col de Verde; sign). The path now runs in a gentle up-and-down through the lovely deciduous forest and 10 mins. later crosses a larger stream again to then ascend steeply up to a small plateau.

The following wetland is crossed along the right-hand edge and some minutes later the hiking path crosses another stream. Shortly afterwards you leave the forest. The path ascends for a short way again and then turns left towards the hillside (after a few minutes at a fork descend steeply for a short way). After a quarter of an hour you arrive at a simply equipped shelter on the top of the pass of **Foce d'Astra**, 1762m. Now descend leisurely all the way across mountain meadows through the Ese valley down to the **ski station** (¾ hr.).

The wetlands above the Bergeries des Pozzi.

The Southern Island

Golfe de Valinco – Ornano – Sartenais – Alta Rocca – Taravu

Since time immemorial, the southern part of Corsica appears to have been the favourite spot to settle for the island's inhabitants. Even the Megalithic and Torrean cultures chose to inhabit this area – »menhir« stones, ceremonial sites and ancient fortifications in *Filitosa, Cauria, Pagliaju, Cucuruzzu, Arraggio, Torre* and *Tappa* today bear witness with artefacts of these native peoples. The southern island, especially the region around Alta Rocca, boasts a fine, bright and sunny landscape. Only in the mountainous areas surrounding the Bavella pass, do the peaks tower and climb to unconquerable alpine summits, otherwise you are presented with leisurely summit paths and curious rock formations.

The **Gulf of Valinco**, where many beautiful sandy inlets flanked by craggy cliffs can be found, is one of the most important bathing resorts on the island. In the hinterland of Propriano, the **Ornano** and **Sartenais** region attracts walkers to panoramic peaks which can be conquered without a great deal of toil and effort. A combined tour can be easily undertaken with *Punta di Muro*, 605m (¾ hr. starting at the crossing of the D 221 and D 321 near Bocca di Giovanella) – a pretty little peak offering a fantastic view of the Bay of Propriano – and ending with an excursion to *Sartène*. A jaunt to the *Punta di Buturetu*, 871m (½ hr. from Miluccia) can be coupled with a visit to *Olmeto*. In any case, make a stopover at the splendid sandy bay at *Roccapina* which sports the renowned »rock lion«.

Menhir in Filitosa.

On the southern tip of Corsica perches *Bonifacio* – the most impressive city on the entire island. Wonderful beaches can be enjoyed along the coast to the north of the city – the best-known being *Plage de Palombaggia*, south-east of Porto-Vecchio. This friendly little

town opens up the way to the sea of boulders of the **Alta Rocca** region. The drive to picturesque *Ospédale*, a village offering a grandiose view of the Bay of Porto-Vecchio, is an experience in itself. Further along, on the stretch of road toward *Zonza* and the *Bavella pass*, you will hardly be able to keep to your seat as your hiking instincts take control. Especially popular and delightful is the Bavella chain, also known as the »Corsican Dolomites«.

34 Monte San Petru, 1400m

3.05 hrs.

Panoramic ridge route above the Taravo valley

The lovely rock formations of Monte San Petru with spectacular views of the island's south, of the Bavella pinnacles and the Gulf of Valinco is enchanting. Unfortunately, the beginning of this walking adventure has been visibly spoiled by a forest fire (2009).

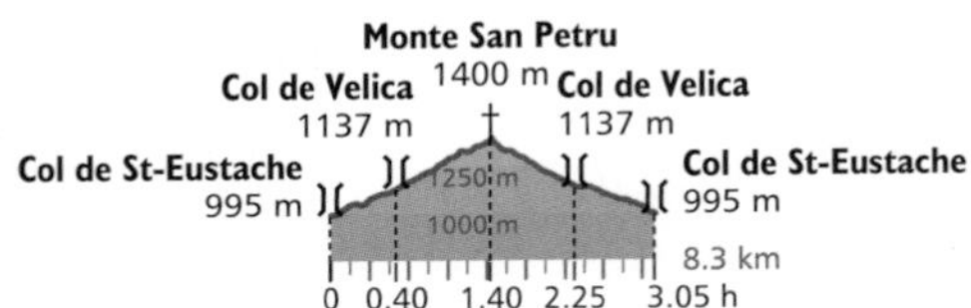

Starting point: Col de St-Eustache, 995m, mountain pass on the D 420 between Petreto-Bicchisano and Aullène.
Height difference: a good 400m.
Grade: easy ridge hike using distinct, mostly marked footpaths (rather overgrown in places).
Refreshment and accommodation: snack bar on the pass. Hotels in Petreto-Bicchisano and in Aullène; campsites on the coast and in Bichisano.
Alternative: ascent from Petreto (a total of 5½ hrs.): at the upper village limits, the main street crosses the main road (fountain). Here, turn right to follow the main street for not quite 100m until a steep, overgrown trail forks away diagonally left (yellow slash). This ascends mostly pleasantly through the wood and forks, 25 mins. later, past a gate – turn left here to follow the fence (yellow waymarkers). At the next fork, at a cattle gate, ascend straight ahead along the ridge. Another 25 mins. more, the trail crosses over a little stream (10m on, ascend to the left!), and 10 mins. after that, on your right, pass a panoramic plateau. Now keep on the level, traverse the slope and cross two more little streams. Then another steep ascent to reach Foci Stretta, and meet up with the circular route.
Map: ign 4253 OT (1:25,000).

You begin your climb from **Col de St-Eustache**, heading west on the gravel road and after 100m turn diagonally right onto the narrower gravel path which, not quite a quarter of an hour later, becomes a broad path (keep straight ahead; yellow-marked). A good half hour more, reach the ridgeline (**Col de Velica**, 1137m). Here take the clearly marked path to the left. You pass the rocky peak of **Punta Pinitelli**, 1201m, to your right, then the *macchia*-covered **Punta di Ziffilicara**, 1207m, to your left, before finally reaching the ridgeline. Ahead you can see Monte San Petru with the village of Petreto-Bicchisano below. Little by little the ferns give way to dwarf junipers, broom and tree heathers. Passing a few boulders to your right, you then skirt around a field of boulders on the right, and finally head towards a prominent free-

Bizarre rock formations near Monte San Petru.

standing boulder. At this point you have to cross over a small hollow with massive stone slabs worn smooth by the elements. Now without any further difficulty, the rocky summit of **Monte San Petru** can be achieved by climbing from the left (south; past this, a peak crowned with aerials).

A lovely alternative route can be taken for the descent: first retrace the path back to **Col de Velica** (¾ hr.), but then continue straight ahead on the right-hand side of the ridge and after a few minutes bear left of the ridgeline through a (forest fire devastated) pine forest. The yellow-marked path was more scenic, in times past, than that of the approach from the Col de St-Eustache. After about 20 minutes a conspicuous, almost mushroom-shaped crag can be seen on the right above the path (somewhat hidden) and a good 5 minutes later, you reach an easily missed junction of the paths on a small meadow plateau (**Foci Stretta**; trail signpost). To the left, a descent could be made to Petreto (→Alternative) – however, stay on the footpath bearing right and, crossing over the ill-defined ridge, descend to **Col de St-Eustache** a short distance away.

35 Capu di Muru

3.00 hrs.

A pleasant ramble between the Gulf of Ajaccio and the Gulf of Valinco

The cape between the Golfe d'Ajaccio and the Golfe de Valinco is the perfect setting for a dramatic and picturesque coastal walk with places for swimming.

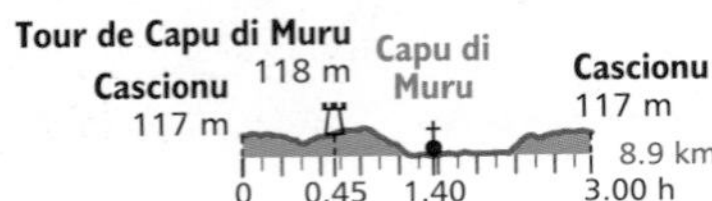

Starting point: Cascionu, 117m. From the D 155 (Bocca di Filippina, sign »Capu di Muru«) drive 4.5km on a narrow asphalt road (after 3.5km, ignore the left turning to Cala d'Orzu) until the road ends at Cascionu where you can park.
Height difference: a good 250m.
Grade: easy walk on footpaths sometimes requiring a good sense of direction in places.
Refreshment: bar-restaurants on the Cala d'Orzu; possibly, a snack bar at the starting point (beverage vending machine).
Map: ign 4254 OT (1:25,000).

At the end of the road in **Cascionu**, a narrow roadway continues straight ahead. Follow this straight on, ignoring the asphalt road forking to the right, and continue by bearing diagonally left after 5 minutes (do not bear right to climb towards the ridge). After an additional 5 minutes, ignore the path descending to the left (alternative return route; extremely overgrown). The route continues across the *macchia*-covered hillside keeping more or less on the level and then descends easily to an ill-defined col (**Chiappa Rossa**,

The dramatic promontory of Capu di Muru.

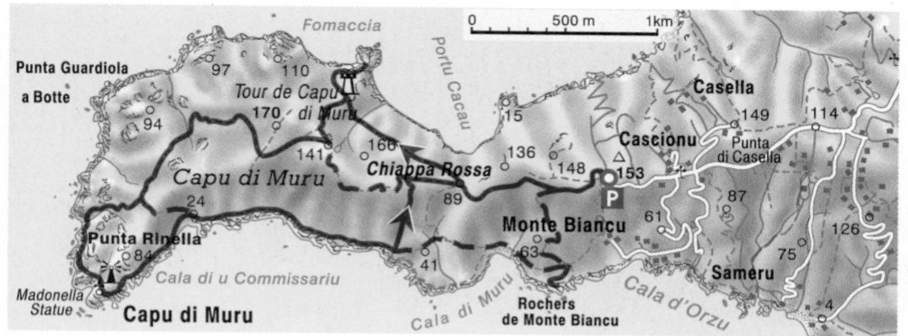

89m; 25 mins.). A signposted path turns off to the right here to the already visible **Tour de Capu di Muru**, 100m, which you reach after 20 minutes. From the platform of the Genoese watchtower, which houses a fireplace with a chimney, enjoy a splendid view over the Gulf of Ajaccio including the island's capital city and reaching as far as Corsica's main ridge.

From the tower follow the ascending path which forks after 15m (on the right a possible descent route to the coast below the tower, a good 10 mins.). Continue left here uphill. At the fork after 5 minutes you reach the Casa de Capu di Muru (141m) on the left after 50m. Cross over the roadway from the approach route and follow the path towards Madonuccia (past a stone oven after 25m). It leads to a large clearing and further on to the ridge. Now begin a steady descent along the ridge. After 20 minutes keep right at the fork (signpost), and again 3 minutes later, and descend through a broad gully, flanked on both sides by intermittent crags, to the sea (10 mins.). Now turn left,

View from the Tour de Capu di Muru of the Gulf of Ajaccio.

taking a footpath to continue along beside the sea. After another 10 minutes, the footpath crosses over a barrier of boulders then leads to a small, somewhat sandy, cove situated below the little lighthouse on **Capu di Muru**. At the cove you will find a statue of the Madonna and a chapel which also serves as a lovely picnic spot – a wonderful place to take a break, a dip and a look-around.

Now continue on towards the Gulf of Valinco and, in a few minutes, pass a building with a mooring – a pretty place for a swim. The route leads in easy up-and-down walking somewhat above the sea and then forks after half an hour (turning right, a worthwhile excursion to the Cala di Muru, a lovely little sandy bay, in 15 mins; just past it, the Rochers de Monte Biancu). We turn left instead to ascend along the signed main trail (some minutes later, at a wall, turn right) to reach a roadway on the ridgeline (¼ hr.); turn right to return in half an hour to **Cascionu**.

Before heading back to the ridge, you could cool off at the Cala di Muru.

0.50 hrs.

Castellu di Cucuruzzu and Capula 36

Educational excursion in Corsica's prehistory

The circular walk to the prehistoric cult sites embraces an exciting insight into the island's history – Cucuruzzu belongs to one of Corsica's most impressive and best-preserved fortification complexes, dating back to the Torrean civilization (Bronze Age).

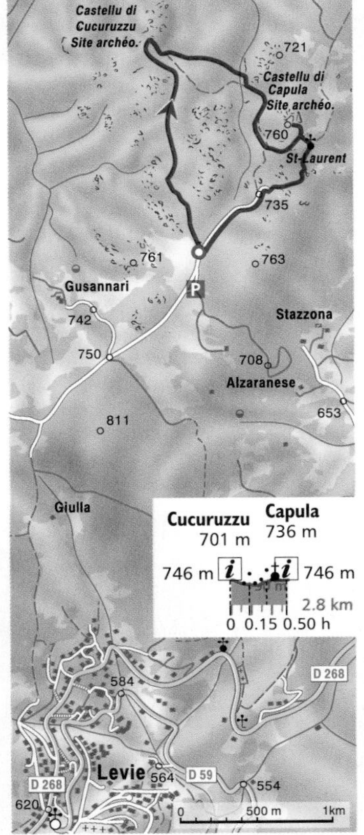

The excursion is entertaining and also ideal for families with children; plan to spend 1½ to 2 hours, including the visit. The walk leads through an enchanting, densely-forested landscape with fantastic granite outcrops. The fee charged for the use of the trail (4 €, open April – October), includes an instructive brochure available at the information office at the entrance (or audio guides are available for an extra charge) listing facts for all of the interesting waypoints, especially those concerning the two cultic sites.

Starting point: information office »Les sites de Cucuruzzu/Capula«, 746m, at the outset of the circular walk: from the D 268 Sartène – Levie, between Sainte-Lucie-de-Tallano (5km) and Levie (3km) a signed access road turns off towards Cucuruzzu. When it ends (4km on), you reach a large car park with the information office.
Height difference: not quite 100m.
Grade: short, easy walk along pleasant trails.
Refreshment and accommodation: beverages/snacks at the information office; Auberge A Pignata near the access road.
Tip: after the walk a visit is worthwhile to the Musée de l'Alta Rocca in Levie, where numerous relics found at the cultic sites are on display.
Map: ign 4154 OT (1:25,000).

From the **information office** (*Accueil*), follow the signed circular walk towards Cucuruzzu. This descends pleasantly through lovely woodland, passing immense granite outcrops, to reach the stone-built fortification of **Castellu di Cucuruzzu**, in a quarter of an hour. This impressive complex of fortifications, which is enclosed by the massive walls, is explored via a little circular route – from here, you can enjoy a marvellous view of the Bavella chain and Monte Incudine.
From Cucuruzzu, the circular route continues by turning sharp right to reach **Capula**. Cross over the course of a stream and, after a total of about 20 mins., meet up with this other, not quite so impressive, fortification complex which, although stemming from the Torrean culture, was mostly built in the Middle Ages. At the foot of the complex, the menhir figure Capula I is standing. From here, it is just a stone's throw to the next destination point, the **Chapelle St-Laurent** (in front of it, tumbledown walls from a medieval church). Meet up with the orange-marked trail *Mare a Mare Sud* to return to the starting point – yet another fabulous forest and granite outcrop trail until it becomes a track.

From Campomoro to the Cala d'Aguglia

37

Fabulous circular walk on the idyllic south-west coast

A picture-book coastal walk: a gentle ascent at first up to a Genoese tower in a picturesque location and then a leisurely walk on the promenade along the bizarre coastline at the end of which you are greeted by a superb sandy beach. The return follows a no less beautiful high path. If you prefer a shorter circuit the walk can be adapted to suit any taste.

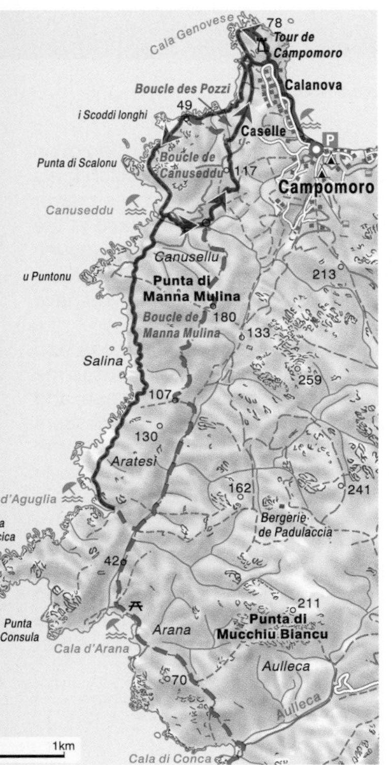

Starting point: car park after the centre of Campomoro, a pretty bathing resort on the southern tip of the Gulf of Valinco (14km south-west of Propriano, at the end of the D 121).
Height difference: 350m.
Grade: easy, leisurely coastal walk – a short section of scrambling can be avoided by walking round to the side.
Refreshment and accommodation: in Campomoro.
Alternative: from the Cala d'Aguglia to the Cala di Conca (1 hr. one way): walk inland along the path beside the stream. The path crosses the stream after a while and then forks: a hiking path turns left via Manna Mulina to Campomoro, straight on goes over a col (42m) to the Cala d'Arana. From a picnic spot under shady juniper trees the path runs for some minutes straight across the sand, then crosses a ridge and leads over to the fabulous Cala di Conca (→Walk 38).
Tip: Campomoro, Cala d'Aguglia and Cala di Conca are visited by excursion boats in the tourist season (from Propriano).
Linking tip: with Walk 38.
Map: ign 4154 OT (1:25,000).

Start the walk from the car park past **Campomoro**'s village centre and continue to follow the coastal road. After 10 minutes it enters the Calanova housing estate (access resi-

The destination of the walk – the marvellous Cala d'Aguglia.

dents only) and just under 10 minutes later you come to the highest point on the road. A hiking path branches off here to the right (signpost) which forks after 10m. Keep right (if you prefer not to do the detour to the Genoese tower you can descend directly to the coast by going down to the left) and at the fork shortly afterwards ascend left to the **Tour de Campomoro**, 78m (go left at the fork at the end). The tower is situated in a panoramic location and is surrounded by a star-shaped wall. Inside there's an exhibition and you have to pay an entrance fee to go up the tower (2.50 €).

The hiking path now descends towards the Cala Genovese (signpost) and after 10 minutes joins the coastal path (*Sentier littoral*). Follow this path to the left, immediately past the marvellous rocky bay of **Cala Genovese** and bizarre *tafoni* rocks. 5 minutes afterwards your path joins the direct descent path. Quarter of an hour later the coastal path forks. If you prefer a shorter circuit turn left here to return to Campomoro (*Boucle des Pozzi*, 2 hrs. in total). Otherwise, turn right onto the coastal path which continues to the right of a huge rock face and then ascends a steep gully with a rock arch – a fabulous section of the path (the somewhat precipitous scrambling stretch is protected by a chain; you could also avoid this by taking the bridle path). After the rock arch the path becomes »tame« again. It runs frequently through stretches flanked by juniper and after a good quarter of an hour at the Punta di Scalonu passes a prominent rocky knoll (fantastic rocky bays down

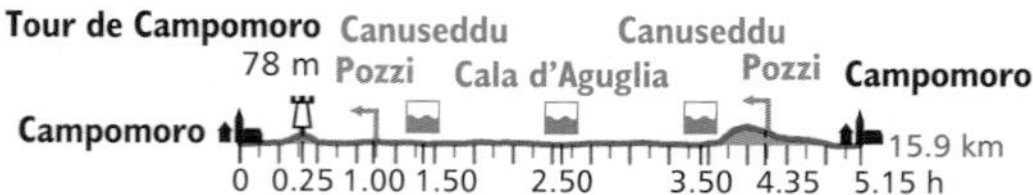

At the Genoese tower on the return.

below it). Continue across a wide expanse of meadowland to **Canuseddu bay** which you reach by the mouth of a stream at a tiny sandy beach – this is a pretty place to stop for a rest and a swim.
As you walk along the left-hand bank of the stream your return path turns off to Campomoro. Fit walkers, however, should continue following the coastal path (straight on through the hole in the wall and then over the stream) even if it's not as spectacular: after an hour you arrive at the idyllic and beautiful **Cala d'Aguglia** protected from the sea by a fjord – the shell-shaped beach with its fine sand is situated at the mouth of a stream along which the coastal path continues (→Alternative).
Back at **Canuseddu bay** follow the hiking path up the stream beside the stone wall. There's a fork after 5 mins. near a pool – continue diagonally right along the path designated for walkers. 5 minutes later a path joins from the right. The path now leaves the course of the stream and ascends in a good quarter of an hour to the mountain ridge above Campomoro. Now in a gentle up-and-down, soon with lovely views of the Genoese tower and the coast (cross over the bridle path), you reach a threshing circle where the Pozzi circular walk joins from the left (10 mins.). 20 minutes later your path joins a hiking path at the foot of the Genoese tower and this brings you up to the right to the fork in the path you will recognise near the road on the Calanova estate (10m on the right) – continue back along this road to **Campomoro**.

In Campomoro, you can bring your day's walk to a pleasant end.

TOP **38** # From Tizzano to the Cala di Conca

5.10 hrs.

Fantastic walk to the Capu di Senetosa for a swim

This walk from Tizzano to the lighthouse of Senetosa and further to the Cala di Conca is one of the most fabulous walks on the island. It spoils you with its marvellous, in places park-like coastal landscapes modelled by nature and idyllic sandy bays, each one more beautiful than the other. It's just a pity that some of the bays are also visited by excursion boats…

Starting point: Tizzano, a small beach resort 17km south-west of Sartène, at the end of the D 48. From Chez Antoine bar-restaurant (end of the asphalt) 4km on a good drivable track (on foot, 1 hr.) to a car park. (Alternatively, you could park after 3.4km at the Cala di Barcaju in the event that the track is in poor condition).
Height difference: 450m.
Grade: easy, leisurely, but rather long promenade by the coast.
Refreshment and accommodation: in Tizzano.
Tip: the Cala di Conca and the Cala di Tivella are visited by excursion boats from Propriano in the tourist season.
Linking tip: with Walk 37.
Map: ign 4154 OT (1:25,000).

From the **car park**, follow the little directional signs and then turn right onto the *Sentier du littoral* (sign). The path leads through *macchia* and, passing blocky boulders, reaches the coast where it forks – turn right to continue along the fantastic blocky boulder coastline. A few minutes later, pass the first lovely little sandy beach. After this, keep to the coastal trail, heading straight on (you could also turn right to reach a track), and soon pass a rocky knoll and, afterwards, another little sandy beach. Continuing past marvellous boulder fields, meet up then with a little rocky bay with the idyllic **Cala di Capicciolu**.

The trail leads to the right to skirt around the sandy beach and then ascends through a valley notch with lovely *tafoni* to reach a ridge. Continue on the other side keeping slightly to the right, with views of the next bays and of the lighthouse on Capu di Senetosa, down into a small valley. Soon afterwards you come to the wonderful sandy bay of **Cala Longa** which reaches far inland and is enclosed by rocks – a fabulous place for a swim. A good 10 minutes later the path crosses over the most beautiful stretch of beach on this coastal walk, the **Cala di Tivella** – the fantastic, coarse sandy beach is divided in the middle by the estuary of a stream. At the end of the beach beyond the dunes there are pine trees offering a shady place to sit (the continuation of the path goes from here).

The hiking path leads through wonderful, in places park-like coastal landscapes – here just before the Cala di Conca.

The walk takes you to two idyllic bays – the Cala di Conca (above) and the Cala di Tivella (below).

Most walkers turn round at this point but the nicest section of the walk still lies ahead, with the exception of the stretch leading to the lighthouse. After 20 minutes the gentle path crosses a stream and a few minutes after that you come to a crossroads at the **Capu di Senetosa**: you could ascend up to the right to the Genoese tower while straight on there's an interesting detour to the lighthouse 150m away. At the crossroads, however, the hiking path follows the roadway diagonally to the left gently downhill. After 2 minutes ignore a roadway branching off left to the boat mooring, similarly at the fork 2 minutes later. A quarter of an hour from the crossroads the waymarked hiking path turns off to the right onto a path that runs somewhat away from the coast with views of a turquoise-blue bay, ideal for a swim. *Tafoni* rocks stimulating the imagination break up the dense *macchia* vegetation. Now

follows the nicest section of the path, the Calanque de Conca: after 20 minutes the path leads across a plateau covered in flowers, then passes a tiny strip of sand. Nature has modelled the landscape now almost like a park. Shortly afterwards you could take a detour on the right to a spring (Funtana di l'Agula, 5 mins.). 10 minutes later go through a stone wall where the path becomes a roadway. After another 5 minutes on the left you will see the derelict house of Casa d'Ana (beautiful view of the Cala di Conca) and shortly afterwards you arrive at the **Cala di Conca**. The idyllic and beautiful sandy beach in the shape of a shell is an inviting place to stop for a swim. The beach is accessible along a track that is full of potholes, so you will rarely find yourself on your own here.
Return route: just past the Cala di Capicciolu, instead of taking the coastal trail, you could follow the roadway. Keep straight ahead and, at the power lines, a good 10 mins. later, turn onto a path next to the fence which skirts around the fence and leads directly to the **car park** nearby.

39 From Roccapina to the Plage d'Erbaju

Short circular walk around the famous rock lion of Roccapina

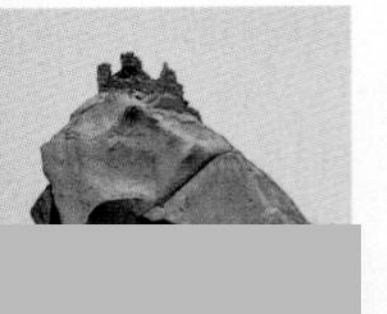

The Lion de Roccapina is one of the biggest attractions in south-western Corsica – this beautiful short walk circumnavigates the rock and on the way goes through some spectacular rocky scenery and to two of the loveliest beaches on the island.

Starting point: Cala di Roccapina, accessible along a 2km washed-out track which turns off at the Bocca di Curali (Auberge Coralli, 19km south of Sartène) from the N 196 Sartène – Bonifacio road. (Keep right at the fork in the track just after the former Roccapina campsite.)
Height difference: 220m.
Grade: an altogether easy walk on clear paths although in places a certain amount of sure-footedness is required.
Refreshment and accommodation: bar-restaurants on the main road, hotels in Sartène or in Pianottoli-Caldarello.
Important advice: the Erbaju beach is largely under the ownership of the luxurious holiday settlement of Murtoli at the north end of the beach – for this reason please keep to the southern half of the beach and do not leave behind any litter.
Map: ign 4254 OT (1:25,000).

From the **car park** at the end of the right-hand track there's a broad path (after 50m your return path joins from the right) that leads below the famous Lion de Roccapina to the western edge of the splendid **Cala di Roccapina**.
From the beach two paths go up to the already visible Genoese tower: a rather adventurous, blue-marked path begins on the right next to the log cabin (at the fork after 20m go left, some easy scrambling in places). However, take the gentler and shorter regular path that starts 30m before the beach next to a large boulder. It runs on the right past the large juniper tree uphill and, at the fork after 30m, keeps left and Roccapina beach is soon lying at your feet. You can also catch a glimpse of the »rock lion« here and there. After about a quarter of an hour the path forks just in front of a

View from the Genoese tower down to the light sandy Cala di Roccapina.

huge rocky knoll: on the right a path continues up to the nearby **Tour de Roccapina**, 130m, which unfortunately you cannot go up. But even so, the panoramic view is breathtaking of Roccapina beach on the one side and Erbaju beach on the other, and as far as Uomo di Cagna and to Bavella – even Sardinia is clearly visible. The lion can only be seen from the side, however. Now turn back and return to the last fork and keep right here. The way-marked path runs at the foot of the rocks and then gradually descends, if a bit slippery over scree, down to **Plage d'Erbaju** where you arrive at a group of rocks at its southern end. The marvellous, about 2km long beach with its sand dunes is without doubt one of the most beautiful – and most remote – beaches on the island. Now continue along the beach. After a good 5 minutes orientate yourself to the right beyond the beach and follow the roadway until, after some minutes of walking through a fenced-in area, a path forks off to the right along the fence (promptly, this leaves the fenced-in area behind; you could also skirt around to the left along an overgrown path). At first the path leads directly towards the Lion de Roccapina and after a good 10 minutes reaches the crest of the ridge on the left of the lion. The hiking path now runs for 5 minutes on the left over the ridge and then gradually descends, in wide loops, down along a former roadway (after a few minutes you can take a shortcut). The roadway is eroded in several places and rather overgrown and joins the track to Roccapina beach after a quarter of an hour near to the **car park**.

Tour de Roccapina
130 m
Cala di Roccapina
Cala di Roccapina
Plage d'Erbaju
Auberge Coralli
Auberge Coralli
114 m
8.8 km
0 0.45 1.30 h

40 *Sentier des Bruzzi*

2.00 hrs.

Circular walk through the nature reserve on the south-west coast

The trail to the Bruzzi peninsula with its offshore island is an especially delightful circular route – bizarre tafoni rock formations, little sandy bays and the marvels of nature satiate all of your senses.

Starting point: the little car park at the outset of the *Sentier littoral des Bruzzi*, 17m: in Pianottoli-Caldarello, turn off from the N 196 along the D 122, heading towards the sea, and follow the signs for »Campings«. 1km further on, just before the church, turn right. A good 2km after that, at the Camping Kévano, turn right again to meet up with the Bruzzi car park after 1.3km (4.6km from the N 196).
Height difference: a good 100m
Grade: an easy coastal walk along distinct paths; some stretches demand a little sure-footedness.
Refreshment and accommodation: in Pianottoli-Caldarello.
Tip: a short distance northwards, you'll find another lovely coastal walk: it sets off at the Anse de Furnellu (turn-off from the N 196, 1km west of the turn-off to Monacia; 1.5km of track) and leads in a south-westerly direction along the coast to the Tour d'Olmeto on the headland (20 mins). From here, you could reach the heavenly Plage Mucchju Biancu (45 mins.).
Map: ign 4255 OT (1:25,000).

From the **car park**, the signed trail ascends pleasantly through the *macchia* to reach a marvellous viewpoint (a stone bench to the left) affording a view of the Bruzzi peninsula with the offshore islands and also the sandy back of Chevanu; in the distance, you can spot Sardinia. Here, the trail forks. Take the right-hand trail which begins in easy up-and-down walking as it passes bizarrely-formed *tafoni* rocks and then gently descends towards the seaside. Still somewhat above, the path veers to the left, crossing over a valley notch,

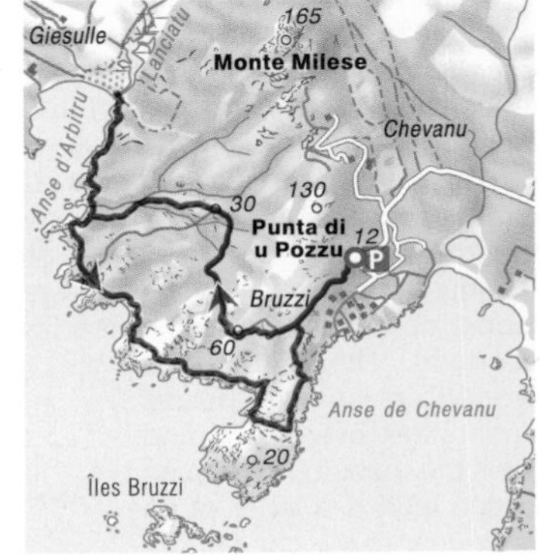

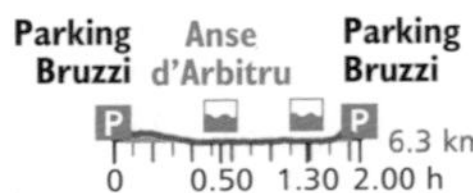

then continues climbing down to the coast to reach the seaside next to a small, pretty, sandy bay.
Before following the coastal trail to the left, a 15-minute excursion to the right is worthwhile, to the sandy bay of the **Anse d'Arbitru**, where you are sure to be tempted to a dip. After this excursion, pick up the *Sentier littoral*, leading pleasantly, almost on the level, along the coast – sometimes through parkland-like hedges, tossed by the wind and sometimes past *tafoni* rock formations and rocky bays. 10 mins. later, pass a »cairn-peppered beach« and 10 mins. after that, reach a »coral beach« at the outset of the **Bruzzi peninsula**.
The trail forks at this point: turn right for a short way, heading out onto the peninsula and then traverse it by following the sign to the left. At another little sandy beach, veer landwards once again. At the merge with the other branch of the trail, the ascent becomes noticeable as it climbs to the viewpoint already met on the approach route. From there, return again to the **car park**.

The Arbitru beach is an excursion not to be missed.

TOP **41** # *Uomo di Cagna, 1217m*

5.15 hrs.

A famous balanced boulder marks the summit

This summit in the island's south is indeed a curiousity: an immense balanced rock – in the past an important landmark for ships at sea – perching precariously on a narrow boulder.

Starting point: car park by the church of Giannuccio, 467m, village 9.5km north of the coast road between Pianotolli and Roccapina.
Height difference: 750m.
Grade: strenuous mountain walk along distinct paths, laborious climb to the summit over boulders, the final leg of the route is not waymarked.
Refreshment and accommodation: snack bar in Giannuccio, hotels in Monacia, campsite in Pianotolli-Caldarello.
Map: ign 4254 OT (1:25,000).

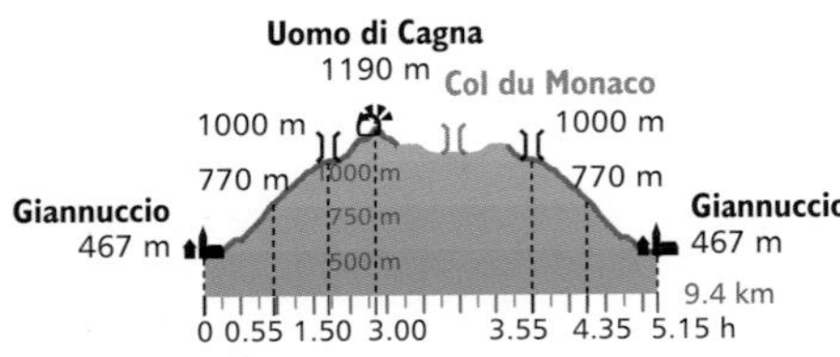

From the church in **Giannuccio**, follow the signs for Omu di Cagna to reach another car park. Sharp to the left here, the *Sentier l'omu di cagna* (sign; yellow-marked) begins. This ascends along a stone wall and, some minutes later, leads past a water house on the right. Shortly after, the path traverses the slope fairly on the level and after crossing a brook, ascends to a **high plateau** covered in tree heather. In the distance the balanced rock comes into view (just under 1 hr. in total). You are surrounded by immense boulders, grotesquely formed and lying one on top of the other and a pine forest shades you from the hot sun. After leaving the pine forest, you reach a **high plateau** (mountain pass) with pretty little picnic spots. The path forks here (a total of 1¾ hrs.; you should turn round at this point if you do not feel confident enough in your footing). The main path leads to the right and after 25m, at a small rock arch and a large cairn, bends

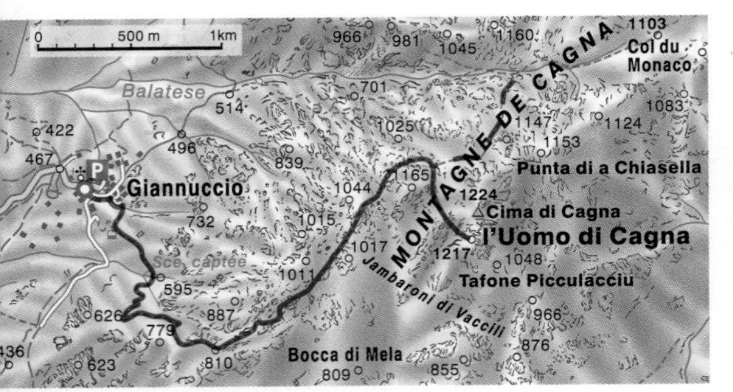

sharply to the left (yellow dots). It leads in a constant up-and-down, while skirting around the mountain lying before us, to reach a sloping high plateau (just under 1 hr.; very strenuous, be sure to follow the yellow waymarkers and cairns). 25m above a trail sign, in front of a small rock face, the path forks again: the path left turns off to the Plateau de Presarella and continues to the Col du Monaco (a very lovely excursion). However, ascend to the right along the yellow-marked path to the top of the ridge next to the southern summit of the Cima di Cagna (10 mins.). The balanced rock once more appears ahead. The waymarkers lead you on the other side of the ridge in a gentle up-and-down to a large rock arch on the ridge (a good 10 mins.), finally diagonally to the right in very strenous scrambling over boulders to the **viewpoint on the rock** directly

The balanced rock of Uomo di Cagna is always in view as you walk across the plateau.

Excursion: the fern-covered plateau (above) – near the Col du Monaco (below).

opposite the balanced rock. From here, there is a breathtaking view embracing the southern part of the island (10 mins., very unclear terrain; the first ascent of the Uomo di Cagna using ropes was in 1970).
Return the same way down the approach route. Walkers wishing to extend the walk, and who have a good sense of direction, can take an excursion to the Col du Monaco on the way back. To do this, return along the approach route as far as the fork on the sloping plateau (see above; ½ hr. from Uomo di Cagna or 5 minutes from the top of the ridge next to the southern summit of Cima di Cagna). Go right here along a clear path (cairns) for a short way uphill to a fern-covered plateau. Cross the full length of the plateau, at first keeping to the right, past a spring, then keeping left all the time along the ridge of the plateau.
10 minutes from the start of the plateau, the path leads downhill on the left-hand side of a rock arch shaped like a handle, always heading for the bouldery summit of the Punta di Monaco. Just under half an hour later the path leads to the **Col du Monaco**, 1103m (a good ¾ hr. from the plateau). Just before the pass, by the way, a path forks off to the left, waymarked with cairns, heading towards Giannuccio (1¾ hr.). The path is, however, barely discernible and, above all, extremely overgrown – so, unfortunately, it cannot be considered as an alternative for the return route.

3.20 hrs.

Bergeries de Bitalza, 1050m 42

Delightful alpine settlement and a rocky summit

Bitalza is one of the most picturesque mountain pastures on the island. The huts, only temporarily inhabited in summer and at the weekend, are grouped like in an amphitheatre around a high meadowland plateau with an altar and a statue of the Madonna – a perfectly harmonious arrangement. This beautiful walk from Vacca to the settlement can be undertaken easily by all walkers. The excursion to the panoramic Capellu summit on the other hand, is only recommended to experienced mountain walkers since the path is rather unclear and a bit of scrambling is required at the end.

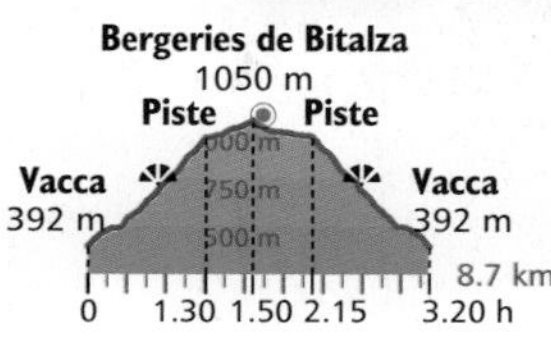

Starting point: Vacca, 392m, small village north-west of Sotta (access along a narrow road via Borivoli, 9km from the D 59 Sotta – Col de Bacinu – Carbini). Park on the road before the village.
Height difference: just under 700m.
Grade: easy walk but at the beginning, sometimes somewhat overgrown.
Refreshment and accommodation: in Sotta and Porto-Vecchio.
Alternatives: 1) from Borivoli to Bitalza (2 hrs.; easy): 5.2km from the D 59 (just past Borivoli) at a roomy lay-by, the yellow-waymarked trail forks away (sign). 15 mins. later, pass a viewpoint with a panorama map board. 10 mins. on, cross over the course of a stream. The trail now ascends in zigzags and, after a total of 1½ hrs., crosses over a track, and crosses it yet again, shortly afterwards (20m left). 15 mins. later, the track is crossed over for the last time. Now follow a roadway which, in a few minutes, reaches the clearing with the Bergeries de Bitalza.
2) from Bitalza to Capellu, 1205m (1¼ hrs. one way; some stretches are extremely overgrown; sure-footedness, a head for heights and orientation skills are required, especially when visibility is poor): 150m from the open-air chapel with the Madonna, a yellow-waymarked trail forks to the left, ascending past the first houses (10m on, a sign »Funtanedda«). Follow the yellow waymarkers (at a fork, pass a bread oven). Just before the crest of the ridge, a path forks away to the left, waymarked with cairns. This ascends, mostly somewhat on the diagonal, traversing the slope and meets up again, after a good ¼ hr., with the ridgeline, just before the Capelluccio. Beyond the ridgeline, continue in a slight descent over a plateau, still heading towards the double peak of Capellu (the path is sometimes extremely overgrown). 10 mins. later, climb up a short gully (easy scrambling), then continue somewhat diagonally through the slope and along the foot of the rock face of the northern peak (1219m), climbing up to the gap between the northern and the southern summits (¼ hr.). From here, soon turn left, climbing over rock to the southern summit of the Capellu where the island's south, as well as Sardinia, lie at our feet (¼ hr., easy scrambling).
Map: ign 4254 OT (1:25,000).

A harmonious arrangement – the settlement of Bitalza on a mountain pasture.

View from Bitalza to Capellu (left).

The starting point is the large old bread oven on the right-hand side of the road in **Vacca**. The path begins on the left next to the oven. You ascend quite strenuously up through *macchia* and mixed forest, later pine forest, sometimes catching glimpses in the direction of the southern tip of the island and the castellated rocks to the side of the path. After an hour, the lovely (but, at the outset, somewhat overgrown) path crosses a stream and half an hour later it joins a forest track (take note of this junction for the descent). Now continue uphill along this forest track. A good 5 mins. later, a distinct path, passing between two cairns and then continuously marked with more cairns, forks to the left. The path crosses a pine forest and, 10 mins. later, reaches a large clearing blanketed with ferns and the **Bergeries de Bitalza**. In the meadow at the foot of the pasturage settlement, an open-air chapel with a Madonna provides a nice spot for a break – but in any case, you should take the time to ramble through the almost-completely abandoned mountain hamlet. We warmly recommend an excursion to the Capellu –the trail leading there is, however, very overgrown and, especially at the outset, not easy to locate (→Alternative).

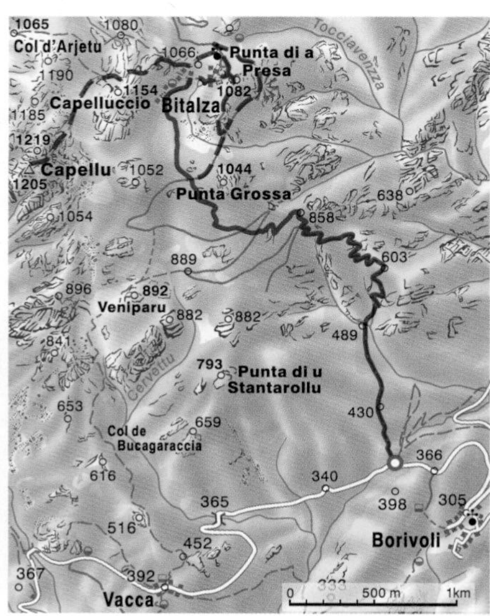

43 From Bonifacio to Paragan beach

3.00 hrs.

Ramble to the sandy bays west of Bonifacio

The coastal trail west of Bonifacio provides the walker with access to a couple of beautiful, sometimes spectacular, sandy bays enclosed by limestone cliffs. Also, along the return route, the trail opens up marvellous views of the harbour town.

Starting point: Bonifacio's harbour. Parking possible at the harbour and in the upper town (signed). Bus connections to Porto-Vecchio and Ajaccio.
Height difference: not quite 300m,

Grade: an easy, thoroughly pleasant ramble.
Refreshment/accommodation: restaurants, hotels, campsites in Bonifacio.
Map: ign 4255 OT (1:25,000).

From the harbour in **Bonifacio**, return along the main street for 200m and, before reaching the Camping l'Araguina, turn left onto the *Sentier des Plages*. This ascends somewhat steeply through the limestone cliffs to reach a high plateau and then cross over a roadway. The broad trail, often cobblestone and flanked by stone walls, drops down to pass through a valley notch down below. At a fork for a path, veer to the right (to the left, a short excursion to the **Plage de la Catena** is worthwhile, a little sandy beach in a secondary bay of Bonifacio). Soon afterwards, the trail continues once again over the high plateau, opening a fleeting view of Bonifacio's upper town. In the following depression, our

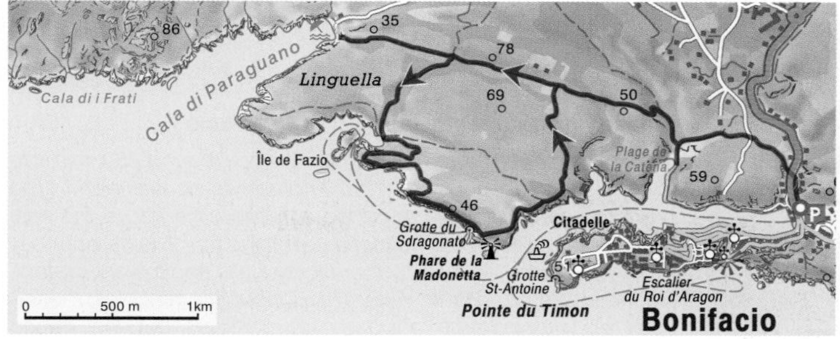

return route later on, forks off left to the Fazio bay and, about 700m past that, you meet up with the **Anse de Paragan** (Cala di Paraguano). An eye-catcher over the white sands and turquoise-blue waters of the bathing bay is the rocky Mont de la Trinité with a hermitage.

Now return along the approach route and, 700m on (10 mins.) turn right onto the path heading towards »Fazio – Madonetta« (shortly after, turn right again). This leads in not quite a quarter of an hour to the fantastic **Fazio bay**, enclosed by limestone cliffs, and the island of Fazio. A small bathing beach is located on the bay – but unfortunately, the popular bay is also the destination for many excursion boats which noticeably disrupts the idyllic setting.

The trail now ascends to the left, following a bend, to reach the next high plateau and then leads constantly close to the edge of the limestone cliffs (the narrow access to Fazio bay can only be spotted by taking a short detour). Soon, a view of Bonifacio opens up. Past the lighthouse **Madonetta** pass yet another marvellous viewpoint with a view of Bonifacio and its harbour fjord, and then the trail veers back towards the interior. After a quarter of an hour, meet up again with the approach route and turn right to return to **Bonifacio**.

44 Capu Pertusato

3.00 hrs.

Cliff walk with a fantastic view of Bonifacio

Founded on the southernmost tip of Corsica around 830, this little town is without doubt the most impressive on the island. The buildings perch on the very edge of white cliffs above the sea, crowded together in a precarious balancing act. The harbour bay (Marine) is watched over by the mighty walls and towers protecting the upper city (Haute Ville). Throughout the centuries, the fortress has withstood the forays of many invaders, but now, during the summer months, the place is overrun by hordes of tourists. Walking round about the old part of town is certainly a must for every visitor, but a quieter and most restful alternative is a stroll along the cliffs to Capu Pertusato.

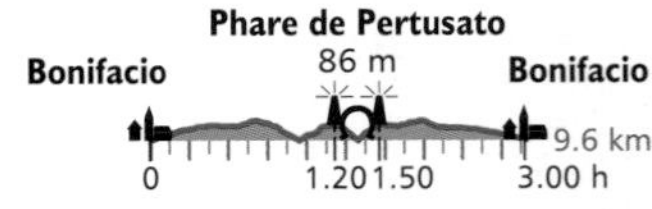

Starting point: harbour of Bonifacio. Car parks at the harbour and in the upper town (follow the signs). Bus service to Porto-Vecchio and Ajaccio.
Height difference: 300m.

Grade: easy stroll. Be careful near the cliff's edge – danger of falling.
Refreshment/accommodation: restaurants, hotels, campsites in Bonifacio.
Map: ign 4255 OT (1:25,000).

Bonifacio, as seen from the path to the lighthouse on Capu Pertusato.

To the left of the Church of **St-Erasme**, the wide steps of Rastello Street climb from the harbour to **Col St-Roch**; from here a descent can be made to the tiny sandy beach, Plage de Sutta Rocca. You choose the path which leads on the left from the col along the edge of the cliff. After a good half an hour the cliff path forks. A steep and overgrown path descends straight on down to a small valley, but keep heading along the path on the plateau and a few minutes later reach a crossroads. Follow the road that leads to the right downhill and leave it after 3 minutes, soon after reaching the valley floor, along a path that branches off to the left and leads up to a derelict fort. Go right here back to the road which

A lovely sandy beach before the Île St-Antoine awaits you at the lighthouse.

you continue to follow past a military tower. The road soon crosses through another small valley – 20m after reaching the bottom of the valley a footpath makes a shortcut to the left and after some minutes joins the road again. 5 minutes later the road ends at the **lighthouse**. At this point only 12km separates you from Sardinia and, also a beautiful sight, are the Lavezzi islands. For those wanting to visit the sandy bay and the little island of St-Antoine below the lighthouse take the path turning off towards it before the lighthouse (steep and slippery!).

On the other side of the lighthouse a path sets off along the cliffs and brings you, in just under a quarter of an hour (at the end a short way steeply downhill) to the foot of an overhanging sandstone cliff directly above Cala di Labra – a considerable number of stalactities hang down from the ceiling and ferns and fig trees have also flourished in this place.

Overhanging cliffs with stalactites at the Cala di Labra.

Lavezzi 45

Island paradise in the strait between Corsica and Sardinia

The island of Lavezzi is a very popular destination offered by excursion boats with a round trip to the grotto and cliffs on the southern tip and to the »millionaire's island« of Cavallo. On Lavezzi you can interrupt the journey for a bathing stop. The island is particularly delightful with its idyllic beaches and fantastic granite formations, and also its very varied flora with some endemic plants.

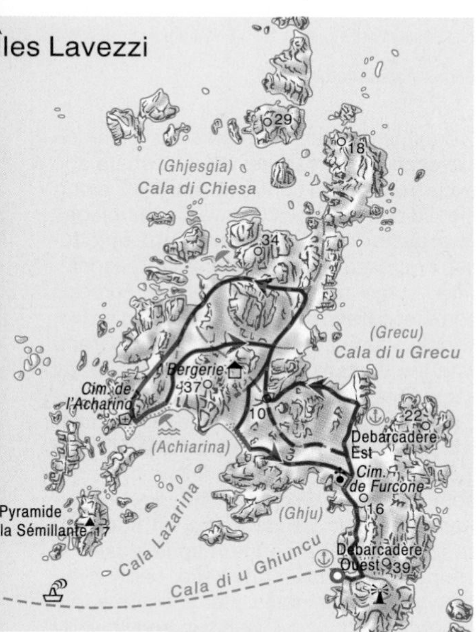

Cala di l'Achiarina
Lavezzu Lavezzu
4.2 km
0 0.40 1.15 h

Starting point: Lavezzi island on the seaway between Corsica and Sardinia, a part of the Bouches de Bonifacio Nature Reserve. From Bonifacio and Porto-Vecchio there are several boat excursions leaving daily to the island.
Height difference: insignificant.
Grade: short, easy coastal walk with places to stop for a swim, no shade (you might need a sun umbrella).
Refreshment and accommodation: restaurants, hotels and campsites in Bonifacio.
Important advice: Lavezzi island is part of the Bouches de Bonifacio Nature Reserve – please make a note of the regulations (e.g. you are not allowed to stray from the paths or pick the flowers).
Map: ign 4255 OT (1:25,000).

Main attraction of the island – the marvellous Achiarina beach.

From the western embarkation point on **Lavezzi** (Debarcadère Ouest) where the excursion boats come in, walk left along the Cala di u Ghiuncu towards the *plages* (the paths to the lighthouse are unfortunately closed for environmental reasons). After some minutes you reach Furcone cemetery. Keep right beforehand to arrive, shortly afterwards, at the **Cala di u Grecu** with the eastern embarkation point (small sandy beach).

Continue towards Achiarina and, after 5 minutes, walk past the ***bergerie*** 50m on the right. At the next fork follow the signpost »Cala di Chiesa«, and soon afterwards the path bends to the left (the path straight on to the northern tip is closed to the public and is, in any case, badly overgrown). A few minutes later you come to a delightful rocky cove with two small sandy beaches, **Cala di Chiesa**.

The path then leads past some marvellous sculpted rocks over to the largest and most beautiful beach on the island at **Cala di l'Achiarina** where there are usually a lot of boats anchored as well. On the right-hand side you will find another cemetery (Cimetière de l'Acharino) and – on an off-shore rocky island – the Pyramide de la Sémillante, in commemoration of the ship-wreck of the Sémillante on 14th February 1855 when 750 people lost their lives.
Here at the latest you should aim to spend some time and go for a swim before returning to the embarkation point. The walk back will take at least half an hour: follow the path round a wide bend to the ***bergerie***. Then you have a choice: either continue straight ahead along the direct path or turn right to walk past more sandy coves and finally past the Furcone cemetery and back to the embarkation point.

The fabulous rocky bay at Cala di Chiesa.

46 Punta di a Vacca Morta, 1314m

3.00 hrs.

Panoramic peak surrounded by a sea of boulders in the Ospédale Forest

Hardly another site on Corsica offers such a sweeping view as this modest summit. To the east, you can admire the coastline of Porto-Vecchio, the Ospédale reservoir to the north as well as the entire Bavella chain and the Gulf of Valinco to the west.

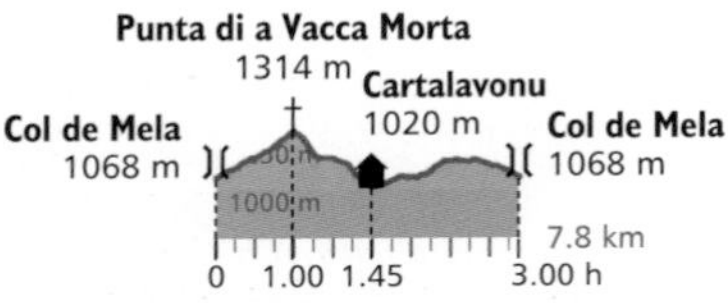

Location: L'Ospédale, daily bus service to Porto-Vecchio and Zonza (→Walk 56).
Starting point: Col de Mela, 1068m. 1km from Ospédale in the direction of Zonza, take the fork to Agnarone, Cartalavonu, Tavogna, then the 1st and 2nd turnings to the left, 3rd and 4th to the right, finally the 5th turning to the left towards Col de Mela. The road ends at a private house (parking places).
Height difference: a good 400m.
Grade: easy mountain hike on adventurous footpaths (possible route finding problems in poor visibility).
Refreshment and accommodation: restaurants in Cartalavonu, Agnarone and Ospédale, hotels and campsites in Zonza and Porto-Vecchio.
Map: ign 4254 ET (1:25,000).

In front of the gate on the **Col de Mela** two orange-marked paths set off – the right-hand one leads to Carbini, the left one via Cartalavonu to Ospédale. Take the left fork. The orange-marked trail climbs to the right of a forestry road and soon crosses over another forestry road into which it merges shortly afterwards. After about 150m, a distinct trail branches off to the right away from the orange-marked forestry road and after 30m runs between two boulders. Cairns now mark the route for the continued ascent. The distinct path follows a fence for a short way along the **ridgeline**, and, 15 minutes later, reaches an open **plateau** (1200m) dotted with enchanting rock formations and wind-twisted pines. From here, cairns mark the route – bearing slightly to the right and, later, more to the left – over a small plateau (turn right here along the ridge; our return route to Cartalavonu turns off immediately to the

Wind-twisted pines and gigantic granite boulders distinguish the unspoilt landscape near Punta di a Vacca Morta. A view of the Ospédale reservoir from the summit.

left) towards the now visible **Punta di a Vacca Morta** (summit cross). All around the peak, beautiful picnic spots can be found and natural playgrounds for children; some boulders also tempt you to a bit of scrambling.

Now walk back along the ascent route for 5 minutes to the small plateau and turn off right here onto the distinct cairn-marked path. It leads quite steeply down through a pine forest to a meadow-blanketed plateau, the **Foce Alta**, 1171m; ¼ hr., where you meet the orange-marked *Mare a Mare Sud* on the left-hand side. Follow this to the right (left goes to the Col de Mela) to **Cartalavonu** where you meet a road next to the Le Refuge Restaurant (a good 20 mins.). Ascend along this road to the left until, after a quarter of an hour on a sharp right-hand bend next to a car park for walkers, a blue and yellow-marked trail turns off left (signpost »*Sentier des Tafonis*«).

The beautiful trail runs gently up and down through a boulder-strewn pine forest and after some minutes crosses a little stream. 25m afterwards at the fork go uphill to the left and after 5 minutes leave a forest road which ends here by going left. 5 mins. later, bear right with the blue waymarkers and 50m on, pass a spring. Some minutes later, meet the orange-marked *Mare a Mare Sud* (left leads in 2 mins. to the Foce Alta) which brings you back to the right to the **Col de Mela** (after 10 minutes it joins a forest road and 2 minutes after that the ascent route).

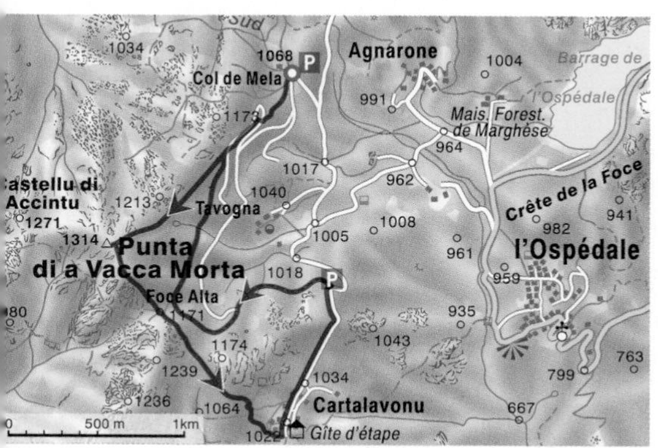

47 Piscia di Gallo

1.50 hrs.

Short walk to the »Rooster's Piss« by the Ospédale reservoir

This route is highly recommended, not only because it passes the spectacular waterfall, the Piscia di Gallo (»Rooster's Piss«) but also, more generally, because of the unique landscape of the Ospédale region. Numerous granite domes and fields of boulders, bizarre rock formations and beautiful forests are in abundance here. However, you won't be alone along this route because it counts as one of the most popular walking paths on the island – in high season, you will most likely encounter hundreds of excursionists and walkers here en route every day.

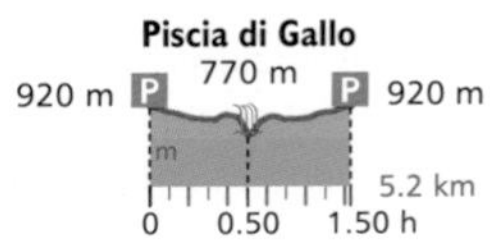

Location: L'Ospédale, a village above the Gulf of Porto-Vecchio with panoramic views south of the Ospédale reservoir. Daily bus service to Porto-Vecchio and Zonza (→Walk 56).
Starting point: at the pay car park (4 €) with snack bars, 920m, 3.5km past the retaining walls of the Barrage de l'Ospédale.
Height difference: about 150m.
Grade: easy walking on well-marked and distinct paths. Sturdy walking shoes are recommended for the steep and slippery descent to the waterfall.
Refreshment and accommodation: there are restaurants in Ospédale, hotels and campsites in Zonza and Porto-Vecchio.
Advice: the best time of the day for the walk is before noon since this is when the waterfall is bathed in sunlight and you can avoid the hordes of tourists. After longish periods without rainfall, the stream dwindles to just a trickle.
Map: ign 4254 ET (1:25,000).

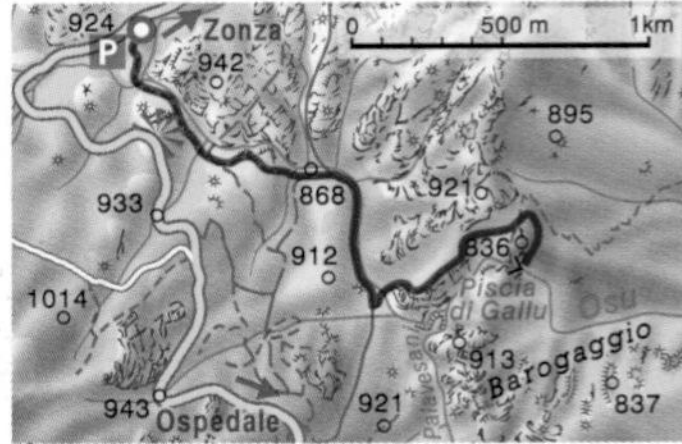

The semi-balanced rock along the path.

Starting at the **car park**, between the snack bars, a trail marked with yellow signs descends to the Oso stream and then continues along the stream and down the valley. A couple of minutes later, cross over a little bridge and then merge later on with a broad gravel track. Some minutes after that, the marked trail forks left and crosses the stream bed. The path now leads through a strange and wonderful landscape of bizarre rock formations mixed with the vibrant green of the pine trees and *macchia* vegetation. The Oso stream below the path which you have just crossed, has bored its way through a rock arch on its journey to the sea which now appears below us. And then you are standing before an immense **rock** that appears to be balanced.

Now the path begins a somewhat steeper descent, passing a huge boulder (almost obscured by the towering pines) with cave-like niches – a paradise for children but not without its dangers! The **waterfall** emerges ahead – shooting out in a single stream from the sheer rock face into the valley below. The final metres of descent clamber down a more difficult and mostly quite slippery path that ends at the rather dirty waters at the base of the waterfall. This stretch, as well as the viewpoint on a sloping rock above the pool, should only be explored by walkers with climbing experience and is not everyone's cup of tea.

Piscia di Gallo.

48 Monte Calva, 1381m, and Punta di u Diamante, 1227m

2.45 hrs.

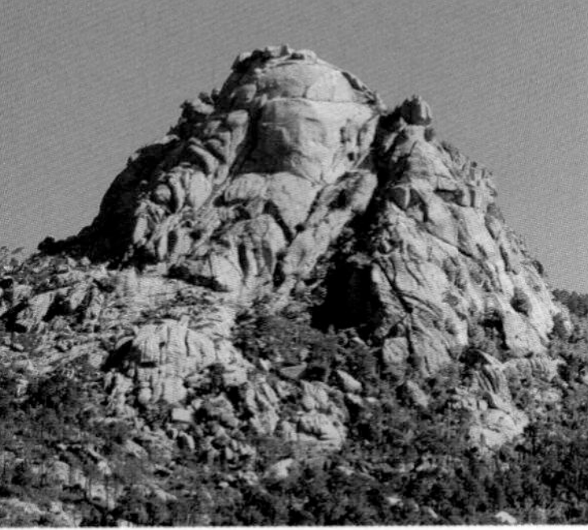

Hike to a congenial panoramic peak with a raw diamond as a bonus

Monte Calva offers an excellent panoramic view which sweeps across Bavella, Incudine, Montagne de Cagna and the Gulf of Porto-Vecchio. However, the climb to the nearby Punta di u Diamante, a peak that truly does honour to its name, is a more exciting adventure in unforgettable scenery. This raw diamond may lack any sign of a cut or a polish, nevertheless the marvellous stony peak possesses a singular charm.

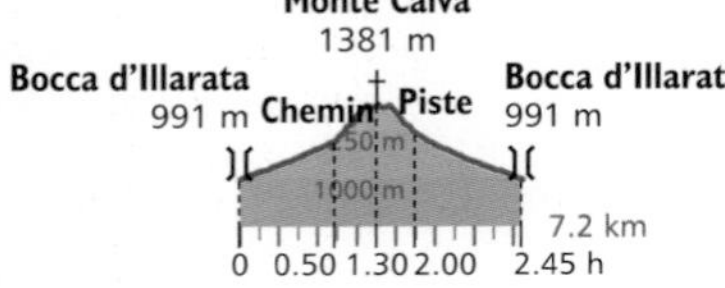

Locations: Zonza, centre for mountain climbers – located below the Bavella pass and Ospédale, beautifully-situated village above the coast Porto-Vecchio. Daily bus service from Porto-Vecchio (→Walk 56).
Starting point: Bocca d'Illarata, 991m, a small mountain pass between Ospédale (10km) and Zonza (11.5km). Parking possible just beyond the mountain pass when approaching from Ospédale.
Height difference: a good 400m.
Grade: easy mountain walk via well-marked paths.
Refreshment and accommodation: restaurants in Ospédale, hotels and campsites in Zonza and Porto-Vecchio.
Tip: the hike can be extended with a detour to the nearby Piscia di Gallo.
Map: ign 4254 ET (1:25,000).

Just before the rocky plateau. – Below: view of Bavella and Incudine from the main peak.

Approaching from Ospédale and just beyond the mountain pass **Bocca d'Illarata** (parking places), a forest track forks off to the right. 15 minutes later, you can already see the craggy summit which is our goal. Continue on the main path. After walking a total of 45 minutes along a stretch with many lovely views of the east coast, the Punta di u Diamante and the Ospédale reservoir, reach the first groups of crags. Now you need to be very careful: soon afterwards, on a right-hand bend, about 50m after skirting a large, furrowed boulder, a distinct cairn-marked footpath breaks off to the left. Keeping right, the footpath ascends along the edge of an area of rock slabs and a gully, to finally reach an exceptionally lovely **rocky plateau**. – By the way, don't worry if you miss the fork for the footpath, since about 5 minutes later and again at a right bend in the track, another cairn-marked footpath forks off to the left climbing even more gently until it merges again on the plateau with the first fork from the main route. – Then skirt around a craggy minor peak by bearing left and later climb over the ridge to the summit next to the radio mast. Just a bit further on you reach the actual summit of **Monte Calva** – a mere four metres higher.

After completing the route, have some fun by exploring the bizarre craggy landscape which surrounds the **Punta di u Diamante**. For this you only need to return to the parking area at Bocca d'Illarata and then continue in the other direction. A distinct, cairn-marked path traverses diagonally along the slope towards the peak. Ascending the bell-shaped crag of the summit should only be attempted by experienced rock-climbers (Grade II).

49 Bocca di Fumicosa, 1335m

2.45 hrs.

At first a pleasant, then a somewhat more adventurous excursion into the craggy paradise of the Bavella

The disastrous forest fires in the summer of 1990 caused serious damage to this beautiful forest and hiking area south of the Bavella pass. Nevertheless, the walk is enchanting as it passes through the untamed, idyllic landscapes, especially on the ridge near the Bocca di Fumicosa.

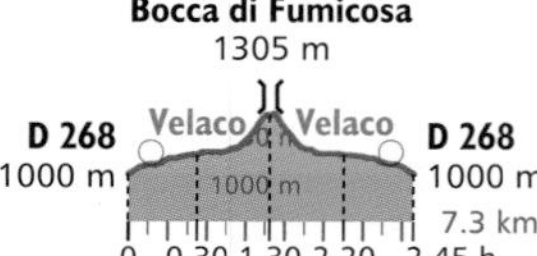

Location: Zonza, 778m. Daily bus service to Porto-Vecchio (→Walk 56).
Starting point: 5km from Zonza, on the D 268 road leading to Bavella pass and 3.7km before reaching the pass, a forest road with barrier forks to the right (1000m).
Height difference: a good 350m.

Grade: remote route for adventurous walkers – the ascent to Bocca di Fumicosa lacks almost any sign of a path and requires some sense of direction.
Refreshment and accommodation: restaurants, hotels and campsite in Zonza.
Map: ign 4253 ET (1:25,000).

Shortly after passing the **barrier** you ascend the narrow forest track to the left, keeping straight ahead and after 10 minutes pass a water reservoir on a bend to the right. 5 minutes later cross the wide forest road (50m on, bear diagonally left) and then after half an hour reach the concreted **Velaco stream** (gate, access for walkers) which you cross immediately by going sharp right. A blue-marked sometimes somewhat overgrown path continues on the opposite side and crosses the slopes in a gentle up-and-down at the foot of

Above: Punta Velaco (centre) and Tour de Samulaghia (right) from the path. Below: Bocca di Fumicosa is a lovely spot for a rest and to enjoy the views.

the rock faces. It takes about 30 minutes until a small **stream** crosses your route. Cairns clearly mark the fork as well as the ascent path that continues climbing, following the right-hand bank of the stream. Always bear slightly to the left in a north-easterly direction keeping an eye out for cairns. After 15 minutes you reach a broad **gully** flanked by rocks where the forest begins to thin out. Not much further on you reach the mountain pass **Bocca di Fumicosa** with a stunning view of the craggy mountain landscape south of the Bavella pass. To the north, you will see the towering Punta Velaco, behind it and to the right, the Promontoire with the pinnacle Campanile de Ste-Lucie. To the right of the Bocca, the sharp-edged peak of Puntu di Ferru and south of this, the slender Tour de Samulaghia can be seen.
On the **descent**, be careful not to miss the blue-marked footpath leading back to the Velaco stream.

50 Trou de la Bombe and Promontoire, 1420m

3.00 hrs.

To the biggest attraction on the Bavella pass

Of the attractions of the Bavella, the hole in the rock of Trou de la Bombe is one of the main ones – and also easy to reach. Because of that, the trail leading there is very busy. The continued route to Promontoire, on the other hand, is a touch more demanding and clearly less frequented – here, the walker can find delight in the unspoilt craggy landscape with nerve-tickling views!

Location: Zonza, 778m.
Starting point: Bavella pass, 1218m. There are car parks located at the top of the pass. Bus service from Porto-Vecchio (→Walk 56).
Height difference: not quite 400m.
Grade: until reaching the Trou de la Bombe, this is an easy walk via good trails; the summit ascent to Promontoire is negotiated along a path waymarked with cairns.
Refreshment and accommodation: restaurants and *auberge* (bunks) in the Village de Bavella; hotels and campsite in Zonza.
Linking tip: with Walk 51.
Map: ign 4253 ET (1:25,000).

At first descend along the road to enter the **Village de Bavella**. At the *auberge*, turn right onto the white/red-marked forest track and a good 5 minutes later, a broad, red/orange-marked trail forks off to the right (immediately afterwards, the white/red-marked *GR 20* forks away to the left from the forest track). The trail ascends pleasantly through pine forest overgrown with ferns and converges with a red/orange-marked footpath after 10 minutes (this is a lovely alternative route for the return, later on, to the Bavella pass; sign »Chapelle«). Just afterwards cross over a small stream by bearing left (the orange-marked trail forks off to the right before that). After ½ hour of walking reach a small rise situated to the right of the striking crag of **Dame-Jeanne**, 1313m.

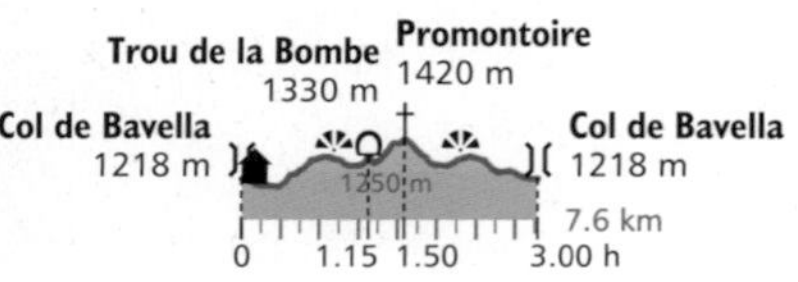

Continue on the red-marked footpath in easy up-and-down walking to reach an open rise (10 minutes), from which you can already take in a lovely view of the mighty rocky summit of Punta Velaco

From left to right: Trou de la Bombe, Promontoire and Punta Velaco.

(easy to spot is the couloir, climbing to the left almost all the way to the summit) and, further to the left, also the hole in the rock, the »Trou de la Bombe« (bomb crater). Now descend to a trail junction situated in the broad meadowland saddle of the **Bocca di Velaco**, 1285m (10 minutes.). The red-waymarked main trail turns to the left here (very difficult to negotiate along the final metres) to reach the **Trou de la Bombe** (U Cumpuleddu, ¼ hr.).

If you also wish to climb Promontoire, just before the Trou de la Bombe, turn right into a gully. After a short ascent, there is a slight descent and, afterwards, you continue again through a valley notch to climb up to the ridgeline. Here at a trail junction, turn left to reach the rocky summit plateau of **Promontoire**. It is worthwhile to roam over the high plateau which boasts some breath-taking viewpoints – to the right and below the sheer drop of the plateau, you can marvel at the quirky rock spire of the Campanile di Santa Lucia.

51 *Punta Velaco, 1483m*

3.00 hrs.

Rocky massif with all the archetypal features

Punta Velaco, combined with Promontoire, make up the central ramparts of the southern Bavella chain. The ascent is negotiated through a steep couloir which, after the easy approach, leaves the walker in a sweat. The summit itself demands some scrambling and a head perfectly free from vertigo. The peak opens up marvellous views of the east coast between Porto-Vecchio and Aléria, as well as the craggy towers of the northern chain and Incudine.

Location: Zonza, 778m.
Starting point: Bavella pass, 1218m. Car park at the top of the pass. Bus service from Porto-Vecchio (→Walk 56).
Height difference: 460 m.
Grade: an easy walk until the Bocca di Velaco. The ascent of the summit, Punta Velaco, is precipitous and includes simple stretches of scrambling (Grade I).
Refreshment / accommodation: restaurants and *auberge* in the Village de Bavella, hotels and campsite in Zonza.
Linking tip: with Walk 50.
Map: ign 4253 ET (1:25,000).

Follow →Walk 50 to reach the **Bocca di Velaco**, 1285m (10 mins.). From here, the red-marked main trail turns left to cross over to the Trou de la Bombe (→Walk 50) – we, however, leave this trail behind already 25m on by

View of the couloir used to ascend to the Bavella's rock spires.

The final metres require some scrambling. A view from the peak towards the north-east and the east coast.

turning right onto the path marked with cairns that leads about parallel to the red-marked trail whilst ascending slightly. After a few minutes, the path forks – here, turn right onto the path marked with cairns that leads into the previously mentioned **couloir** flanked by mighty rock faces.

After 30 minutes of steep climbing (halfway along, passing through a rock arch), finally reach the end of the gully. From here, bear to the right by scrambling (Grade I) onto the other side of the ridge and continue (somewhat precipitous) to the nearby summit of **Punta Velaco**, marked with a cross.

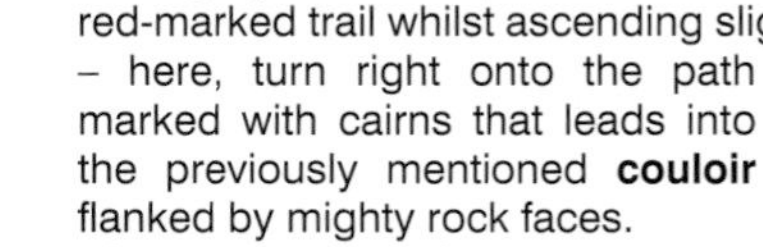

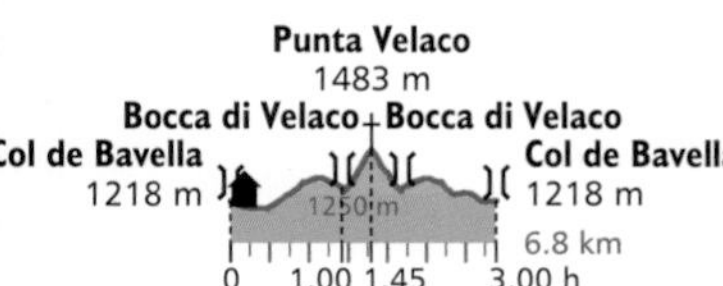

52 Refuge de Paliri, 1055m

4.15 hrs.

Forest walk along sections of the GR 20

The main attraction of this lovely although sometimes strenuous forest hike is the climber's paradise of Punta Tafunata di i Paliri – a climbing crag sporting a huge rock window – just north-west of the Paliri mountain hut. For a view of the rock window, you have to persevere all the way to the hut, but you will be rewarded with a cosy sojourn, food and beverage.

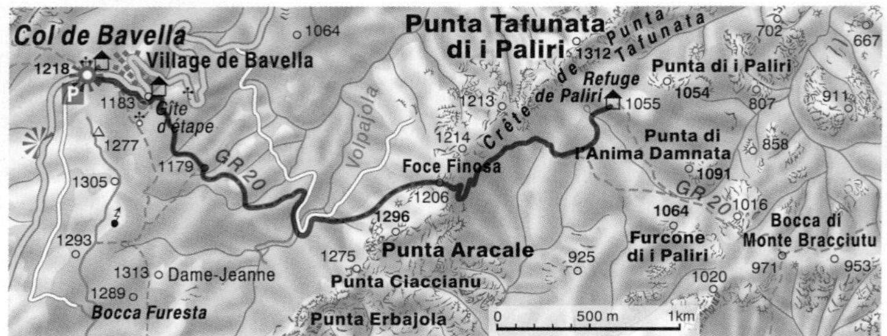

Location: Zonza, 778m.
Starting point: Bavella pass, 1218m. There are car parks located at the top of the pass. Bus service from Porto-Vecchio (→Walk 56).
Height difference: a good 600m.
Grade: arduous, although not difficult, walk along the well-marked *GR 20*.
Refreshment and accommodation: Refuge de Paliri (beverage and simple fare); restaurants and *auberge* (bunks) in Village de Bavella, hotels and campsite in Zonza.
Map: ign 4253 ET (1:25,000).

From the Bavella pass, walk down the main road to the **Village de Bavella**. On the hairpin bend at the *auberge* turn off to the right onto the white/red-marked *GR 20* following a forest track at first. After 5 minutes the *GR 20* forks

The Paliri hut with the Punta Tafunata di i Paliri – in the upper-left, centre of the photo, the rock window.

to the left, climbing down a steep slope via a footpath that can be quite unpleasant when wet. 15 minutes later, the path crosses a small stream and in another 15 minutes reaches a forestry road at the valley floor. Take this road to the right, cross the Volpajola stream and a little later on turn right again onto another footpath (signpost) that climbs in zigzags to the **Foce Finosa**, 1206m (sign, nice resting places). The path leads over the col, descends steeply and after ¼ hr. traverses the slope to the left, passing a prominent crag and then reaches the wonderfully situated **Paliri hut** (at the end, passing a spring).

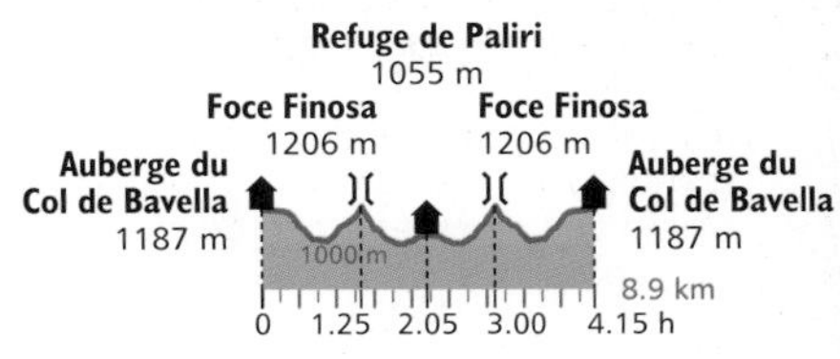

TOP

53 Cascades du Polischellu

Adventurous cascade walk through a delightful mountain landscape

This is certainly the most beautiful and adventurous cascade walk on the island. Time and time again, crystal-clear pools must be swum across, cascades scrambled round and gorges negotiated. If children are along, only the first stretch to the 3rd, at the latest, the 5th cascade should be attempted, since numerous difficult sections lie ahead. Bravehearts could shorten the descent by jumping over the cascades.

696 m
D 268 480 m
D 268 480 m
500 m
2.7 km
0 2.25 4.30 h

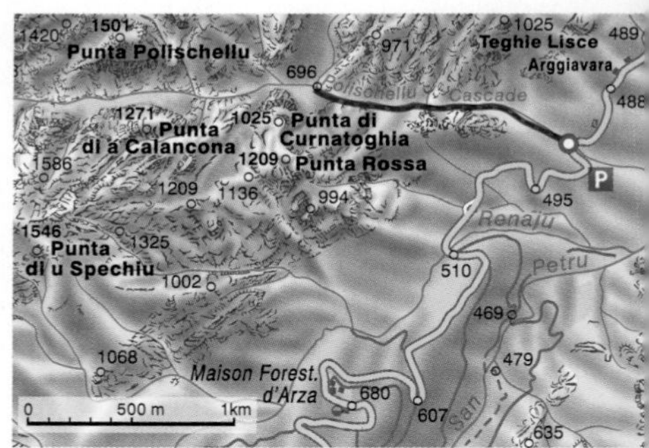

Locations: Solenzara, small seaside resort on the east coast. Zonza, 778m, centre for mountain climbers in the Massif de Bavella.
Starting point: bridge which spans the Polischellu stream, 480m, on the D 268 between Col de Bavella (9.5km) and Bocca di Larone (3.5km). Parking possible on the road or in the large car park south of the bridge.
Height difference: 200m.
Grade: walk combining lots of scrambling and a swim. The path is usually distinct, in prominent places marked by cairns – nevertheless, from time to time, the path must be rediscovered. The necessary equipment includes swimwear and water sandals with straps (do not attempt it barefoot). Provisions and valuables must be carried in waterproof and sealed packs. Take note: attempt this hike only during stable and rain-free weather conditions as thunderstorms can turn the stream into a roaring torrent. In the case of an emergency, return to paths located high above the stream to follow a route back to the bridge.
Refreshment and accommodation: an *auberge* at the Col de Bavella, restaurants, hotels and campsites in Zonza and Solenzara.
Tip: those courageous enough can shorten the descent considerably by jumping down the up to 10m high cascades.
Map: ign 4253 ET (1:25,000).

To the left of the **bridge** spanning the Polischellu stream, a footpath descends following the left bank in 10 minutes to the **1st cascade**. The cascade falls in two steps and can be skirted round by keeping left. However, it is much nicer to swim across the large pool at the base, then scramble to the left of the cascade to reach the first step, then cross over to the right side to

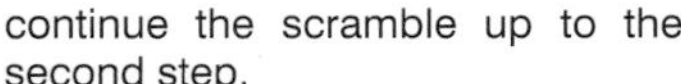

continue the scramble up to the second step.

Immediately afterwards, reach the base of the **2nd cascade**. Swim across the pool and scramble up to the right of the waterfall.

The **3rd cascade** is bypassed at the same time.

The descent to the **4th cascade** requires negotiating a small, but steep sloping rock face. In return for your efforts, the cascade itself presents no problems. Swim across the narrow pool and continue along the stream bed.

Just in front of the **5th cascade** a footpath climbs to the left to skirt around the waterfall. Once again, a difficult scramble follows down to the stream, this time using widely-spaced handholds and footholds.

6

7

8

9

11

Only hikers with climbing skills should try to negotiate this section and children should be secured with a short length of rope.

Arriving at the **6th cascade**, first swim across the crooked and elongated pool and then scramble up the boulder to the left of the cascade. However, it is easier to skirt around the cascade to the left via the gorge.

The **7th cascade** presents no real obstacles and can be easily climbed.

The easiest way to bypass the **8th cascade** is by taking the short, in places steep path to the left slightly above the valley.

The **9th cascade** can be easily bypassed to the left.

In front of the **10th cascade** wade through the pool and climb up to the right of the waterfall.

About 50m before reaching the impossibly sheer rock faces that surround the **11th cascade**, climb up from the valley via the path to the right (steep and requiring some easy scrambling) to bypass the waterfall.

In this way you have also skirted around the **12th cascade**.

To accomplish the detour around the **13th** and the **14th cascade**, climb

to the left over an unpleasantly steep slope. The rest of the trip presents no difficulties if you don't count the steepness of the descent. The **15th cascade** as well as the **16th cascade** can be easily bypassed.
The **17th cascade** is a proper waterfall, about 25m in height that is, however, often dried up in mid-summer. You can climb to the right of the waterfall through a rock arch to reach the top and enjoy a view of the cascades below.

Now the valley clearly begins to level out. There are, in fact, a dozen or so more pools, but these are too small and too shallow for bathing.

17

12

13

14

15

54 Cascades de Purcaraccia

2.45 hrs.

Demanding half-day walk to the famous cascade slides

The cascades of Purcaraccia are probably the most renowned destinations in Corsica for canyoning fans – the chutes and cascades are among the best on the island. Consequently, the cascades are very popular, both for hoards of canyonists and for walkers with bathing in mind who can thoroughly enjoy the beautiful rock pools.

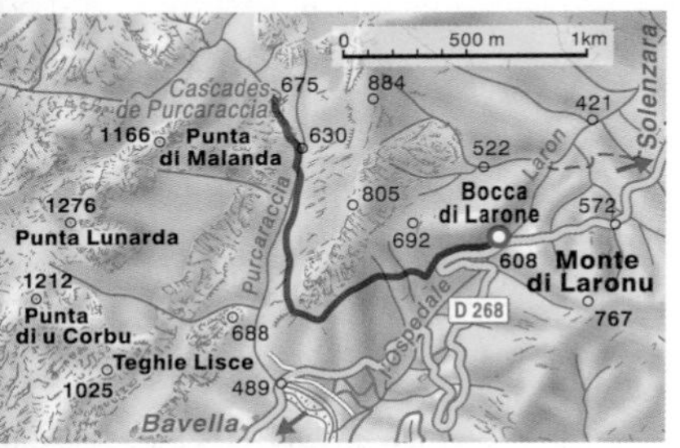

Starting point: Bocca di Larone, 608m, the pass on the D 268 between Solenzara (17km) and Col de Bavella (13km).
Height difference: not quite 150m.
Grade: a demanding walk, some stretches require a fair head for heights, some easy scrambling (beware: tilted precipitous rock slabs!). Only suitable for children and walkers with mountaineering skills!
Refreshment and accommodation: at the Col de Bavella *auberge*; in Solenzara restaurants, hotels and campsites.
Map: ign 4253 ET (1:25,000).

From the top of the pass at **Bocca di Larone**, follow the road for 300m towards Bavella pass until reaching the first hairpin bend (parking also possible here) – at this point, the trail forks to the right. It leads along the slope

Striking pinnacles of granite tower over the Purcaraccia valley.

in light up-and-down walking, usually through a shady scrub and pine forest. After a quarter of an hour, the path leads up the valley above the Purcaraccia stream, opening up views of the spectacular granite pinnacles on the opposite side of the valley and especially of the Punta di Malanda. Half an hour later, the path forks – here, you could descend left to a lovely rock pool. We keep straight on, however, along the path crossing the slope, also straight at

The Cascades de Purcaraccia is a very popular destination for canyonists.

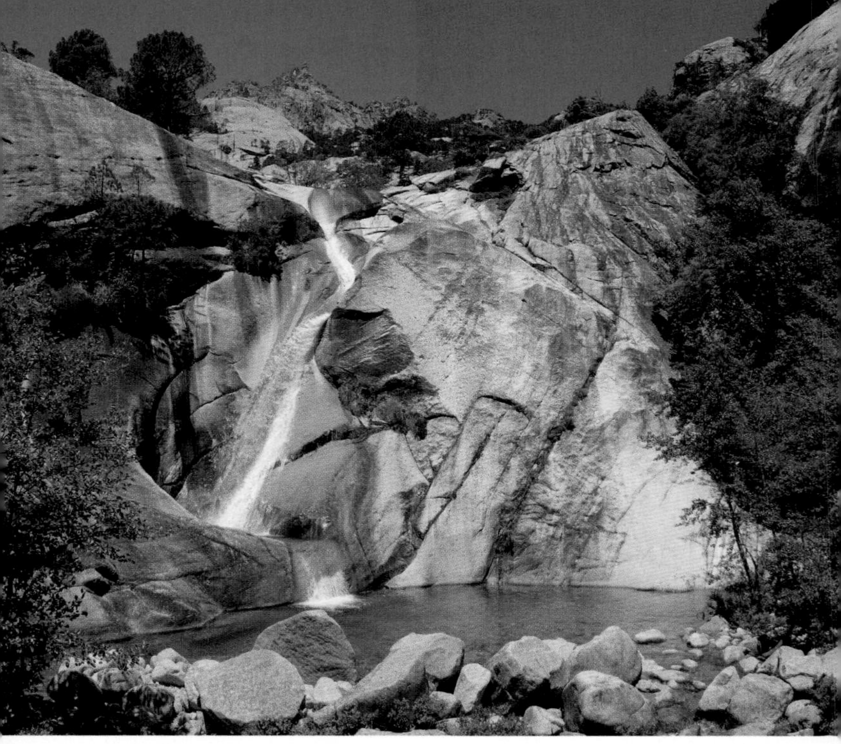

End of the trail – the final waterfall of the Cascades de Purcaraccia.

the following forks and then, 10 minutes later, we reach the **Purcaraccia stream** directly at a 20m high rock face.

The trail now crosses to the other side of the valley, passing a lovely rock pool and an overhanging rock and also the first cascades. Almost a quarter of an hour later, in front of a rock face, a path forks to the right and leads, in 5 minutes, to the upper step of the largest and most beautiful waterfall of the **Cascades de Purcaraccia**. From here, you can continue on for a couple of minutes along the right bank until the path ends at the last major cascade (see photo above).

Cascades de Purcaraccia
675 m
Bocca di Larone 608 m
Bocca di Larone 608 m
3.9 km
0 1.25 2.45 h

3.15 hrs.

Fiumicelli valley 55

Adventurous stream route with stretches of swimming

The Fiumicelli valley is an ideal introduction to anyone interested in learning canyoning. Typically, the Bavella valley offers both a gentle landscape, as well as a dramatic one, in the gorge at the valley's end. Pleasant stretches of wading through the stream are combined with short swims through crystal-clear rock pools; time and again, cascades require a short hop into the water. An occasional sandbank is a welcome invitation to a bathing break. Naturally, the route is also popular with regular bathers who only wish to wander a short way into the valley and who usually prefer to start at the Fiumicelli bridge.

Location: Solenzara, a little seaside resort on the east coast.
Starting point: Rocchiu Pinzutu, 337m, a large, tumbledown house with the inscription »Corsica Canyon« on the D 268 Solenzara – Bavella pass, car park (15km from Solenzara or 2km from the Bocca di Larone).

Destination: Pont de Fiumicelli, 158m, at Km 12 on the D 268 (3km/45 mins. along the road to return to the starting point; alternatively, you can hitchhike or park a second car here before the walk).
Height difference: 200m in descent.
Grade: easy canyoning route with a few jumps and swims, also suited to families with children, nevertheless, some stamina and climbing skills are required. Equipment needed consists of swimwear and water sandals, securely strapped (do not go barefoot!). Provisions and valuables should be packed in water-tight containers. Caution: attempt this route only during dry and stable weather – if a storm should strike, the stream can become a raging torrent! Not suitable for dogs!
Refreshment and accommodation: in Solenzara restaurants, hotels and campsites.
Tip: if you only want to get a sample of the route, start at the Fiumicelli bridge and walk upstream.
Map: ign 4253 ET (1:25,000).

Rocchiu Pinzutu 337 m — Fiumicelli 290 m — Pont de Fiumicelli 158 m
4.4 km
0 0.35 2.40 3.15 h

During the Fiumicelli walk, numerous bathing pools await us, some of them trimmed with inviting »sandy beach«.

The trail begins past the building **Rocchiu Pinzutu** (to your right) below the road. Unfortunately, this is private property and, because of that, you must continue along the road for 50m until, at the crag, an unpleasant, slippery path forks away to the right and descends. This leads fairly on the level through the scrub forest and crosses the Laron stream not quite half an hour later. A good 5 minutes after that, reach a sandbank on the **Fiumicelli river**.

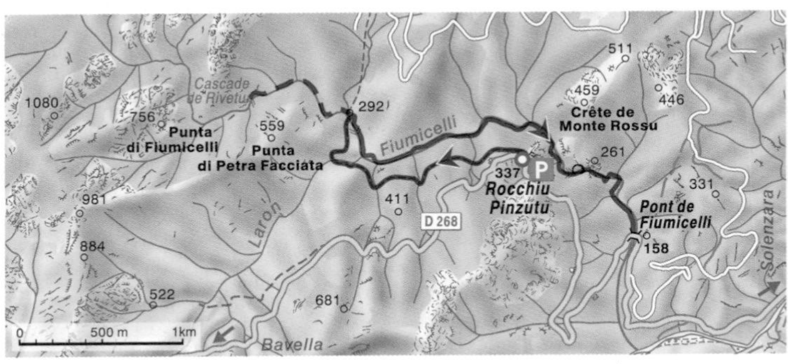

The adventurous cascade tour begins here. Very fit walkers can take an excursion upstream to the spectacular, about 80m high, Rivetu waterfall (about 1 hr., each way; demanding scrambling section) however, we follow the stream down the valley taking the most »direct way«, that is, through the stream bed. This is usually quite easy to negotiate but from time to time, there are slight challenges to be met. Thus, the first small waterfall soon requires your attention; and almost ½ hr. after that, an even higher cascade is met, but this one could also be skirted around by scrambling. Not quite an hour later, we are left without an alternative: we must swim across a deep pool (skirting around would be extremely difficult) – but this is exactly what makes this tour so exciting! Gradually, we enter into a gorge where another cascade must be skirted around: scramble down to the left to swim across the pool and then, on the opposite bank, pass through a rock arch. The cascades that follow can also be skirted around to the left. Later on, the walls of the gorge widen out somewhat but, nevertheless, there are still some pools to be swum and cascades to be negotiated. Finally, we meet up with the **Fiumicelli bridge**.

What you have to get through – wonderful rock pools enclosed by rock walls – perfect for novice canyonists.

56 Tower III (Punta di a Vacca), 1611m

Enthralling ascent through a wild and rocky landscape

The approach to the Col de l'Oiseau, the gap before Tower I, is one of Corsica's most picturesque ascents. Near the summit, in the middle of a splendid rocky landscape, numerous easy scrambles must be negotiated.

Location: Zonza, 778m.
Starting point: Bavella pass, 1218m. Parking possible at the top of the pass.

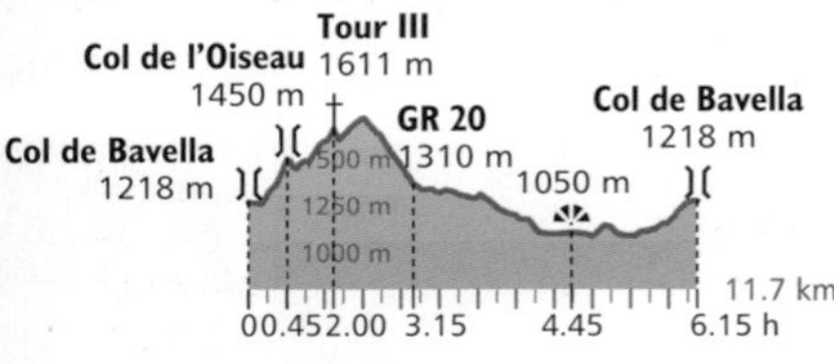

Daily bus service from Porto-Vecchio (Porto-Vecchio 7:00 a.m., Ospédale 7:20 a.m., Zonza 8:05 a.m., return at 6:05 p.m.).
Height difference: a good 850m.
Grade: strenuous walk with some sections of scrambling; well-marked footpath.
Refreshment and accommodation: restaurants and *auberge* in Village de Bavella, hotels and campsite in Zonza.
Map: ign 4253 ET (1:25,000).

At the **Bavella pass**, take the white/red-marked *GR 20*, passing the statue of Notre-Dame-des-Neiges. After 5 minutes you reach a signposted junction and turn onto the *alpine variant of the GR 20* marked with two yellow dashes – a strenuous climb! The ascent takes 45 minutes, leading through an incredible backdrop of wind-tossed pines, bizarre rock pinnacles and fields of scree until reaching the **Col de l'Oiseau** (Bocca di u Truvone), 1450m, with a beautiful view of the towers which are your goal, as well as the southern Bavella mountain chain. Crossing to the other side of the gap, the footpath begins an immediate descent, bearing to the left at the foot of the face of **Tower I** (Punta di l'Acellu). The terrain that follows is somewhat difficult, therefore be sure to follow the yellow markings. The path leads along the foot of the crags, ascending slightly, and then crosses over

The towers of Bavella as seen from the Col de Bavella.

to the base of the rock wall of **Tower II** (Punta di l'Ariettu; do not climb to the gap between Tower I and II). During this stretch, descend over an unpleasant, steeply-sloping area of rock slabs that is fortunately secured with steel chains. After this section, climb to the **gap** between Tower II and III and enjoy a magnificent view of the east coast near Solenzara. Skirt around the rocky base of Tower III by following the yellow markings to the right, until you reach the **col** to the north of the tower (the gap between Tower III and Tower IV, 1 hr. from the Col de l'Oiseau). From here you only need about a quarter of an hour to climb to the highest point (cairns; easy scrambling. Grade I+) of **Tower III** (Punta di a Vacca; marked by a heap of stones). From this lofty eyrie, enjoy a bird's-eye view of the dramatic mountain landscape.

It is best to return via the ascent route, but if you still feel fit enough, follow the alternative return: from the col north of Tower III, continue the ascent along the foot of the awe-inspiring Tower IV (Punta di u Pargulu, ¼ hr.) via the yellow-marked path. Here bear left to descend to the white/red-marked *GR 20* (¾ hr.) and then continue along this route to the left in a never-ending trudge down the slope back to the Bavella pass (3 hrs.).

From Col de l'Oiseau, you can already spot Tower II (left), III (centre) and IV (centre right).

57 *Monte Incudine, 2134m*

8.15 hrs.

Phenomenal 360° view from the southernmost 2000 metre summit

Monte Incudine is a fantastic panoramic summit that offers a view embracing the Bays of Ajaccio and Valinco as well as the east coast – in good visibility you can even make out Monte San Petrone.

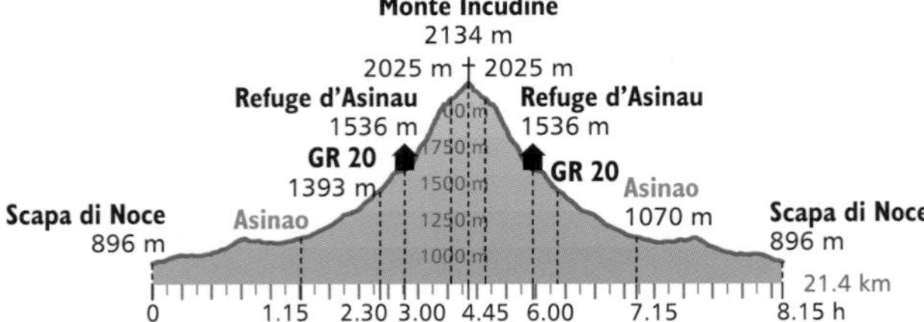

Locations: Quenza, 813m, village south-west of the Bavella chain. Zonza, 778m, at the foot of the Bavella pass.
Starting point: about 4km from Zonza on the main road to Quenza, turn right on the D 520 towards Prugna to reach the last houses of Scapa di Noce (3km). Parking possible at the highest point on the road, 896m (electricity pylon; junction with the forest road to Refuge d'Asinau, sign).
Height difference: a good 1300m.
Grade: easy mountain hike along a forest road and well-marked footpaths. Good physical condition is required.
Refreshment and accommodation: overnight stay in the Asinau mountain hut (beverages, simple food, mattress dormitory). Restaurants, hotels and campsites in Quenza and Zonza.
Alternatives: ascent to Monte Incudine also possible starting from the Bavella pass or from the Plateau du Coscione along the *GR 20*.
Map: ign 4253 ET (1:25,000).

The kick-off begins via a gravel road, with a view of the Bavella towers.

Take the **gravel road** that forks off to the right from the main road leading into the valley. Heading toward the Bavella mountain chain, you pass a few houses. The forestry road is marked in yellow at the beginning and leads predominantly through a pine wood. After a good hour of walking, another forestry road merges from the right; continue straight ahead. 10 minutes later, cross the Asinau stream (1065m) and then reach the end of the gravel road near a small **dam**.

Before the dam cross over to the left-hand bank of the stream, following the yellow-marked path. Ahead and to the left you catch your first glimpse of Monte Incudine, while to the right, there's a view of the Bavella pinnacles. After a total of 2½ hours of walking – the pines have given way to scrubby broom in the

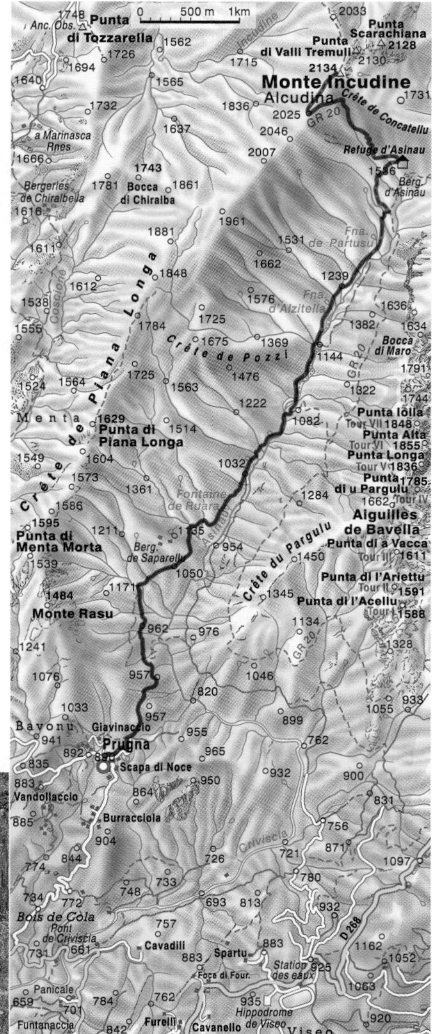

The Asinau hut burnt to the ground in 2016 and is to be built anew; at the moment, a temporary shelter serves walkers. – Photo below: just before reaching the summit.

meantime – you meet up with the white/red-marked *GR 20* (signposts), which takes you to the left and ascends in a half hour to the **Asinau mountain hut**, 1536m (you could, instead, take the trail that leads straight on, via the Bergerie d'Asinau, which is somewhat more pleasant). Continue along the *GR 20* (sign »Alcudina«) which ascends over scree and rock slabs and through alder scrub in a north-westerly direction, then swing to the west to reach the **south-west ridge** (1½ hrs. from the hut). On the other side of the ridge, the *GR 20* turns left, but take the right-hand trail instead and climb along the ridge for a good 20 mins. to the summit of **Monte Incudine**.

1.30 hrs.

Monte Santu, 599m 58

Panoramic rocky peak with a small bouldering area for climbers

This mountain has something for everyone: for the hiker, an easily-reached viewpoint with an awe-inspiring view of the craggy peaks gathered around the Bavella pass as well as a bird's-eye view of the east coast; for the rock climber, some nice little bolt-protected routes on the 20 metre high south face. After completing the route, there is time enough for a refreshing dip in the Solenzara stream (about 6km west of Solenzara) or in the sea.

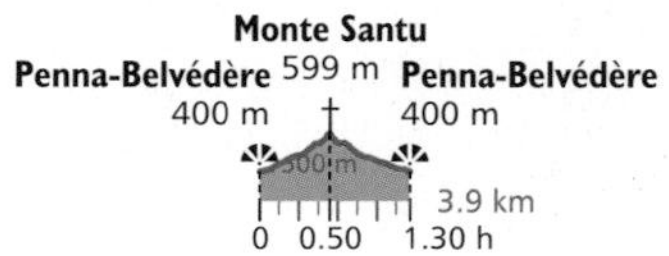

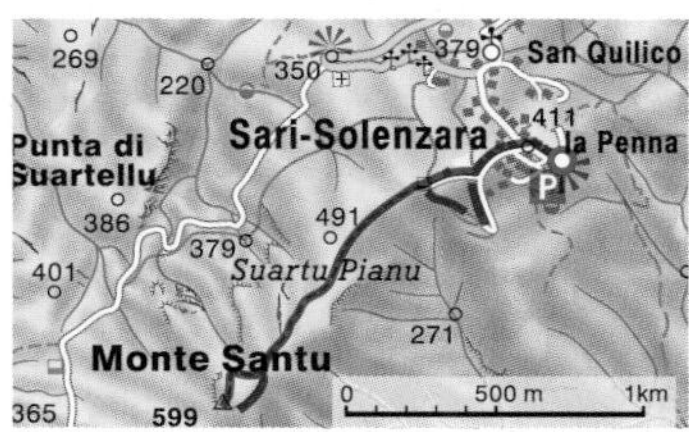

Location: Solenzara.
Starting point: Belvédère la Penna, 400m, in the mountain village of Sari-Solenzara, 7.5km south-west of Solenzara.
Height difference: 200m.
Grade: easy walk via a distinct footpath.
Refreshment and accommodation: in Solenzara restaurants, hotels and campsites.
Map: ign 4253 ET (1:25,000).

From the **Belvédère la Penna** in Sari-Solenzara (lovely view of the east coast), walk 50m back along the road and turn left onto a road (sign »Monte Santu«) that leads uphill round bends (after 150m on the right an old oven). 10 mins. later, the track reaches a **water reservoir**. Here the yellow-marked trail forks away, heading straight on. This ascends along the *macchia*-covered mountain ridge. After just under half an hour there's a fork in the path (sign).

Along the right-hand path, across a rather rocky hillside, covered in grass and *macchia*, you reach the summit of **Monte Santu** in a good 5 minutes. The left-hand path leads up to a cave and the climbing routes on the south face. Shortly after the summit you can also descend a mini *via ferrata* (only for walkers with climbing experience) to the foot of the rock and at the fork after 25m walk back to the left to the junction.

59 Étang d'Urbino

Leisurely beach walk to a lagoon – also perfect for a barefoot stroll

If you like beach walks you will find a considerable number of opportunities on Corsica's eastern coast in particular. Almost the whole of the coastline between Bastia and Solenzara is one long sandy beach interrupted only by river estuaries and almost purpose built for lengthy strolls along the sand. Particularly lovely is the section of beach to the north of Ghisonaccia. Here you quickly leave civilisation behind and experience a wonderful, to a large extent isolated beach. An idyllic beach lagoon, the Étang d'Urbino, also awaits you there. The path is ideal for walking barefoot – not only the way there across the beach, but also the return over mostly sandy or loamy paths and tracks are a delight for rather »hardened soles« (take shoes with you as well, to be on the safe side).

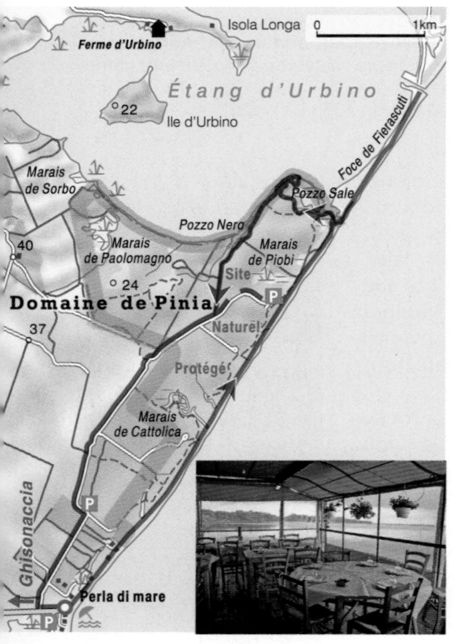

Starting point: Ghisonaccia beach, at the end of the D 144 (4.5km from the roundabout at the southern edge of the village, signposted). If you want to shorten the length of the walk by a good hour, turn left 200m before the beach onto the D 444 – after a good 200m the road turns into a badly eroded track in places and forks after 1km at a car park with pine trees. Go left/straight on here for another 3km; keep along the track straight ahead (right) at all junctions and following the wave signs to a car park/turning round place with shady pines behind the beach.
Height difference: insignificant.
Grade: easy beach walk.
Refreshment and accommodation: in Ghisonaccia.
Tip: trip to the Ferme d'Urbino, a floating restaurant on a peninsular projecting a long way out into the lagoon. The restaurant serves really fresh oysters and mussels which have been bred in the lagoon (from Ghisonaccia about 6km on the N 198 to the north to the signposted turn-off, from here, about 3km to the restaurant).
Map: ign 4352 OT (1:25,000).

Pozzo Sale – full of atmosphere – a little bay in the Étang d'Urbino.

Follow the **beach** in a northerly direction and you soon leave the last houses and beach facilities behind. The beautiful sandy beach is for the most part left in its natural state – only quad bikes occasionally disturb the tranquillity. There are some extensive pine and scrub forests behind the beach that are under environmental protection. After about an hour, pass a car park (behind the beach) and a good quarter of an hour after that, reach the **Étang d'Urbino** (Pozzo Sale). A path branches off left along beside the lagoon full of reeds (your return path), but before you turn back, you should walk further along the beach. You now find yourself on the narrow strip of land although, after another 15 minutes, you end up back at the lagoon. 10 minutes later the beach walk comes to an end at a canal, a good 10m wide, which is the inlet from the sea to the lagoon.

Walk back to the start of the lagoon (25 mins.) and turn right here onto a roadway from which a narrower path turns off immediately right. It leads up to the lagoon, then turns away from it again. At the fork after 5 minutes keep to the right, and do the same again 5 minutes later. Just under 10 minutes after that a path joins from the left (the continuation of your path later on). Soon afterwards keep right at the fork. After 5 minutes you arrive at a bend in the path where a path branches off right to a solitary **pine tree** from where there's a fabulous view across the lagoon to the strip of land. A few minutes later you reach the crossroads again and continue straight on (after 3m there's a path to the right to the shores of the lagoon, lovely view across to the peninsula with the restaurant). After 5 minutes ignore a path turning off left and 5 mins. after that, at a barrier, you meet a roadway which you follow to the right (an immediate view of the section of the lagoon called **Pozzo Nero**). After a quarter of an hour your roadway joins a track coming from back left (left goes in 20 mins. to the beach car park). As you continue along your route keep straight on at all junctions and after about a good three quarters of an hour you arrive back to your starting point.

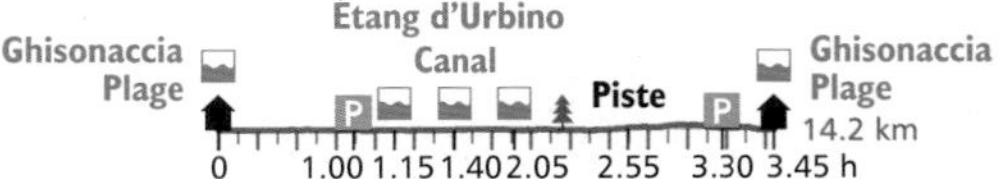

The Central Region

Fiumorbu – Venachese – Cortenais – Boziu – Niolu – Ascotal

In the heart of the island, nature's blessings have filled Corsica's treasure chest to overflowing. Sparkling lakes, thunderous streams, endless forests, sleepy valleys, and last but certainly not least, the majestic peaks of the two-thousanders provide a paradise for every walker and mountain climber. Corte is the most important town of the region, situated between Monte Padru to the north and Monte Renoso to the south.

The **Fium'Orbu valley**, with its numerous gorges, is one of Corsica's most peaceful mountain valleys. Especially around the *Col de Verde*, 1289m, surrounded by deep deciduous and pine forests, a multitude of beautiful walks can be undertaken. The most popular walk in the region is the ascent of the easiest of the 2000m/plus peaks, *Monte Renoso*, 2352m. North of Ghisoni, *Punta Muro* towers up 1565m, a fantastic panoramic peak offering splendid views of Monte d'Oro, Rotondo and Renoso (¾ hr. from Col de Sorba, 1311m).

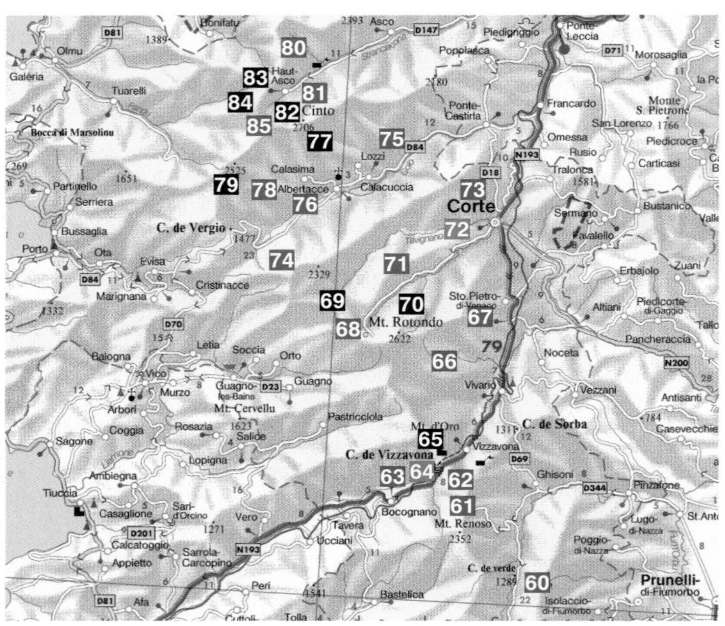

The Pic Lombarduccio as seen from the car park at the Bergerie de Grottelle (Restonica valley). Below: the Cascade du Voile de la Mariée (»Bride's Veil Waterfall«) near Bocognano.

Down the other side of the Sorba pass brings you to the **Vecchio valley** with the villages of *Vizzavona, Tattone, Vivario* and *Venaco*. The vast deciduous and pine forests of the area offer pleasant walking opportunities – nearly all the villages are connected by well-maintained trails. Apart from this woodland walk and the Punta di l'Oriente, we also recommend an excursion into the unique craggy kingdom of the Migliarello chain.

In Corte you find two of the most famous valleys on the island, the **Restonica valley**, and the **Tavignano valley** which is closed to traffic. Magical pine forests, cheery crystal-clear streams and fantastic mountain scenery all combine to create the special charm of the Restonica valley. Just as gentle as it can be wild, this picture-book valley, lying between Corte and the *Melo* and *Capitello lakes* attracts many tourists – and without exaggeration earns the prize as the most beautiful mountain valley on the island. Because of the sometimes chaotic traffic conditions on the narrow road, one should be sure to begin an excursion here starting early in the morning – otherwise the trip could easily turn into a nightmare. Experienced mountain hikers should not fail to tackle the classic walk onto *Monte Rotondo*, Corsica's second highest peak.

The picturesque town of Corte is the region's capital.

The **Niolu** region is the actual nucleus of the island. Around the *Calacuccia reservoir* you will experience Corsica in its most pristine form: small, simple villages surrounded by open pastureland, pine forests and a few outstanding mountain peaks – Cinto, Paglia Orba and Tafunatu. The high valley in the upper reaches of the *Golo* is bordered to the west by the *Col de Vergio* and to the east by the wild *Santa Regina Gorge*. Niolu is traditionally pastoral countryside, where pigs, cows and horses graze freely – a perfect landscape for lengthy walking routes. As well as the routes described here we also recommend the shepherds' path from the Calacuccia reservoir to the *Bocca â l'Arinella*, 1592m, which offers breathtaking views of the lake, Niolu and the Cinto massif.

Finally, the **Asco and Stranciacone valley** is Corsica's most alpine of the mountain valleys as well as the island's centre for mountain climbers. A visit to this rugged valley is very worthwhile if only to enjoy the valley head at *Haut-Asco* with views of the inimitable double-peak of *Capu Larghia*, and *Monte Cinto* whose ascent is one of the most challenging climbs on the island. In addition to these and the following routes, we recommend an excursion to the *Pinara valley* (starting at the old Geonese bridge below the upper end of Asco village to the Bergerie de Pinara, 937m, 3 hrs. one way).

5.15 hrs.

Refuge de Prati, 1830m, and Punta della Cappella, 2041m

60

Hut and summit walk with fantastic views above the Col de Verde

The Col de Verde is one of the most tranquil – and at the same time most lovely – hiking areas in Corsica. On both sides of the pass you are presented with wonderful beech and pine forests and panoramic two-thousanders. Particularly beautiful and varied is the walk along the GR 20 to the »memorial ridge« with its quirky rock figures and the simply equipped Prati hut. Fit mountain walkers will also want to add on the detour onto Punta della Cappella which provides a short adventurous scramble.

Locations: Ghisoni, 635m, and Zicavo, 730m.
Starting point: Col de Verde, 1289m.
Height difference: 1000m.
Grade: as far as the hut, simple but strenuous walk on a mostly steep path. The summit ascent to Punta della Cappella requires a bit of scrambling.
Refreshment and accommodation: snack bar on the Col de Verde, in the Refuge de Prati (simple bunks) drinks, cheese and sausage. Hotels in Ghisoni and Zicavo.
Map: ign 4252 OT (1:25,000).

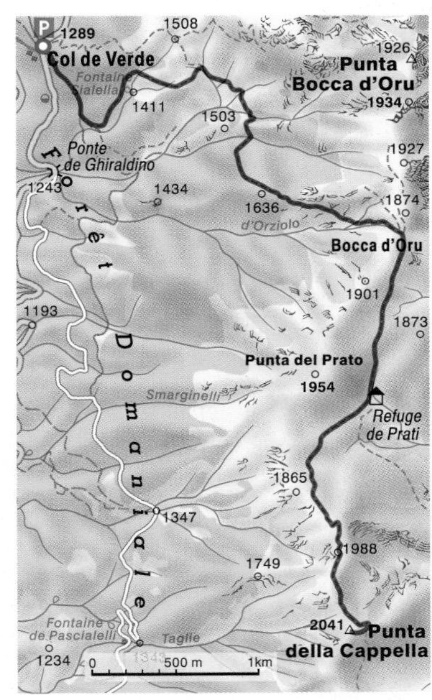

At the **Col de Verde** the white/red-marked *GR 20* crosses over the main road – follow the famous long distance path in an easterly direction. It runs along a forest track and ascends gently through lovely beech and pine forest. After 5 minutes it crosses over a forest road. A good 5 minutes after that, the *GR 20* turns off left onto a trail but leaves it behind again, a few minutes later, by turning right onto a path. This

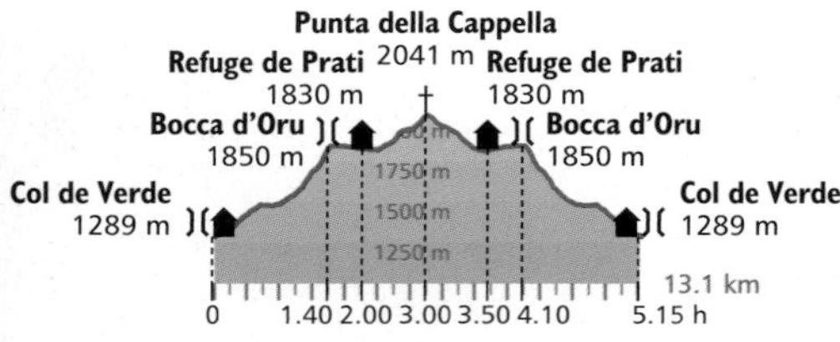

path crosses another forest path 5 minutes later, then the forest thins out somewhat and dwarf gorse and juniper are proliferating along the edge of the path. After a good half an hour's walking, you come to a ridge from which a view opens out of the »memorial ridge«. The path then descends on the left into a **hollow** and crosses it by keeping on the right (on the left you could walk a bit further on to explore the fabulous rock formations and figures along the ridge).

After a few minutes the path, which continues to cross the hillside on a gentle incline, crosses a stream bed and shortly afterwards, another one. Then it runs uphill more clearly again through beech forest. After about 20 minutes you have come to the end of the steep section. The forest thins out once more – you can see the main ridge ahead and on the right, Taravo valley. The *GR 20* then ascends on the right across the hillside and finally heads directly up towards the **Bocca d'Oru**, 1850m, on the main ridge (35 mins.) from where you can enjoy a superb view of the neighbouring 2000 metre peaks of Monte Renoso, Monte d'Oro and Monte Rotondo, and an especially spectacular view of the east coast. The path now runs on the right more or less

After a good hour the main ridge with Bocca d'Oru appears right in front of you.

The panoramic ridge path to the Punta della Cappella adorned with a cross.

on the level along the left-hand side of the ridge. You can already see Punta della Cappella ahead of you. After 10 minutes the path gradually descends along beside a small stream down to the beautifully situated **Prati hut**, 1830m, a welcome sight where you can find refreshment. Some horses and cows graze the meadows and the alder scrub around the hut.

10 minutes after the hut the *GR 20* ascends more steeply over the ridge to a small elevation on the crest. After another short descent with one or two quite exposed and airy sections over the rock the path climbs steeply up towards the Punta della Cappella and contours round the summit on the left across the hillside. After about 2 minutes a path, marked with cairns, turns off on the far side of the summit up to the summit cross of **Punta della Cappella** – a lovely, but tricky and adventurous ascent with some easy scrambling (Garde I) over boulders (10 minutes). The views from the summit are unparalled – you can see Monte Incudine in the south, other two-thousanders in the north, the east coast and, in good visibility, even the west coast and, down below, the Taravo valley.

61 Lac de Bastani, 2089m, and Monte Renoso, 2352m

4.15 hrs.

Two-thousander without difficulty

Out of the »Big Six« – Monte Cinto, Monte Rotondo, Paglia Orba, Monte Padru, Monte d'Oro and Monte Renoso – Monte Renoso is certainly the easiest to reach. The route is worth taking if only to experience the idyllically situated Bastani lake and to enjoy sweeping views of Southern Corsica and also of Monte d'Oro and Monte Rotondo.

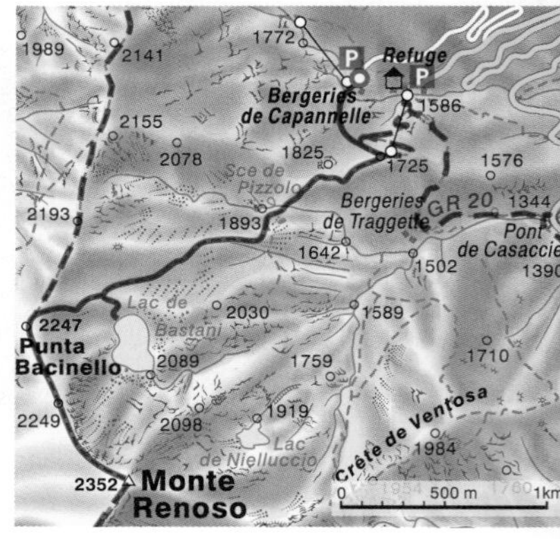

Location: Ghisoni, 635m.
Starting point: *Gîte* U Renosu, 1670m, at the Capannelle ski resort. From Ghisoni drive 6.5km towards the Col de Verde, turn right towards the ski resort (11km), and just before reaching it, at the fork in the road, turn right to ascend to the upper car park with the *Gîte* U Renosu.
Height difference: 750m.
Grade: easy, but somewhat strenuous walk; the path is well-marked.
Refreshment and accommodation: *Gîte d'étape* U Fugone by the ski resort, hotel in Ghisoni.

Alternatives: the route can also be started from the *Gîte d'étape* U Fugone (add 20 mins. to the overall time). Circular route: Renoso – Col de Pruno – Bergeries des Pozzi – Plateau de Gialgone (then via the *GR 20*) – car park (total time 9 hrs.).
Map: ign 4252 OT (1:25,000).

Idyllic meadowed plateau half way along the path to Bastani lake.

Bastani lake with Monte Renoso.

Start off from the **car park** at the end of the road by the *Gîte* U Renosu to continue along the broad gravel road and cross over the wooden bridge. 200m after that, turn diagonally right onto a narrower trail that leads somewhat above a mountain station for a ski-lift. When the trail ends, a cairn-marked path continues to the right, following the ascending ridgeline to reach, after a total of 45 minutes, a small **meadowland plateau** (1893m) where the Pizzolo stream flows along its course. Pass a basin, criss-crossed by rivulets, on its left side (a pretty spot for a picnic), cross over the stream and climb easily to the left along an almost imperceptible ridge. Soon the ridge appears which will lead to the summit. Cross over another high valley bearing left (if you continue straight on through the valley you can ascend directly up to the Renoso ridge) and after 1½ hrs. reach the shores of **Bastani lake**, 2089m, nestling in a hollow.

Now continue right, up along the ridge and before the next hollow, ascend to the right, up to the ridge (just under ½ hr.; make a note of the path for the descent in case the mist comes down suddenly). The broad desert-like ridge leads left uphill to reach the summit of **Monte Renoso** (½ hr.; metal cross).

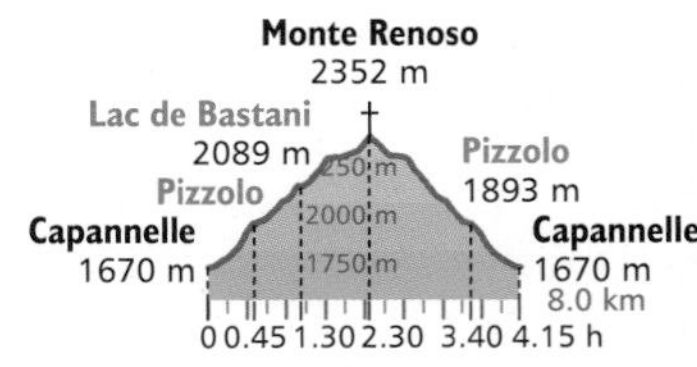

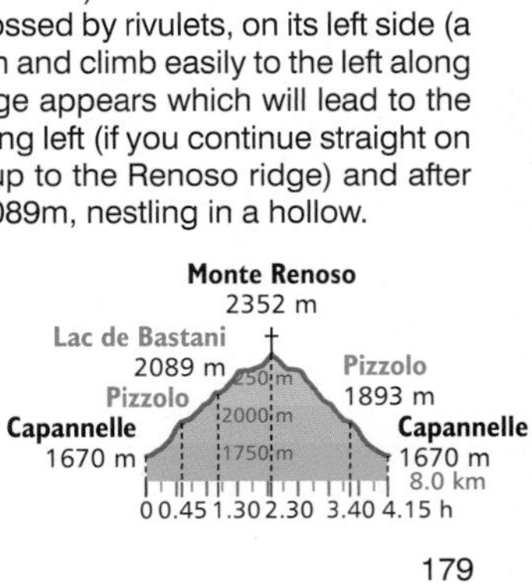

62 Punta di l'Oriente, 2112m

5.30 hrs.

Panoramic ascent to the southern pillar of the Vizzavona Pass

The walk to Punta di l'Oriente counts as a pleasure tour par excellence: passing through an enchanted beech wood, meet up with a bergerie and then ascend along an open mountain ridge which presents marvellous views of Monte d'Oro and of the Migliarello chain on the other side of the valley.

Starting point: Col de Vizzavona, 1163m, alternatively the transmission station, 1198m, at the end of the access road (350m) that turns off and heads southwards at the pass.
Height difference: not quite 1000m.
Grade: this is a strenuous mountain hike but leads along well-marked paths; the ascent to the summit requires light scrambling.
Refreshment and accommodation: restaurants and hotels in Vizzavona, campsites in Tattone.
Map: ign 4252 OT (1:25,000).

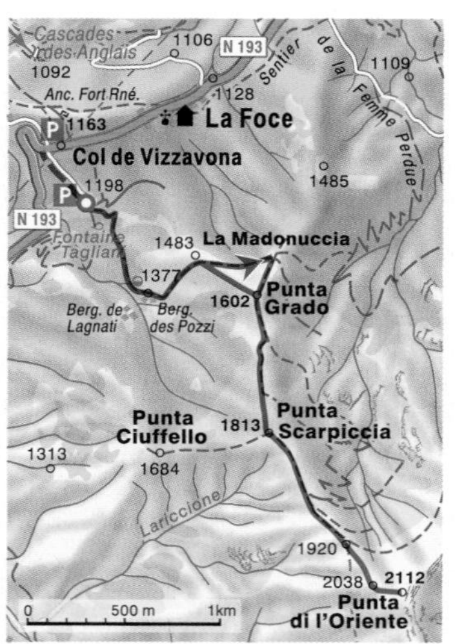

The broad, marked trail begins behind the fence in the car park for the **transmission station**. This ascends through a lovely beech forest and then narrows some minutes later. A few minutes after that, the trail passes below power lines (here, straight ahead). 10 mins. later, the trail leaves the forest behind and then passes the **Bergeries des Pozzi**, 1377m, with several stone houses. Now we turn left towards the slope, ascending steeply, sometimes with scree underfoot, while enjoying a fantastic view of the Gravona valley and Monte d'Oro as well as Pointe Migliarello. 20 mins. later, reach the ridgeline – now with a view towards Tattone and Monte Cardo. Through a little beech wood,

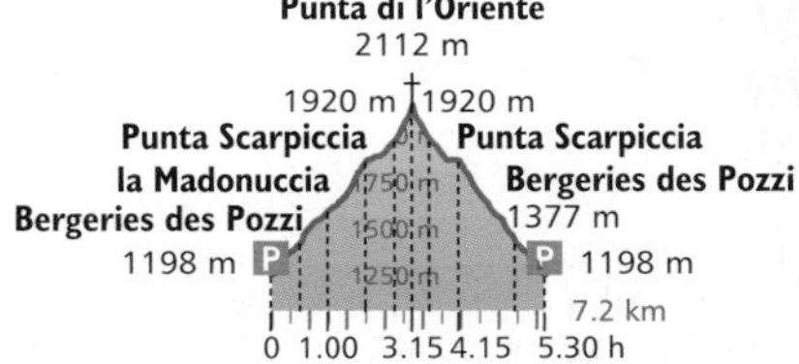

the trail crosses over to the neighbouring ridge, to reach this at the prominent boulders of **la Madonuccia**.

From now on, continue along the ridge uphill, crossing alpine meadows and flanked by alder trees. 10 minutes later, pass the Punta Grado, 1602m, and a good half an hour after that, the Punta Scarpiccia, 1813m – the ridge hooks to the left here. Consequently, the trail leads a few metres below an only somewhat pronounced summit rise (1851m), and then forks, not quite half an hour later, at a height of 1920m. The main trail veers to the right away from the ridge and continues towards Monte Renoso. We, however, continue ascending to the left, somewhat away from the ridge. At the foot of a rock face (¼ hr.), cairns mark the path heading left, which keeps close to the ridgeline, ascending along the edge of a row of rock faces and then crossing over to the ridge – from here, enjoy a marvellous view of Fium'Orbu and »monument ridge«; Monte Rotondo appears as well. From the rocky summit of the **Punta di l'Oriente** (far to the left and marked by a cross), which can be reached through some easy scrambling (Grade I–II; at the end, keep left), a view to Monte Renoso also opens up.

After an hour's walk, reach the boulders of la Madonuccia with a view of Monte d'Oro.

63 Richiusa Gorge

Short walk to one of the most spectacular ravines on the island

The Richiusa Gorge at the foot of the fabulous Migliarello mountain chain is an absolute natural gem – the impressive ravine is just 3m wide and enclosed by over 50m high rock walls. It is a popular destination for canyonists, while walkers on the other hand, are content to make a short trip to the start of the gorge to take a refreshing dip in one of the wonderful pools to be found there.

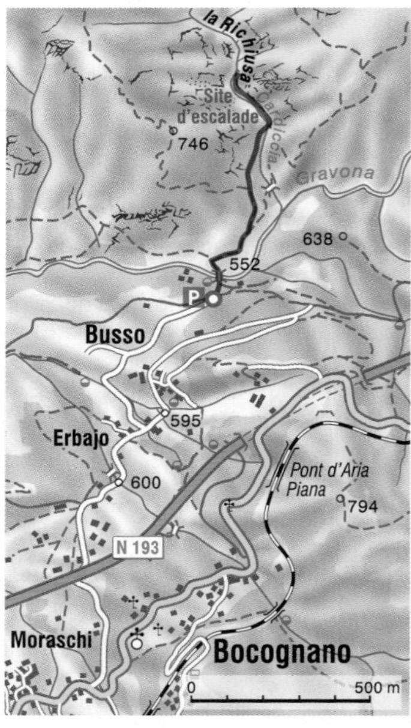

Starting point: walkers' car park in Busso, 570m, suburb of Bocognano (1.6km from the old main road at the upper village limits of Bocognano; signposted).
Height difference: a good 100m.
Grade: not difficult, only the last part requires a bit of scrambling.
Refreshment and accommodation: in Bocognano.
Alternative: walkers with more stamina are recommended to follow the signposted Richiusa circuit (3½ hrs.).
Tips: canyonists continue by ascending the path on the left from the head of the gorge to then descend through the impressive gorge (consult the information board at the car park Busso). After the walk (in the afternoon), a rewarding experience is an excursion to the Cascade du Voile de la Mariée (from Bocognano via the D 27; 10 mins. from the road).
Map: ign 4252 OT (1:25,000).

From the walkers' car park in **Busso**, descend along the road for 50m until, before reaching a waterworks, a yellow-marked trail forks off to the left. 50m further on, the trail turns right to cross over the Gravona via a bridge (Pont de Busso) and then forks – here, turn right towards Richiusa. After a good 5 minutes there's a fork in the path (signposts) – continue left here. 2 minutes later, keep to the path heading straight on towards »Site d'escalade«. After a few minutes it crosses the Cardiccia stream, shortly afterwards leads on the right, up

ONSORT *Direttore:* **Matthew Rudd**

hias Krella *Concerto d'organo*

ppe Lefebvre *Concerto d'organo*

Josef Stoiber *Concerto d'organo*

do Ciampa *Concerto d'organo*

hard Ascherl *Concerto d'organo*
(Toscana Organ Festival)

ranz Hauk *Concerto d'organo*

Spanu *Concerto d'organo*
(Toscana Organ Festival)

OSAIC Canadian Vocal Ensemble
ettore: **Gordon Mansell**

www.musicaincattedralelucca.com

n Martino - Lucca

VIVI LUCCA

Novembre 2022

Con il patrocinio e il contributo

pila il formulario! Grazie

ARBOUROUGH SINGER CHOIR

corale strumentale

Biagetti *Concerto d'organo*

nmaso Mazzoletti *Concerto d'organo*

ard Marx *Concerto d'organo*

sław Kapitula *Concerto d'organo*

Cattedrale di Sa

Cathedr

Da Giugno a

Con il contributo

Dopo il concerto con

Venerdì 3 Giugno, ore 21.00 The HA
Concert

Venerdì 17 Giugno, ore 21.00 Giulia

Mercoledì 22 Giugno, ore 18.30 Ton

Giovedì 30 Giugno, ore 18.30 Bernh

Martedì 5 Luglio, ore 18.30 Przemy

Venerdì 15 Luglio, ore 21.00 ELY C

Domenica 17 Luglio, ore 18.30 Matt

Domenica 31 Luglio, ore 18.30 Phili

Domenica 7 Agosto, ore 18.30 Franz

Giovedì 25 Agosto, ore 18.30 Leonar

Lunedì 5 Settembre, ore 18.30 Burk

Domenica 25 Settembre, ore 18.30

Mercoledì 5 Ottobre, ore 18.30 Ugo

Martedì 22 Novembre, ore 21.00 M

Di

ingresso libero

At the entrance to the Richiusa Gorge you will find some refreshing pools.

through the small side valley and turns left back to the stream. After this, leave the climbing area on your right and continue following the waymarked path which ascends to a spur, then leads steeply down to the stream and on the right-hand bank of the stream goes over rocks to the start of the **Richiusa Gorge**. The entrance to the gorge is closed off by a beautiful pool. Continuing beyond the next pool of water is only possible for experienced climbers.

64 Cascades des Anglais

1.30 hrs.

The Agnone waterfalls – a miracle of nature

Nowhere else on Corsica can be found such a wealth of natural bathing pools, sculpted out of the rocks by the waters, like here at the cascades of the Agnone stream. It is hard to imagine a more beautiful experience than to walk through the shady beech forests along the Cascades des Anglais and enjoy this natural wonder to its utmost. However, you cannot ignore the fact that the cascades are no secret and are a very popular island attraction indeed. Anyone wishing to enjoy this amazing adventure in solitude will have to start off very early in the morning.

Starting point: train station at Vizzavona, 915m, on the Corte – Ajaccio line.
Height difference: 200m.
Grade: easy walk on a well-marked route.
Refreshment and accommodation: kiosk at the cascades, restaurants/hotels in Vizzavona, campsites in Tattone.
Alternative: the Cascades des Anglais may also be reached from La Foce located at Col de Vizzavona, 1163m (signposts; 20 mins. one way to the kiosk).
Maps: ign 4251 OT, 4252 OT (1:25,000).

Begin the walk heading south from the **train station** via a small tarmac road which ascends to the »Casa di a natura«. Here you take the white/red-marked *GR 20 Nord* forking off to the right and soon cross over two

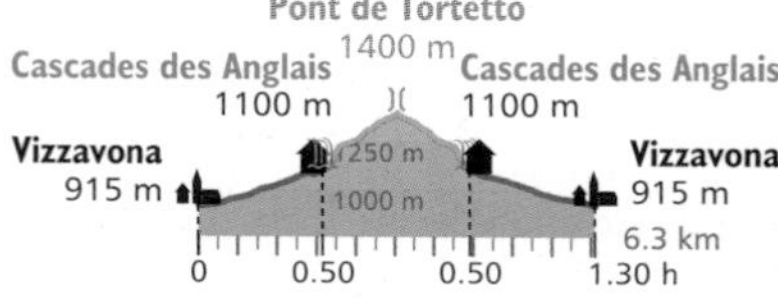

bridges. After the second bridge but before crossing a third, the *GR 20* bends to the left joining a forest road (10 mins.). 10 mins. later the *GR 20* turns off from the forestry road again to the left, crosses a small footbridge and follows a lovely, gently ascending forest path. A good quarter of an hour after crossing the footbridge you can see the first waterfalls; after another bend in the path, you have arrived at the lower end of the Cascades des Anglais. Below the waterfalls there are only ruins left of the bridge which was replaced with another one near the kiosk at the start of the **waterfalls** where the *GR 20* crosses the Agnone stream. Subsequently, more than twenty waterfalls can be enjoyed – each with bathing pools hewn from the rocks and filled with crystal-clear mountain water which offers an opportunity for bathing. If you feel like walking a bit further on, you come to the Tortetto bridge after a total of 2 hours and on the way, take an optional detour (left) to the beautifully located **Bergerie de Porteto**, 1364m. Another waterfall can also be reached in just under a quarter hour from the Tortetto bridge.
Alternative return route (1¼ hrs.): past the kiosk, follow the forestry trail along the right bank, soon passing an aerial adventure park (at the fork, turn diagonally right), to reach the main street in La Foce. Turn right here and, 40m on, before reaching the Auberge A Muntagnera, turn left to climb over the low wall (blue dots) along the ascending trail, to reach a broad intersecting trail. Turn left and, 20 minutes later, at the fork, turn left again to descend (sign »Vizzavona Gare«) to the main road. Turn right for 200m until, past a lay-by for parking, the trail continues on to the left. This crosses a forestry trail and soon after, passes by a little forestry house – here, continue by descending along the broad forestry trail. It merges into the *GR 20* at the Casa di a natura and the street that returns to the train station.

The Cascades des Anglais are one of the showpieces on the island.

TOP

65 *Monte d'Oro, 2389m*

9.00 hrs.

Pinnacle paradise above the Col de Vizzavona

It's possible to ascend one route up onto Monte d'Oro and descend another, which significantly adds to the experience of a summit ascent already rich in panoramic views.

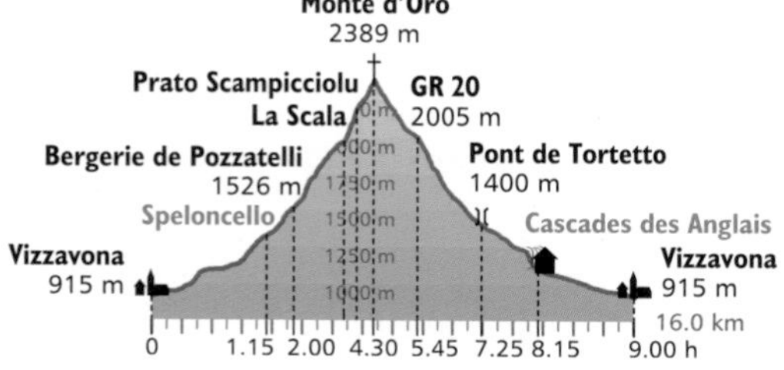

Starting point: train station at Vizzavona, 915m, on the Corte – Ajaccio line.
Height difference: 1500m.
Grade: strenuous mountain hike on well-marked footpaths (however, pay close attention to the waymarkings!); the ascent to the summit requires basic climbing skills (Climbing Grades I–II).

Refreshment and accommodation: restaurants and hotels in Vizzavona, campsites in Tattone.
Map: ign 4251 OT (1:25,000).

Begin the walk heading south from the **train station** via a small tarmac road which ascends to reach the »Casa di a natura«. Here you take the white / red-marked *GR 20 Nord* forking off to the right and soon cross over two bridges in succession. After the second bridge but before crossing a third, the *GR 20* bends away to the left; here turn right crossing the little stone bridge and then turn immediately left after the bridge onto the yellow-marked path (signpost »Monte d'Oro«). Some minutes later, the path crosses over a forest road, and in another 10 minutes meets an intersecting path which you follow to the right. Soon after crossing a stream, the path merges with a forest road

Panoramic summit view stretching from Monte Renoso (left), over the Migliarello chain, all the way to Monte Rotondo (right).

Even well into July, snowfields can make the ascent from the cirque through the couloir (left) to the summit of Monte d'Oro very difficult.

which you leave about 7 minutes later by turning left on the yellow-marked path. Subsequently, cross over the forest road twice more, then turn away and leave it behind you (signpost). After a total of 1¼ hours, the path crosses the Speloncello stream and shortly afterwards climbs along the right bank of the stream winding upwards in a series of zigzags. Just before reaching the **Bergerie de Pozzatelli**, 1526m, you cross a tributary stream and the houses of the mountain pasture can already be seen to the left (2 hrs.). The path stays besides the stream, sometimes passing through scrub alder, until reaching a splendid natural amphitheatre surrounded by towering crags and scree slopes. Here the marked path takes a bend to the left and leads into a narrow gully filled with rocks and scree; once inside, keep always to the left. Aptly named »La Scala« (the Ladder), the gully is very steep and can be covered in snow into July. There are also a few sections of scrambling to overcome (I). After 4 hours of walking you reach a grass-covered terrain (mountain spring). Another ½ hr. of scrambling over scree and boulders (II) leads to the summit of **Monte d'Oro**. If the sky is clear, enjoy a view embracing the

The grassy terrain and the summit peak.

rugged Migliarello mountain chain and sweeping all the way to the Gulf of Ajaccio. After a well-deserved rest, descend for a good 10 minutes until reaching the scree-covered terrain of the »Shoulder of Unification« (**Épaule de la Jonction**). Here continue along the right-hand path at the fork towards »Muratello« (arrow painted on a boulder) always following the yellow waymarkers (some stretches

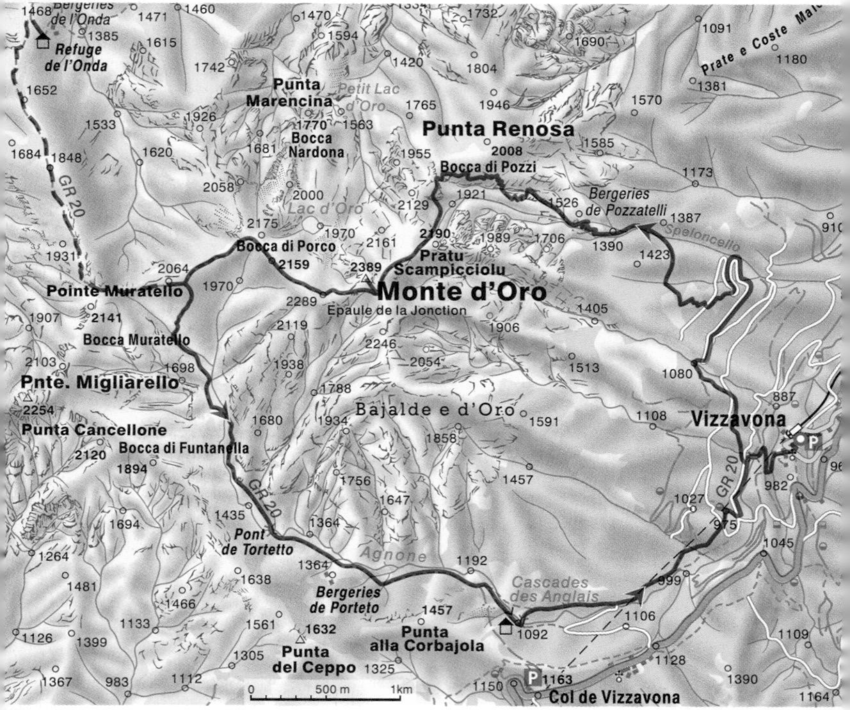

Descent from the Bocca di Porco into the Agnone valley. Above: the Migliarello chain.

meagrely marked; when in doubt, keep to the ridge). After a short descent, the path crosses a steep scree slope. Afterwards follow the ridgeline in a continuous up-and-down to the **Bocca di Porco** (not quite 1 hr.; lovely view of the Lac d'Oro), and shortly after descend to the left to join the white/red-marked *GR 20* (20 mins.) and follow this in a southerly direction to the left. You pass a waterfall and after walking for a total of 3 hrs. cross over the Agnone stream via the **Tortetto bridge** and soon pass by the marvellous **Cascades des Anglais** whilst crossing through shady beech forests. Just under 1 hr., at a kiosk, the *GR 20* returns to the left bank over a bridge. Now walk along a lovely forest path, which finally crosses over a footbridge and merges with a forest road. This road leads in 10 mins. to the second bridge that you met on your original approach. Turn right here to return to the train station at **Vizzanona**.

66 Manganello valley

7.00 hrs.

Waterfall walk through a fairy-tale mountain landscape

This lovely walk through the Manganello valley has something for everyone: families can play happily by the stream that is your constant companion; fit walkers will want to make the long ascent up to the Petra Piana hut at the foot of Monte Rotondo, the second highest summit on the island.

Location: Tattone, train station on the Corte – Ajaccio line.
Starting point: Canaglia, 720m, road from Tattone. Car park at the start of the path. From Tattone train station ½ hr. on foot.
Height difference: 500m to the cascades; 1150m to the Petra Piana hut.
Grade: easy valley walk; strenuous ascent to the Petra Piana mountain hut.
Refreshment and accommodation: Bergeries de Tolla, Petra Piana mountain hut, bar-restaurants in Canaglia and Tattone, hotels in Vivario and Vizzavona; campsites in Tattone.
Alternatives: starting at Bergeries de Gialgo make the descent to Pont du Vecchio. From Petra Piana mountain hut (overnight stop) to Monte Rotondo (2 hrs., →Walk 70) or to the Onda mountain hut. From the Onda hut (overnight stop) to Vizzavona (→Walk 65) or via the Grottaccia valley to return to Canaglia.
Map: ign 4251 OT (1:25,000).

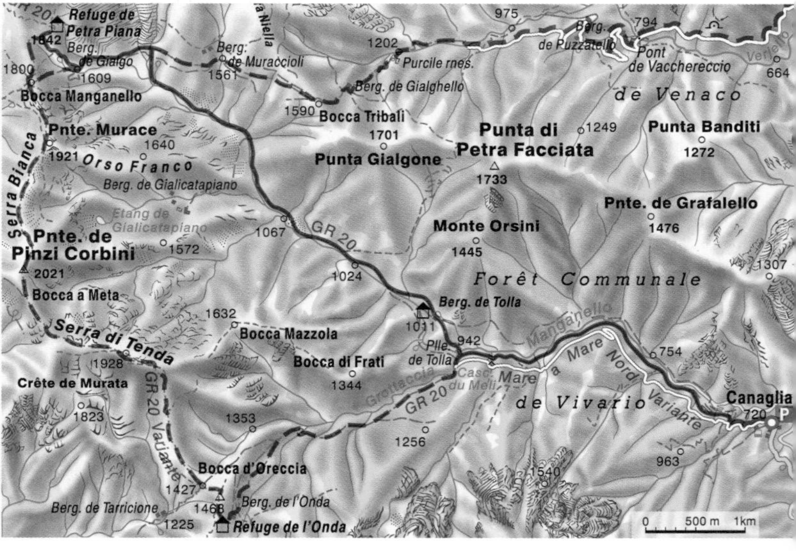

At the Bergeries de Tolla, the view opens up to Monte d'Oro.

From **Canaglia** gently ascend via the orange-marked gravel road through a chestnut and pine forest. Cross a bridge (gate; 50m afterwards go straight on at the fork along the footpath) and reach the **Manganello stream** after a good quarter of an hour. Follow the stream past inviting bathing pools, crossing over another bridge by the Meli waterfall until reaching the Tolla bridge (1¼ hrs.). The loveliest bathing pools can be found between the Meli bridge and the **Tolla bridge** where you meet up with the white/red-marked *GR 20*. Follow this path to the right, crossing the Manganello, and ascend through an open forest of tall trees to the nearby **Bergeries de Tolla**, 1011m, (in tourist season: cheese, snacks, drinks). Afterwards, you reach a splendid high valley where you can amble along without much effort through woods and over meadows. After three quarters of an hour, you arrive at a **series of cascades**, some of Corsica's most beautiful. The stream splashes from pool

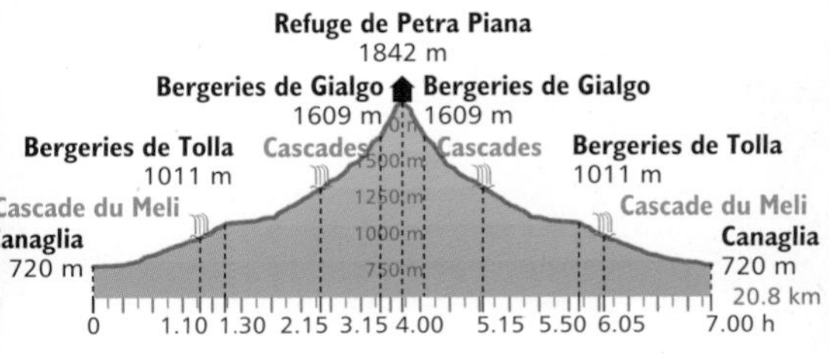

to pool over wide rock slabs and over terraces, providing bathers with a shower or a slide. In the background, the Rotondo massif completes a perfect picture. Continuing on along the path through the high valley – almost completely lacking in trees and in charm – is very strenuous. It is no wonder that most hikers turn back after enjoying a dip at the cascades. After a total of 3¼ hrs. you cross through the scrub alder-blanketed high plain at the Bergeries de Gialgo, 1609m. Another ¾ hour of walking brings you to the marvellously located **Refuge de Petra Piana**, 1842m, used by many mountain climbers as a base before climbing Monte Rotondo.

The captivating series of cascades. Below: the annex for the Petra Piana hut.

5.00 hrs.

Chapelle Santo Eliseo, 1555m

67

Delightful circuit route at the foot of Monte Cardo

The chapel of Santo Eliseo is the goal of a pilgrimage taking place every year on August 29. The chapel is situated in a marvellous panoramic position at the foot of the mighty Monte Cardo (2453m) and can be taken in along a lovely circuit route, passing several rustic and idyllic bergeries.

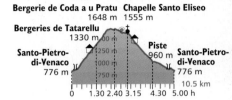

Bergerie de Coda a u Pratu 1648 m
Chapelle Santo Eliseo 1555 m
Bergeries de Tatarellu 1330 m
Santo-Pietro-di-Venaco 776 m
Piste 960 m
Santo-Pietro-di-Venaco 776 m
1500 m
1250 m
1000 m
750 m
10.5 km
0 1.30 2.40 3.15 4.30 5.00 h

Starting point: the church of Santo-Pietro-di-Venaco, 776m; from the N 193 near Venaco, the church can be reached via the D 350.
Height difference: 900m.
Grade: easy but a somewhat long and strenuous circular walk via marked walking trails.
Refreshment and accommodation: restaurants, hotels and campsites in Venaco.
Map: ign 4251 OT (1:25,000).

From the church of **Santo-Pietro-di-Venaco**, ascend along the village street. 5 minutes later, reach a fork at a bridge (parking possible; wash-house) – turn left here and then right at the following junction (orange waymarking) and continue uphill until the end of the street where the walking trail forks off

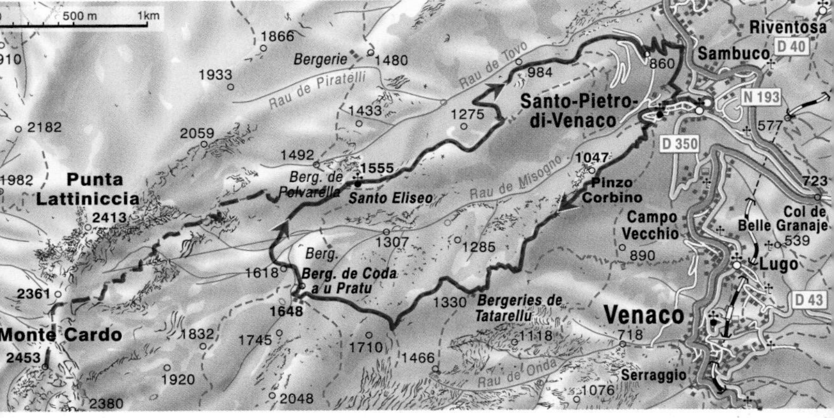

The Bergerie de Coda a u Pratu at the foot of the Monte Cardo massif.

to the right. 50m on, keep following the orange markings by turning diagonally left, and soon afterwards, past a building, diagonally right climbing up through a little chestnut wood. The lovely old trail winds somewhat steeply through the shade of a scrub forest that soon opens up. After half an hour, the trail levels out leading somewhat to the side of the ridgeline for some minutes and presenting a marvellous view over the spacious valley terrain surrounding Venaco (pay close attention to the waymarking!). About 20 minutes later, pass by a hidden away cave dwelling (shelter) then not quite half an hour afterwards, reach the splendid panoramic vantage point where the **Bergeries de Tatarellu**, 1330m, lie.

Past the last building, the trail passes a mighty beech tree. 5 minutes later, pass by yet another hut (just after, ignore a trail forking off to the left to the Bergeries Ubuli/Venaco). Soon afterward, the trail veers to the right towards the beech forest and crosses over a brook to continue a steep ascent. A quarter of an hour later, leave the beech wood behind. Continue ascending over the steep grassy ridge until, 20 minutes later, the orange-marked trail hooks to the right, somewhat below a group of crags, and then crosses over the ridgeline (on the other side of the valley, we can already spot the Chapelle Santo Eliseo). The trail now leads through the slope keeping on the level through alder thicket and then, 20 minutes later, reaches the **Bergerie de Coda a u Pratu**, 1648m, situated centre stage of a cirque with boulders.

50m before reaching the hut, the trail forks – turn right here following the orange markings to descend. Soon after, the trail crosses over the Misogno stream and then traverses the slope to reach the next ridgeline where we meet up with the Bergerie de Polvarella, and just after, the **Chapelle Santo Eliseo**, 1555m. The panoramic view from here is spectacular, taking in the eastern coast, Monte San Petrone and a backwards view towards Monte Cardo, which can be climbed in 3 hours starting from here (cairns; demanding, sometimes somewhat precipitous).

The trail now descends steadily over the boulder-strewn ridge, presenting a continuous view of Venaco. A quarter of an hour later, the trail enters a wood, and then some minutes later, passes an overhanging rock (shelter; shortly after, bear right at the fork for l'Ernacce). Half an hour later, cross over terrain belonging to a *bergerie* (Stazzalellu di i Culletti), and afterwards, ignore a path forking off to the left (*Sentier botanique du Caracutu*). 5 minutes later, pass by an old stone house in the middle of a wood (Stazzu di L'Abertina) – here, ignore a trail forking off to the right. Shortly afterwards, meet up with a track and follow this to the right. Not quite half an hour later, in **Santo-Pietro-di-Venaco**, at the road bridge, the track merges with the approach trail – on the other side of the bridge, turn left onto the village street to return to the church.

The Chapelle Santo Eliseo perches on a panoramic ridge.

Lac de Melo, 1711m, and Lac de Capitello, 1930m

Via Melo lake to the basin of Corsica's most beautiful mountain lake

No other mountain lake in Corsica is so dramatically surrounded by crags and fields of snow – even up to early summer – as Capitello lake, lauded by many as the most beautiful on the island. Melo lake is a perfect place for a picnic – indeed, the soft, green alpine meadows on the shore count as one of Corsica's most popular hiking destinations during the summer months.

Starting point: Bergerie de Grottelle, 1370m, at the end of the road into the Restonica valley (15km from Corte, pay car park, July 15 – Aug 15. Shuttle bus from the info point between Corte and Tuani).
Height difference: just under 600m.
Grade: easy but strenuous well-marked walk with short stretches of secured scrambling some of which (on the way to Melo lake) can be bypassed.
Refreshment and accommodation: Bergerie de Melo, Bergerie de Grotelle; restaurants, hotels and campsites in the Restonica valley and in Corte.
Alternative: from Capitello lake via the *GR 20* to Melo lake (2½ hrs.): ascend with the yellow markings to the *GR 20* on the central ridge, 2090m (a good ½ hr.; to the right, a possible ascent to Punta alle Porte, 2313m, 1 hr., or to Pointe des Sept Lacs, 2266m, with seven mountain lakes lying at your feet). If you follow the *GR 20* on the other side of the ridge to the left (at first, some scrambling, a good head for heights is required), you will reach the Bocca a Soglia, 2052m (¾ hr.,sign). From there, descend to the left to Melo lake (yellow markings, 1¼ hrs.; striking streams, ravines and an alpine lake are off-trail).
Linking tip: with Walk 69.
Map: ign 4251 OT (1:25,000).

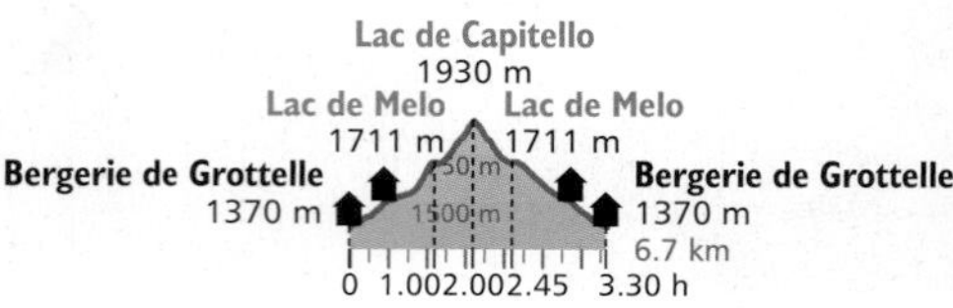

A PLACER A L'AVANT DU VEHICULE, BIEN LISIBLE DE L'EXTERIEUR

FIN DE STATIONNEMENT AUTORISE

DATE HEURE

16/09/22 17:59 STD

GJ793VJ

16/09/22 13:5? 3,00€ B23OPU

PRIX

LE FORFAIT EST DÛ EN CAS DE PAIEMENT INSUFFISANT

Fabrication Imprimerie Nouvelle +33 (0)5 63 76 52 48

Patent / Brevet : FR 2607610 - EP 274294 - US 4945213 - CA 1318887 - Certificat n°/ Attestation INKP460 - KZ PREMIUM

The route starts at the end of the narrow road leading through the Restonica valley, at the **Bergerie de Grotelle**, 1370m. The well-marked footpath (yellow) climbs fairly easily on the right-hand side of the valley. After 25 minutes you pass the Bergerie de Melo (snack bar Chez Félix), and a good 5 minutes later the path forks at a large cairn. Here you either continue diagonally left along the more leisurely main path which immediately crosses over the stream and then ascends the left-hand side of the valley to the lake – or go right along the more demanding path that requires some scrambling in a couple of places protected with chains and up two steel steps. Both paths join up again at

On the way to the lakes there are some easy sections of scrambling to overcome. In early summer you must expect to be walking over snowfields.

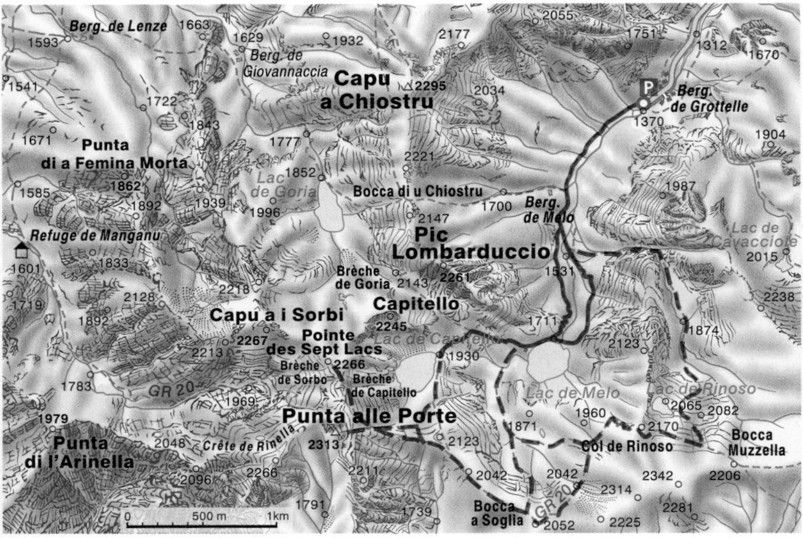

Above: there's a lovely view of Melo lake from the path up to Capitello lake.
Below: lovely spots to take a break can be found on the shores of Melo lake.

Melo lake, 1711m (a good hour, spring before the lake).

If you want to continue further to Capitello lake keep along the right-hand shore of the lake to the nature reserve administration building, where the yellow-marked path forks off. Keep on the right-hand bank of the stream with a view of the marvellous craggy backdrop of Pointe des Sept Lacs and Capu a i Sorbi. The at times unpleasant stony and rocky footpath climbs steeply and is, just past the fork to Goria lake, protected by a chain for some metres. Shortly before reaching the lake, cross over the stream (the rocks are a bit tricky if they're wet). Eventually you arrive at **Capitello lake**, 1930m (1 hr.). The yellow-marked path leads to the *GR 20* that runs high above the lake (→Alternative).

Ascent from Capitello lake to the ridge along the GR 20 (Alternative).

69 Lac de Goria, 1852m

6.30 hrs.

This lake is a remote jewel away from the tourist paths

Only a stone's throw from the much-visited Capitello lake can be found Goria lake, a wonderful mountain lake which, with a bit of luck, you will be able to enjoy in complete solitude. However the path to this idyllically situated spot requires quite a lot of effort: the path over the Brèche de Goria is very steep added to which the couloir is often covered in snow right into summer.

Starting point: Bergerie de Grottelle, 1370m, at the end of the road into the Restonica valley (15km from Corte, pay car park, July 15 – Aug 15. Shuttle bus from the info point between Corte and Tuani).
Height difference: just under 1100m.
Grade: long, demanding mountain walk which requires good fitness as well as sure-footedness and a lack of vertigo (some scrambling (Grade I), route finding from the Goria notch not always clear). Only to be recommended in absolutely stable weather conditions, at the earliest from June/July onwards.
Refreshment and accommodation: Bergerie de Melo, Bergerie de Grottelle, restaurants, hotels and campsites in the Restonica valley and in Corte.
Alternatives: from the Brèche de Goria there's an ascent possible to the western summit of Pic Lombarduccio, 2261m (20 mins.). Also a circular walk: outward path (turn-off at the Bergerie de Melo) or return via the Bocca di u Chiostru, 2147m.
Map: ign 4251 OT (1:25,000).

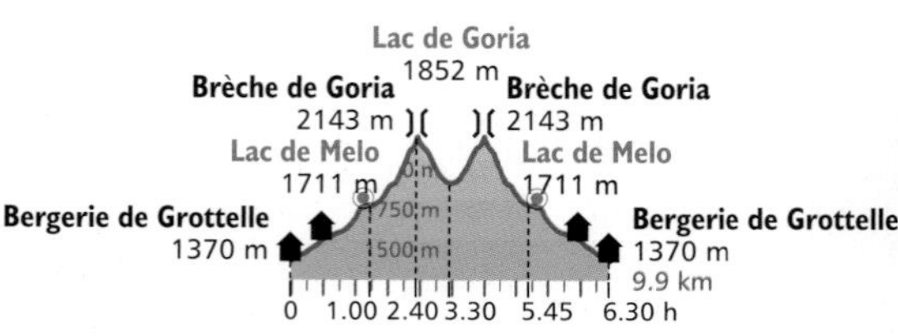

The route is at first identical with →Walk 68. So, from the **Bergerie de Grottelle** ascend to **Melo lake**, 1711m (a good hour). Follow the hiking path on the right-hand banks of the lake towards Capitello lake. After half an hour the path crosses a stream and a few minutes later you come past a pile of stones. One minute afterwards a clear cairn-marked path turns off right before the next steep incline over a stream. It ascends steeply and in a direct line up to the notch between Pic Lombarduccio (on the right) and Capitello

The steep ascending couloir to the Brèche de Goria.

(left) – in places requiring some easy scrambling (I). In early summer you might also have to take into account numerous snowfields as well. The laborious ascent takes about an hour to the striking notch, no more than two metres in width, of the **Brèche de Goria**, 2143m, from where you are rewarded with a fabulous view of Goria lake and across Nino lake to Paglia Orba and Monte Cinto (see photo left).
After a short and steep descent the path runs on the right, away from a steep scree and rock gully. After that it's a steady descent keeping diagonally right across the hillside, mostly over scree and rock debris. After about three quarters of an hour from the notch you arrive at the eastern shore of **Goria lake**. The valley basin with the lake is enclosed on the far side by the impressive rocks of Capu a i Sorbi and Pointe des Sept Lacs (see photo below).

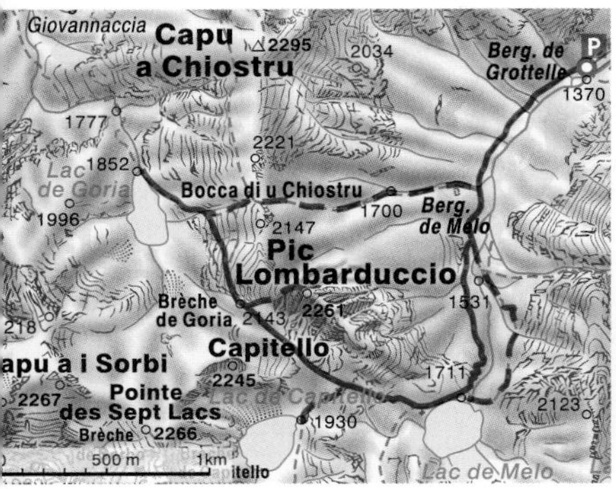

TOP 70

Lavu del'Oriente, 2061m, and Monte Rotondo, 2622m

An adventurous mountain walk with a variety of scenic features

Monte Rotondo is a scenically very impressive walk and at the same time one which requires the greatest of challenges that Corsica has to offer mountain walkers, anyhow one which involves a steep ascent of a good 1600m. Therefore start this walk as early as you can in the morning but also because of the views. Ferdinand Gregorovius extoled its virtues in his descriptions from 1852: »The horizon which you can see from Rotondo is more fabulous and beautiful by far than from Montblanc.« In fact in good visibility there's a superb view of all the significant peaks and mountain lakes (with the exception of Melo lake) on the island. If you prefer not to go to the summit you should at least make a visit to the idyllic Oriente lake. Here you are presented with an incomparable high mountain landscape: lush green meadows, burbling streams, sparkling white snowfields. It's as if you are standing in a gigantic amphitheatre with the summit of Rotondo at its apex.

Location: Corte, 396m, train station on the Bastia – Ponte Leccia – Ajaccio line.
Starting point: Pont du Timozzu, 1000m, 11km to the west of Corte, on the road into the Restonica valley. Bus service from Corte in the tourist season. Only very few little lay-bys; parking also possible at the Pont de Tragone which crosses the Restonica just beforehand.
Height difference: 1100m to Oriente lake, 1650m to Monte Rotondo.
Grade: easy, but laborious walk to Oriente lake on well-marked paths, sure-footedness (I+) and good fitness required for the summit ascent. The couloir to the summit is usually covered in snow into July.
Refreshment and accommodation: bivouac hut on the summit, restaurants, hotels and campsites in the Restonica valley and in Corte.

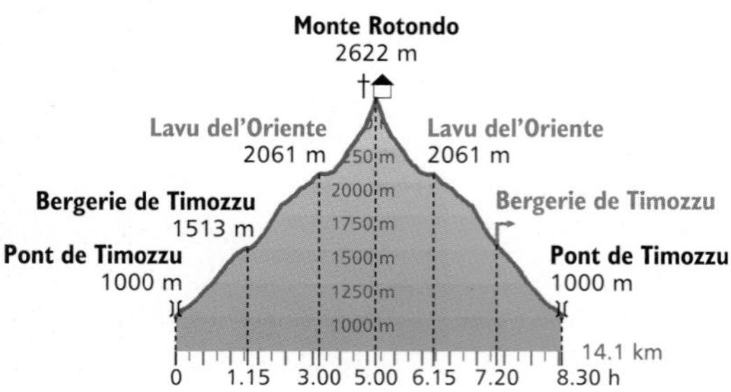

Alternative: recommendable two-day trek: from Corte to Tattone by train, ascend from there as in →Walk 66 to the Petra Piana hut (overnight stop); the next day climb to the summit and descend into the Restonica valley.
Map: ign 4251 OT (1:25,000).

The bivouac at the summit. Below: Bergerie de Timozzu.

From the **Timozzu bridge** walk a little way up the road until a steep forest track with a barrier turns off left (»*Timozzu/Rotondu*« written on a boulder). After just under a quarter of an hour there's a fork in the track. Continue right here. After another 10 minutes the shady forest path becomes narrower and is marked with cairns and leads uphill in steep bends on the right of the stream through the wonderful forest which gradually thins out. After a total of 1¼ hrs. you reach the stone buildings of the **Bergerie de Timozzu**, 1513m (cheese for sale in July/August). Then (before the *bergerie* to the right) follows a strenuous ascent along a high ridge covered in alder scrub and juniper.

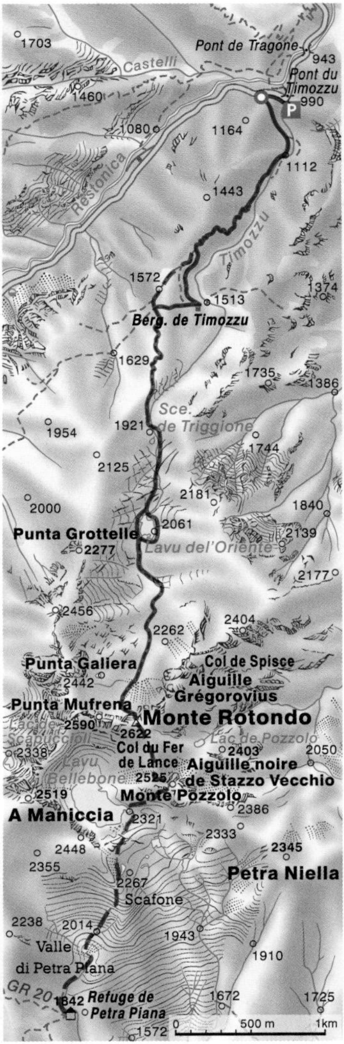

The idyllic Oriente lake opens up a huge amphitheatre whose apex is formed by Monte Rotondo. To the right of the blocky summit (centre / left of photo), the couloir for the ascent can be seen.

Only after one hour does the path run somewhat more gently along the right-hand side of the lively **Timozzo stream**. Just before a waterfall you cross over the stream (20 mins.). The path now keeps left and leads up to a col (10 mins.) and on the right cross the hillside back to the stream. A good

10 minutes later it changes again onto the other bank and finally brings you across luxuriantly green meadows to the **Oriente lake**, 2061m, with its delightful islands covered in grass and rocks.
From the lake you already have a good view of the ascent path ahead. The cairn-marked path at first takes you on the left across meadows, rock slabs and the stream to the edge of the Oriente valley basin. Then an unpleasant section follows over rock ledges, scree and boulders and heads south towards the clearly pronounced **couloir** coming down the right-hand side of Rotondo. At the foot of the broad scree gully cross over, or go around, a snowfield which is usually still covered in snow even in the summer months. The only bright spot on the subsequent steep climb up the rocks (in places, I) and scree is the little Galiera lake, which appears sidewise behind you. Be careful: there's a risk of rocks falling in places on the steep ascent path in the couloir. After 1¾ hours you finally reach the **notch** on the right of the summit block and directly above the Bastani lake. Now, you only need to turn left to ascend to the nearby summit of the **Monte Rotondo** (a final easy scramble, I+) and the bivouac hut with a corrugated-iron roof.

71 Bergeries de Cappellaccia, 1650m

4.00 hrs.

Alpine plateau with rustic huts and a fabulous view

You will be enchanted by the original stone huts of the Bergeries de Cappellaccia which huddle together, at times appearing like little castles. You find yourself here at the highest point of the extensive Alzo plateau where you can enjoy fabulous panoramic views reaching from Monte Rotondo across Punta Artica and Paglia Orba as far as Cinto.

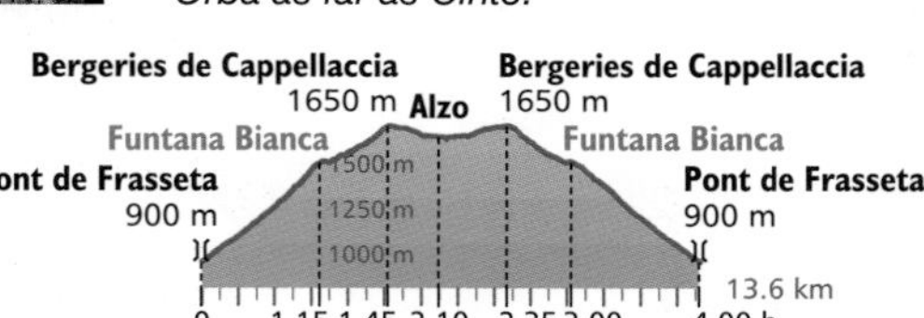

Location: Corte, 396m.
Starting point: car park on both sides of the road at the Pont de Frasseta, 900m, about 350m before the Pont de Tragone (first road bridge over the Restonica, 11km from Corte).
Height difference: a good 800m.
Grade: mostly comfortable ascent on a well-marked mule path.
Refreshment and accommodation: in the Restonica valley and Corte.
Alternatives: ascent to the summit of Forcelle, 1765m (see photo below; ½ hr.). From the Bergeries de Cappellaccia, head in an easterly direction, somewhat to the left and below the ridge, to meet the saddle at the ridgeline on the way to the peak (¼ hr.); continue through a couloir and then, in a direct line, ascend to the summit (the final metres require easy scrambling).
The walk can be extended to a two-day trek: from the Bergerie d'Alzo via the forestry house of Alzo to the Refuge de Sega (1 hr., overnight stop), from there either through the Tavignano valley down to Corte (→Walk 72), via Bocca â l'Arinella to Casamaccioli or via the Lac de Nino to the Poppaghia forestry house (→Walk 74).
Map: ign 4251 OT (1:25,000).

A **signpost** and orange waymarkers indicate the path. It leads at first in wide bends up through the pine forest which, however, soon thins out. After a quarter of an hour ignore a path turning off diagonally left to the Bergerie de Grotelle. A good 5 minutes later the orange-marked path again bends to the right. You are soon afforded a view of Pic Lombarduccio at the end of the Restonica valley. Gradually, too, the rocky summit of Rotondo with its snowfields lasting into early summer appears above the surrounding mountain peaks. After not quite three quarters of an hour, arrive at a high mountain ridge where the path zigzags uphill. A good half an hour later, leave the ridge behind by heading right and then cross two small streams, one after the other (Funtana Bianca), and then a hillside. You also now catch a glimpse of the first chimney and ascend the bends up to the **Bergeries de Cappellaccia**, 1650m (1¾ hrs.), with a well. The unusual **Bergerie de Colletta** is situated not far away. If you wind your way down the plateau along the red-marked path you come to the **Bergerie d'Alzo** in just under half an hour where, if you're lucky, you will be able to buy some cheese. If you wish to continue from here there's another hut a little further on, the Alzo forest house. A clearly marked path leads from here, keeping slightly to the left, down to the Sega hut.

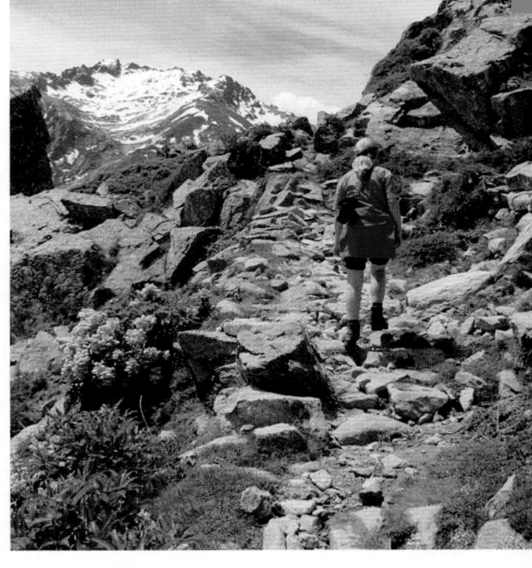

The lovely walking trail – in the background, the snow-capped Monte Rotondo.

72 Tavignano valley

Mule path to the Russulinu bridge

The Tavignano valley is one of Corsica's most captivating valleys. Although lacking the lovely pine forests found in the Restonica valley, a deep gorge with a multitude of bathing pools surrounded by rocks awaits you. Most importantly – this valley is the exclusive domain of the hiker.

Starting point: pay car park, 450m, either at the end of Rue St-Joseph or Chemin de Baliri in Corte. Approach: at the roundabout at Corte's southern village limits (towards Ajaccio; Casino supermarket) turn off onto the Av. du 9 Septembre and, 650m on, cross over the Restonica and, shortly after that, the Tavignano. Just afterwards, turn left to ascend along the Chemin de Baliri (D 823) which then ends at the car park.

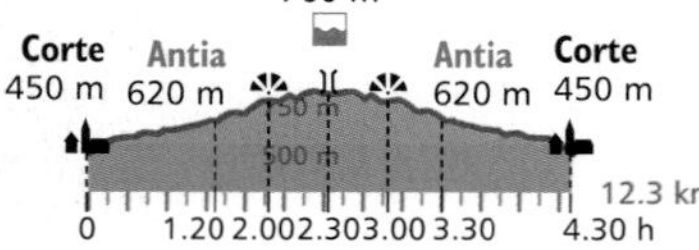

Height difference: about 450m.
Grade: leisurely hillside walk (but exposed to the sun) on a well-marked mule path; numerous ascents and descents.
Refreshment and accommodation: in Corte.
Alternatives: from the bridge and along the left bank of the Tavignano river, an ascent can be made to the Refuge de Sega, 1166m (2½ hrs., →Walk 71).
Maps: ign 4250 OT, 4251 OT (1:25,000).

The **signposts** (»Passerelle Russulinu«) at the car park clearly indicate your route. The excellently maintained, orange-marked mule path ascends gently

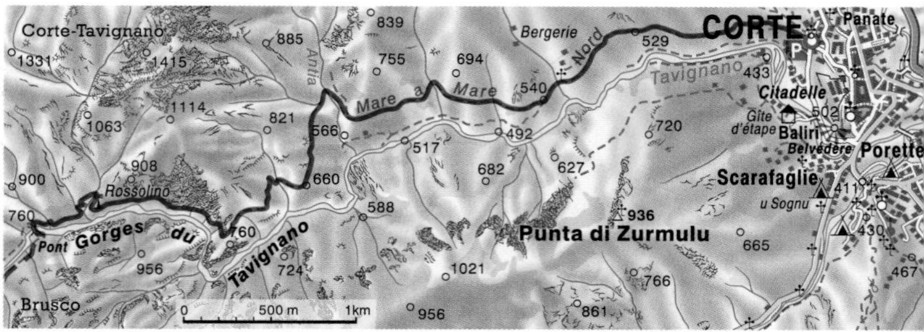

The wonderful, in most places stone-paved path through the Tavignano Gorge.

to the right above the Tavignano river and into the valley (after a few minutes, go right!). White rock roses and bushes of purple lavender line your path – not until after an hour of walking do you meet up with a couple of pine trees. Near two chestnut trees, cross a **stream bed** and then after another 20 minutes, cross the Antia stream near a **stone hut** – lovely spots to take a break. Take a last look at the attractive bathing pools below before the Tavignano disappears into a gorge; but shortly afterwards and at the end of a rather more steep ascent, you reach a **rocky plateau** (760m) with wonderful views of the river, surrounded by rocks enclosing splendid bathing pools. Gradually your path approaches the Tavignano again; this is the prettiest stretch of the route with marvellous *tafoni* rock formations at the edge of the path. Shortly after crossing yet another stream, reach a **bridge** (Passerelle Russulinu; a spring next to it) spanning the Tavignano. Here, you can select a lovely place next to the inviting pools for a spot of sun-bathing and a swim.

73 Arche de Corte

4.50 hrs.

Unique: the rock arch high above Corte

The Arche de Corte (Arcu di u Scandulaghju) is a very special natural monument: quite unexpectedly, this impressive arch of granite rock towers up alongside the trail, accompanied by a fantastic view of the Rotondo massif. In this rocky amphitheatre, you feel yourself transported into the Bavella! The trail leading to the arch is strenuous, however, and also somewhat monotonous during the first stretch. But it's worth the effort – and if you boast the necessary physical fitness, you really should pay a visit to the Bergerie U Padule.

Starting point: pay car park, 450m, at the end of Rue St-Joseph or the Chemin de Baliri in Corte. Approach: →Walk 72.

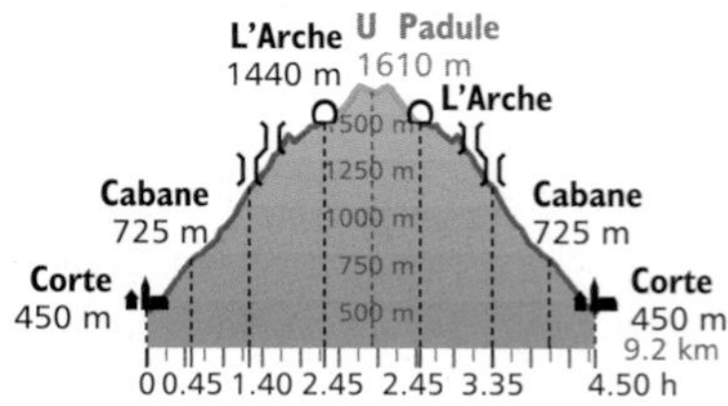

Height difference: not quite 1100m.
Grade: a long, demanding hike along a very good and distinct, but sometimes very steep, path. The primary ascent is very exposed to the sun.
Refreshment and accommodation: in Corte.
Alternative: a circular walk: from the Bergerie U Padule, you could descend via the (tumbledown) Refuge forestière de Forca into the Orta valley and use it to return to Corte (demanding; 6½ hrs).
Map: ign 4250 OT (1:25,000).

From the **car park**, follow the street, passing the turn-off for Tavignano and 25m further on, turn left before reaching the gate, along the trail heading towards »L'Arche«. The red-marked trail traverses the slope diagonally. Just past a gate, ascend to the right over slabs of rock to the ridgeline. Continue ascending steadily along the ridgeline. After ¾ hr., reach a stone-built **shelter** and, 10m further, the trail forks (to the left, a trail descends into the

Tavignano valley) – keep to the trail heading straight on which now veers to the right along the slope. At the next ridgeline (here, 15m to the right of the trail, a tiny, stone hut) the trail begins to wind up steeply again. Some minutes later, meet up with an intersecting trail (take note for the return!) which soon afterwards enters a forest. Through the steep slope, now ascend to a saddle on the ridge – a lovely place to take a break while enjoying a view of the Rotondo massif and the Monte San Petrone. Now the trail continues on over the ridge and skirts around the rocky outcrops that follow by veering to the right along the slope, once again, ascending steeply. At a spreading pine tree, reach yet another ridgeline saddle. Past the pine, ignore a trail forking off to the right and, instead, continue the ascent along the right-hand side of the ridge. 20 mins. later, the path crosses over the ridge and leads along the other side of the ridge, traversing the slope, at first climbing down, and then undulating. From the landscape of pine-spotted rock faces and crags, you can almost imagine being transported into the Bavella! Not quite half an hour from the ridge, the trail passes the mighty stone arch of the **Arche de Corte** – a fantastic place for a rest and to enjoy the views!

If you still feel fit, you could continue on to the **Bergerie U Padule** (¾ hr., a good 200m of altitude) – the meadowland slopes surrounding the marvellously situated alpine pasturage, boasting numerous stone huts, is the summer haunt of countless cows. Directly at the spot fording the stream in front of the *bergerie*, you will find a spring.

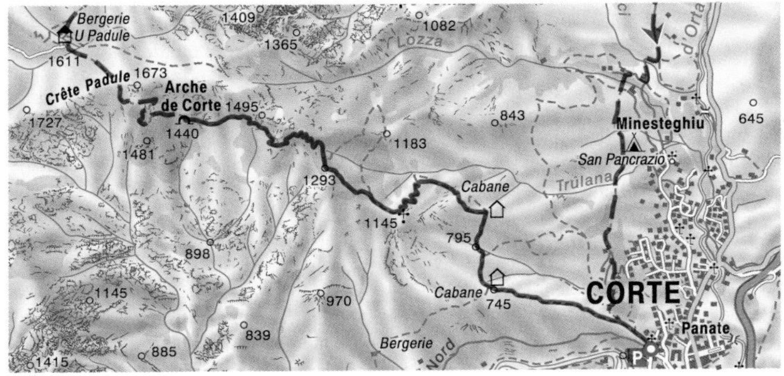

TOP 74 *Lac de Nino, 1743m*

A mountain paradise surrounded by deep-green meadows

This idyllic blue lake lies hidden in a gentle hollow framed by emerald-green mountain meadows and veined with meandering rills of dark water. In summer the lean feral pigs root around for tender morsels, while the more boisterous of mountain walkers pursue a half-hearted chase to catch these nimble-footed, curly-tailed porkers. Cowbells sound out from the bushes along the lake; horses graze peacefully on the close-cropped pastures and are spoiled by the attentions of horse-loving hikers – neither fence nor herdsman in sight. Thanks to the marvellous laricio pines that make up Valdu Niellu (black forest) and the unique views of the ridge between Paglia Orba and the Cinto massif this hike is a real treat – despite the steep climb during the second leg of the route.

Starting point: Poppaghia forestry house, 1076m (next to it, an aerial adventure park), 11.5km east of Col de Vergio or 9km west of Albertacce (Niolu).
Height difference: about 730m.
Grade: moderate walk; from the Bergerie de Colga complicated and strenuous (rock slabs, unpleasant when wet). Only suitable for children with mountaineering experience!
Refreshment/accommodation: Castel di Vergio hotel-restaurant on the road to Col de Vergio; in Albertacce and Calacuccia.
Alternatives: Nino lake can also be approached from the Castel di Vergio hotel, 1404m (3½ hrs.). The route can be extended to a 2-to-3-day trek by either following the Tavignano downstream to the Refuge de Sega (stay overnight, →Walks 71 and 72) or along the *GR 20* via the Refuge de Manganu with overnight stop and finally reaching the Restonica valley or continuing on even further to reach Rotondo. A possible ascent from the lake to the panoramic Punta Artica, 2327m (3 hrs. there and back).
Map: ign 4251 OT (1:25,000).

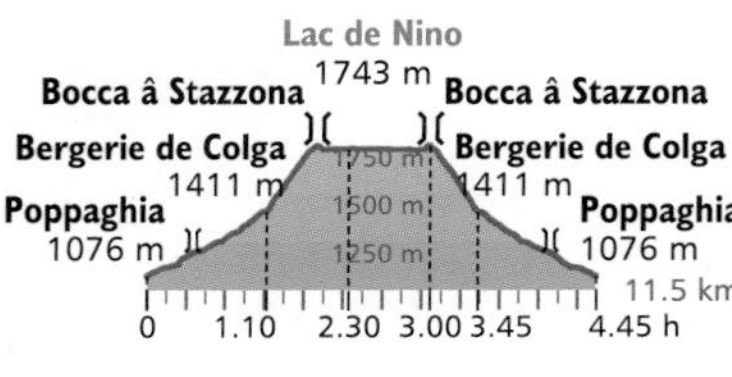

At the Bergerie de Colga – a view of the Cinto massif (in the background to the right).

Begin the walk near the **Poppaghia forestry house** on the road between Col de Vergio and Albertacce. The well-marked path climbs rapidly through the majestic pine forest and, after a short time traversing a hillside, follows the right bank of the Colga stream. After about an hour of walking, and shortly after crossing over to the left bank of the stream through alder scrub, you reach the **Bergerie de Colga**, 1411m.

Now a strenuous climb begins over scree and slabs of rock to reach the col of **Bocca â Stazzona**, 1762m (about 1¼ hrs. from the *bergerie*). Take a break here and enjoy a view of the Cinto massif and of the mountain paradise lying below before descending in a quarter of an hour to **Lac de Nino**, 1743m, and finding a comfy spot on the lush mountain meadows (sometimes a bit too lush).

The shores of Nino lake are grazed by free-ranging cows, pigs and horses. Monte Rotondo in the background (left).

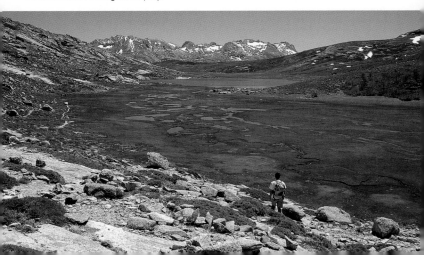

75 Scala di Santa Regina

4.15 hrs.

Spectacular goatherd's trail through the famous gorge

The Scala di Santa Regina is one of Corsica's most impressive gorges. Since time immemorial, it has provided an important route between the northern central island and the Niolu – in former times, during the summer, goatherds drove their flocks along the »Sentier de la Transhumance« into the Niolu but, today, it is the walker who enjoys the spectacular, sometimes cobbled, mule path that is set apart from the noise of road traffic.

Starting point: the church in Corscia's highest-lying district, 889m. Approach via the D 84, Calacuccia – Scala di Santa Regina (– Castirla).
Height difference: a good 600 m.
Grade: the approach route is easy for the most part, but the return route is often steep and somewhat overgrown (some route-finding skill is demanded).
Refreshment/accommodation: Calacuccia, Albertacce. *Gîtes d'étape* in Corscia.
Map: ign 4250 OT (1:25,000).

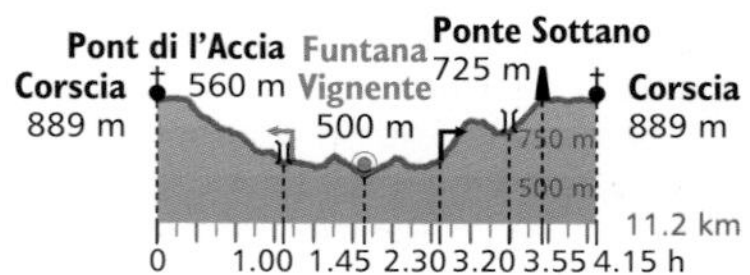

Park near the church in **Corscia's** highest district (you could also set off instead at the town hall with the *Gîte*) and walk along the narrow street, passing the cemetery, to reach the houses of **Costa**. Past the little square, continue straight ahead along the trail that traverses the slope. A few minutes later it merges into the trail that starts off at the town hall. At the crossroads above the electricity pylon take the path forking diagonally right (weathered sign, orange/red-marked). For the first few metres, the path is covered in shards as it descends gently in zigzags – already, the Scala di Santa Regina appears down below as does the road. Ten minutes later, another trail from Corscia merges into ours – here, the ancient, sometimes stone-cobbled, mule track veers to the left and continues a pleasant descent through the slope. Scattered, bizarrely-formed boulders flank the trail and, from down below, the traffic noise blares with the hooting and honking horns of trucks and busses. Afterwards, the trail hooks at the edge of a terrain and drops down in tight zigzags to reach the **Pont di l'Accia** – the middle pillar of the two-span arched bridge rests on a mighty boulder. A wonderful place for a dip!

The trail through the Scala di Santa Regina is incredibly scenic.

Now the cobbled trail ascends somewhat again. 150m on, at the highest point of the trail, a path forks off to the left – our return trail (50m after that, a trail forks away to the right to a road bridge). But before continuing, you really must take an excursion along the trail heading straight on that leads to the

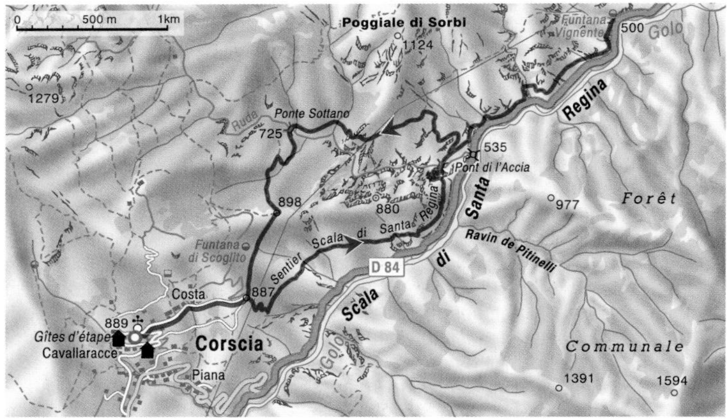

The ancient mule track is one of the island's most beautiful walking paths.

Funtana Vignente (¾ hr. one way) – the marvelous walking path leads steadily above the road, passing through rock faces; a short stretch is even secured by a cable, with views of inviting rock pools. The trail doesn't merge with the road until reaching the spring (down below, a couple of lovely rock pools that are, however, only accessible via an overgrown path).

Now head back again. At the turn-off for the return route pick up a path marked with cairns that is somewhat overgrown at the outset. This is not always completely distinct as it steeply ascends, bearing slightly to the right and passing through rock rose and rosemary bushes, then bearing somewhat to the left a few minutes later. After ½ hr., not quite 100m of altitude below a power pylon, the path veers away to the left towards the slope. During this traverse, pass a mighty, flat-topped crag, ideal for a break (an undercut rock face next to it). Shortly afterwards, the trail leads through a **breach in the rock**. The rock face trail high above the tumultuous Ruda stream with its marvellous rock pools is yet another »cherry on the cake« for this circular walk – and is a perfect reward for the ordeal of the ascent. Unfortunately, this pleasure doesn't last very long because soon the trail continues on through woodland to the Ruda stream which we cross upstream from an impressive string of cascades via the **Ponte Sottano**. The trail now ascends in zigzags through a romantic deciduous forest, sometimes following a secondary stream which, later on, the trail crosses over. The trail now continues, flanked by stone walls. 50m before a high voltage power pylon, reach a high terrain. Here, pass a memorial for a pilot (turn left afterwards). Some minutes later, meet up with the trail junction already met on the approach route. Turn right onto it to return to **Corscia**.

2.25 hrs.

Golo circular walk from Albertacce 76

Pleasant circular route with numerous bathing spots

The splendid rock pools of the Golo above Albertacce are amply renowned. At the road bridge, you can expect a serious hustle and bustle. Further upstream, this quickly peters out because the stretch that follows is more or less difficult to negotiate due to the lack of a distinct path. Because of this, we propose a short circular walk that leads past a couple of lovely bathing spots and, on top of that, a couple of options for the more adventurous walker.

Starting point: D 84/junction of the Mare walking path at the western village limits of Albertacce, 854m (900m before the Golo road bridge).

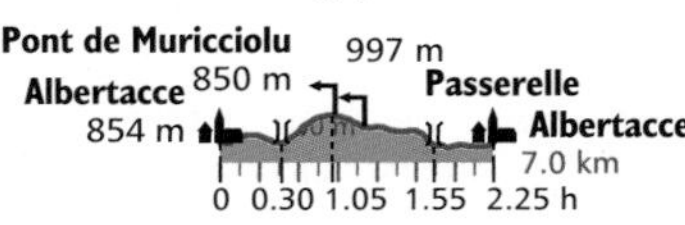

Height difference: 250m.
Grade: an easy circular walk throughout. The descent to the Golo bridge, without a distinct path, demands some route-finding skill as well as sure-footedness but this could be left out of your itinerary.
Refreshment/accommodation: in Albertacce and Calacuccia.
Map: ign 4250 OT (1:25,000).

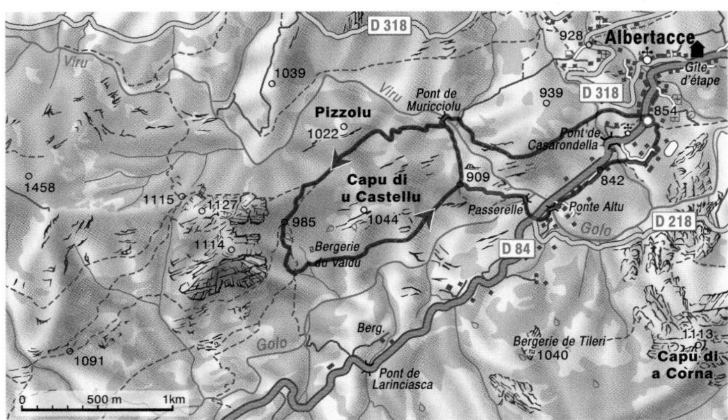

After only half an hour, you reach one of the first lovely bathing spots at the Pont de Muricciolu, where an ancient mill is located next to it.

Begin the walk at the western village limits of **Albertacce** at the turn-off of the orange-marked *Mare a Mare Nord* towards Evisa (sign). This leads almost on the level, opening up a lovely 360º view of the mountains. A few minutes later, cross over a stream. Dwarf broom, pines and chestnut trees now flank the trail – a backwards view takes in the Calacuccia reservoir and, shortly after, a frontwards view of the impressive Paglia Orba opens up. The trail now descends gently (to the right, a trail forks away towards Lozzi). Next to an old mill, you cross over an ancient stone bridge (**Pont de Muricciolu**) spanning the Viru stream (marvellous spots to relax and enjoy a dip).
30m past the bridge, the trail forks – bearing diagonally right, keep to the orange/purple-marked *Mare* trail that steadily ascends to a high plateau with pine trees. The trail now leads on the level over the high terrain next to the Capu di u Castellu. Ignore a left-hand fork with faded dark green waymarkings (arrow). 3 minutes later, the trail forks again – bear diagonally left to pick up a distinct path that, 15m on, enters a recently planted dense forest. The path leads in a long curve, steadily descending and is soon waymarked with pale orange markings. At a tree trunk marked with a blue square, meet up with an ancient trail, sometimes flanked with tumbledown stone walls – turn sharp left onto this trail to continue. The path crosses over a brook and soon leaves the forest behind. In front of us, take in a view of the Calacuccia reservoir and, below, a view of the Golo with its numerous inviting rock pools and cascades (if you are confident walking cross-country, 5 minutes later at the next ridge you could descend to the stream; about 60m of altitude). The lovely high trail clearly veers away from the Golo and then leads, flanked by stone walls, through a picturesque landscape with gigantic boulders. After a total of

20 minutes walking, reach a **knoll** in front of two chestnut trees to our left. If you prefer an easy circular route, keep along the trail that leads to the right of a spherical boulder and descends to the Pont de Muricciolu nearby. However, anyone who is not opposed to a uncomplicated cross-country stretch lasting about 15 minutes can turn right onto the trace of path that leads from the knoll, just past the stone wall to the right. The path promptly disappears – now continue, always keeping somewhat to the left and crossing over the ridge, with the last stretch situated to the right of the ridgeline. Descend to the **Golo bridge** that spans a long, narrow rock pool, enclosed by rock faces (→photo above). Cross over the bridge and follow the trail to the nearby **D 84**. Cross over the road and then continue diagonally left via the roadway that becomes the **Ponte Altu**, the old Golo bridge, situated directly adjacent to the road bridge. After this, either continue along the main road or take the trail that runs parallel to it; this becomes a narrow road later on (right). When the road hooks in front of a football pitch, continue straight ahead along the path that, at the end, slightly veers to the left and then turns right to merge onto the *Mare* trail – turn left onto it to return to the **starting point** on the main road.

Below the walking path, you can discover a number of splendid rock pools on the Golo.

TOP **77**

Monte Cinto, 2706m

8.30 hrs.

Pleasant footpaths onto the king of Corsica's mountains

Monte Cinto is the king of Corsica's mountains. In clear weather, the summit view stretches from the east to the west coast. All the peaks – at least all those of Northern Corsica – are spread out below. The walk is very strenous; this counts for the ascent from Haut-Asco as well as for the ascent from the south which is, however, thoroughly enjoyable except for the climb over scree during the first stage. Scrambling is easy due to the solid, easy-to-grip surface of the rock. Anyone aspiring to conquer the summit should start off early in the morning to avoid the midday heat and to better the chances of a clear view from the top.

Starting point: Lozzi, 1080m, a tiny Niolu village perched above the Calacuccia reservoir. From the D 84 Calacuccia – Albertacce drive 3km to the end of the asphalt by two campsites. The continued drive along the 7.5km long, washed-out track is reserved for the locals (gate).
Height difference: about 1750m.
Grade: a footpath, usually well-marked with cairns. A sense of direction, stamina and sure-footedness are necessary; but the stretches of scrambling (Grade I) can be easily negotiated and are barely exposed.
Refreshment and accommodation: Refuge de l'Ercu (small self-catering hut, open in the tourist season), hotels and restaurants in Albertacce and Calacuccia, campsites in Lozzi at the start of the track.
Alternative: the path leading upstream from the Ercu hut to the very tiny Cinto lake is well worth a detour (an ascent is possible via the Pointe des Eboulis to Monte Cinto).
Map: ign 4250 OT (1:25,000).

Ascent from Lozzi – the hillside is covered in flowering gorse in early summer.

View from the hiking path to the Ercu hut of Monte Cinto (centre left). The ascent goes up the large scree slope on the right and continues along the rocky ridge that leads left up the summit.

Starting off at the Camping L'Arimona at the end of the asphalt in **Lozzi** (car park) continue for a good 5 minutes along the gravel track until a signposted roadway on the left turns off to the Refuge de l'Ercu and soon becomes a path (left). The orange-marked hiking path runs somewhat parallel to the track, touches it briefly on the next bend and then after a quarter of an hour, once more joins the track. 5 minutes later the signposted hiking path turns off right again. It ascends across a hillside covered in gorse with its wonderful blossom in early summer and affords fabulous views of the Calacuccia reservoir and Cinto. After 5 minutes it crosses the track and a few minutes later runs along the track for 3 minutes to then turn left onto a path beside a fence. It crosses the track once more and after a good 10 minutes passes the foundation walls of the **Capella a sa Lisei**, 1383m. Not quite a quarter of an hour after that the hiking path joins the track again which you now follow to its end (20 mins.). A clear path leads from the car park in a north-westerly direction across a high ridge downhill to the **Refuge de l'Ercu**, 1667m (½ hr.). You can

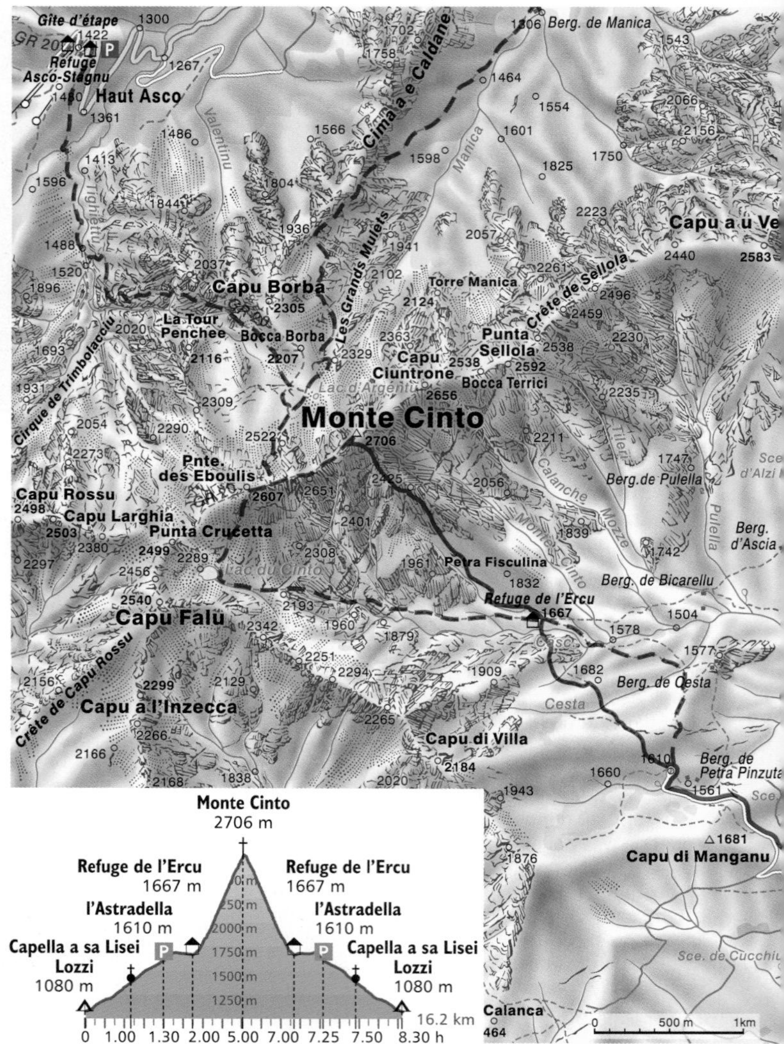
Gîte d'étape
Refuge Asco-Stagnu
Haut Asco
GR 20
Cima a e Caldane
Berg. de Manica
Valentinu
Manica
Tighiettu
Les Grands Mulets
Capu a u Ve
Crête de Sellola
Torre Manica
Capu Borba
La Tour Penchee
Bocca Borba
Cirque de Trimbolacciu
Punta Sellola
Capu Ciuntrone
Bocca Terrici
Lac d'Argentu
Monte Cinto
Tilleri
Calanche
Berg.de Pulella
Pnte. des Eboulis
Capu Rossu
Capu Larghia
Punta Crucetta
Monte Cinto
Mozze
Pulella
Berg. d'Ascia
Lac du Cinto
Petra Fisculina
Berg. de Bicarellu
Refuge de l'Ercu
Capu Falu
Crête de Capu Rossu
Berg. de Cesta
Cesta
Capu a l'Inzecca
Capu di Villa
Berg. de Petra Pinzuta
Capu di Manganu
Sce. de Cucchiu
Calanca
Monte Cinto 2706 m
Refuge de l'Ercu 1667 m
l'Astradella 1610 m
Capella a sa Lisei Lozzi 1080 m
Refuge de l'Ercu 1667 m
l'Astradella 1610 m
Capella a sa Lisei Lozzi 1080 m
2500 m
2250 m
2000 m
1750 m
1500 m
1250 m
16.2 km
0 1.00 1.30 2.00 5.00 7.00 7.25 7.50 8.30 h
0 500 m 1km

now clearly see the first third of your ascent path which runs on the right across a broad band of scree up to the prominent rocks. Many of the stretches over scree and rock are difficult to discern and require a good sense of direction to follow.

The view from Cinto summit to Paglia Orba.

At first, the climb is strenuous, leading over a **band of scree** to ascend to the rocks. The footpath is mostly marked by cairns (also white and red dots in rocky parts) and skirts around the crags by bearing left at first, and then leads across gullies and crevices along the **south-east ridge** towards the crest. About 2¼ hrs. after leaving the Ercu hut and shortly after passing a small **terrace** with a view backwards of the Calacuccia reservoir, your rocky ascent path merges with the **regular approach** from Haut-Asco (pay attention on the descent). Now continue to the right without great difficulty over the south-west ridge to the summit of **Monte Cinto**.

It is best to make your **descent** using the same route, but you can also return to the Ercu hut via Lake Cinto. However this alternative is one hour longer and demanding.

The ascent route from the north, from **Haut-Asco** (Plateau Stagnu) is considerably longer, more strenuous and more difficult in the rocky areas, but the fascinating scenery makes it a worthwhile choice. You can expect the ascent to take about 5½ hrs. The ascent follows the white/red-marked *GR 20* via **Bocca Borba** (→Walk 82) to the main ridge with the Pointe des Eboulis, where you turn left and continue along the south-west ridge to reach the summit (2 hrs. from Bocca Borba).

78 Viru valley

3.45 hrs.

Hiking along waterfalls and through forests at the foot of Paglia Orba

The route through the Viru valley to the Auberge U Vallone offers stunning views of Paglia Orba, the island's most beautiful mountain.

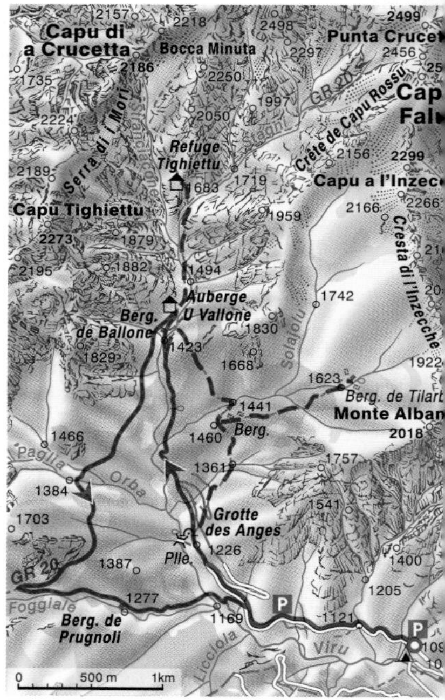

Location: Calasima, 1095m, Corsica's highest village in the Niolu region.
Starting point: after about a 2km drive into the Viru valley, at the end of the asphalt road, 1096m (parking possible; a campsite by the stream below, the track that follows is very bumpy).
Height difference: a good 400m.
Grade: easy valley and hillside walk on forest roads and well-marked paths.
Refreshment/accommodation: staffed Auberge U Vallone (bunks); Auberge i Milari (shortly before the end of the road); restaurants and hotels in Albertacce and Calacuccia; campsite in Lozzi.
Alternatives: just past the Grotte des Anges a possible ascent onto Monte Albanu, 2018m (2½ hrs., very indistinct, sometimes very overgrown). An ascent is possible from the Bergerie de Ballone along the *GR 20* to the Refuge de Tighiettu, 1683m (40 mins.). Continuing on the *GR 20* through the Foggiale valley, you could reach the Refuge de Ciottuli di i Mori in 2¼ hrs. (→Walk 79).
Map: ign 4250 OT (1:25,000).

Follow the **gravel road** up the valley. After about 15 mins. pass a large orientation board »Forêt communale d'Albertacce Calasima« (car park). Subsequently, ignore the roadway that forks to the left and 5 mins. later, our road takes a sharp bend to the right. A path marked with cairns continues straight on and leads directly above the **Grotte des Anges**, 1226m, which is formed by three large boulders and after 10 minutes joins the gravel road again. However, you leave the gravel road almost im-

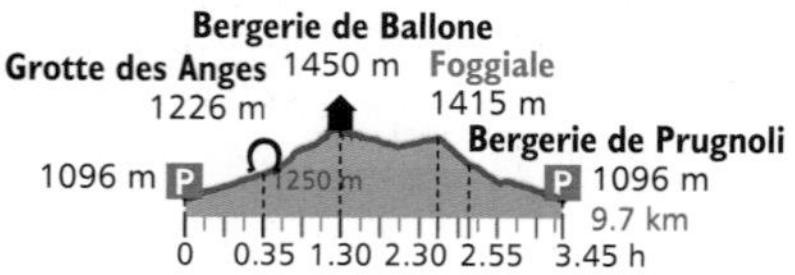

The striking Paglia Orba reigns over the Viru valley (here at the Grotte des Anges).

mediately by turning left on the yellow-marked path which forks a few minutes later – here follow the yellow waymarkings to the right (do not continue straight on to the stream). 5 minutes later you meet the forest road once more at a parking bay below a water tank. Now follow the forest road. Some minutes later, the road becomes a trail which, shortly before the **Bergerie de Ballone**, 1450m (food and drink available during the tourist season, bunks), and near the **Auberge U Vallone**, crosses over the Viru stream. Pleasant bathing pools can be found not far away.

Beside the *auberge*, turn left on the *GR 20* (white / red). The beautiful high path runs along the right-hand side of the valley through an open pine wood. After ½ hr., the path crosses over a stream right at the foot of Paglia Orba and then leads directly into the **Foggiale valley**. Just before you reach the stream (1 hr.), a footpath marked with large cairns branches off to the left and follows the left bank of the stream down the valley. Bathing pools invite you again for a break and a cool swim – the largest pools, with a natural slide, are at the end of the cascades. After about half an hour, reach the stone walls of the **Bergerie de Prugnoli** situated near a gigantic boulder. Just after passing the *bergerie*, the path forks – here, continue descending along the main trail above the stream (some stretches are a little confusing). Somewhat above the mouth of the Foggiale, the path crosses over the Viru stream at a lovely rock pool. On the opposite flank of the valley, meet up with a gravel road. Turn left to ascend to a track and then turn right to return to the **starting point**.

79 Paglia Orba, 2525m

Demanding mountain hike onto Corsica's »Matterhorn«

This majestic peak with a magnificent view embracing Cinto, Rotondo, Lake Calacuccia and the Gulf of Porto is surely the island's most beautiful mountain. Less-experienced mountain climbers should only climb as far as the Ciottuli di i Mori mountain hut or to the Col des Maures.

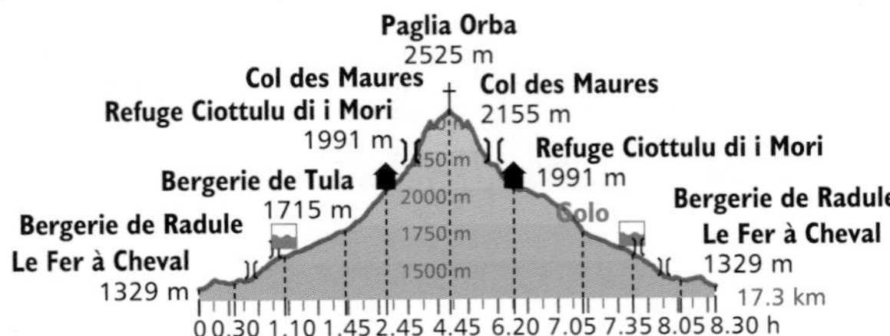

Locations: Evisa, 829m, a village at the western foot of the Col de Vergio. Albertacce and Calacuccia, villages in the Niolu region.
Starting point: bend in the road known as »Le Fer à Cheval«, 1329m (parking on the side of the road), 2km below the Castel di Vergio hotel, on the road leading to the Col de Vergio.
Height difference: 1350m.
Grade: easy mountain walk along well-marked footpaths until reaching the Col des Maures; the ascent to the summit involves a couple of quite difficult scrambling sections (in places Grade II) added to which there are some very steep and sometimes icy snowfields in early summer.
Refreshment and accommodation: simple food and bunks in the Ciottuli di i Mori hut (end of May to the start of October); the Castel de Vergio hotel provides a restaurant, rooms and bunks; *buvette* for refreshment on Col de Vergio, campsites in Evisa and in Lozzi by Albertacce.
Alternatives: this walk can also be started from Col de Vergio (¼ hr. longer to reach Bergerie de Radule, yellow-marked path) or at the end of the road into the Viru valley (→Walk 78). Recommended two-day trek: ascent from the Viru valley to the Ciottuli di i Mori hut (with overnight stop) and descent via the Golo valley (Radule waterfall – Bergerie d'Alzetu) into the Viru valley.
Map: ign 4250 OT (1:25,000).

Many walkers are content to walk along the valley as far as the Ciottulu hut and then turn back.

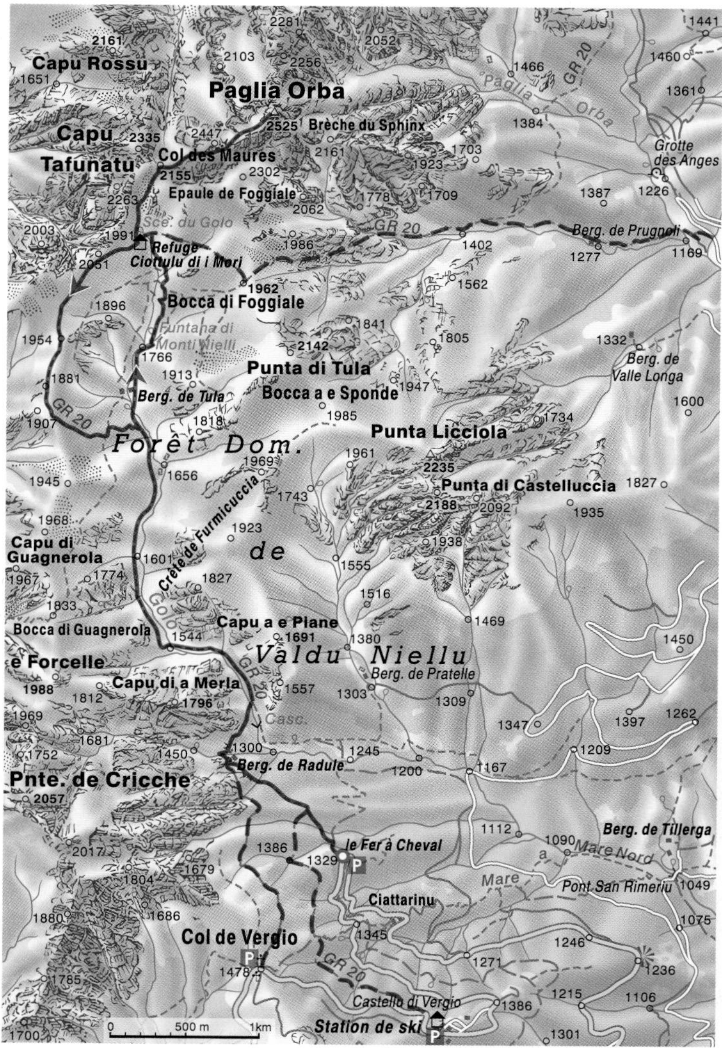
Paglia Orba
Capu Rossu
Capu Tafunatu
Col des Maures
Brèche du Sphinx
Epaule de Foggiale
Sce. du Golo
GR 20
Refuge Ciottulu di i Mori
Bocca di Foggiale
Funtana di Monti Nielli
Punta di Tula
Berg. de Tula
Bocca a e Sponde
Forêt Dom. de Valdu Niellu
Punta Licciola
Punta di Castelluccia
Crête de Furmicuccia
Capu di Guagnerola
Bocca di Guagnerola
e Forcelle
Capu a e Piane
Capu di a Merla
Berg. de Pratelle
Casc.
Berg. de Radule
Pnte. de Cricche
le Fer à Cheval
Ciattarinu
Col de Vergio
Castello di Vergio
Station de ski
Berg. de Tillerga
Mare a Mare Nord
Pont San Rimeriu
Grotte des Anges
Berg. de Prugnoli
Berg. de Valle Longa
Golo
Paglia Orba
0 500 m 1km

In the Golo valley near the Bergerie de Tula.

Follow the *Sentier de Radule* (blue waymarkers and two yellow dashes, go left after a few minutes) which leads in a northerly direction through a lovely little birch forest to the white/red-marked *GR 20* (10 mins.). Turn right and continue to the **Bergerie de Radule** (20 mins.). 10 mins. later cross the **Golo** via a bridge above the **Cascades de Radule** where erosion has created numerous pools in the rocky valley. Follow the *GR 20* on the left uphill to reach an enormous **area of rock slabs** with a bathing pool (the *GR 20* skirts around this point to the left over a bridge; ½ hr.). This is a pleasant stretch, leading up the valley towards the soon visible peaks of Paglia Orba and Capu Tafunatu. After a total of 1½ hours, the *GR 20* turns away from the Golo stream and climbs the hillside to the left. It is better to continue straight ahead at this point to reach the **Bergerie de Tula**. Shortly before the derelict stone hut, the path changes over onto the right bank of the stream. A good 10 minutes later, the path again crosses to the left bank and climbs the steep bends up to the clearly visible **Ciottuli di i Mori mountain hut**, 1991m (2¾ hrs. from »Le Fer à Cheval«).

Behind the hut a signposted, white-marked footpath leads through a scree-filled cirque to reach the **Col des Maures** (20 mins.). Shortly before reaching

The Ciottulu di i Mori hut with Capu Tafunatu (left) and Paglia Orba (right).

the crest of the pass, a cairn-marked path forks off to the right towards Paglia Orba, at first skirting round some small rock walls. Shortly afterwards, a difficult stretch of scrambling must be negotiated (Grade II) and then the scrambling continues steeply through crevices and gullies (I–II). Just about an hour after leaving the mountain pass, you reach a small **plateau** affording views of the gigantic hole (measuring 30 by 12m) piercing the peak of Capu Tafunatu as well as of the north-west face of Paglia Orba. Now there's a short traverse across an exposed ledge leading to a climb through a crevice. After this section the most difficult leg of the route is behind you and, in just another 10 minutes, you are standing on the western summit of the **Paglia Orba**. Here at the top there are some little patches of beautiful alpine flowers. Now only a deep-cut notch separates you from the main summit. You therefore have to descend 45 metres of height and then continue your climb along the broad ridge to the summit, 2525m.

At first, you **descend** the same way down as you came up. – On the way (from Col des Maures) you can also bag the **Capu Tafunatu** rock window (¾ hr., II). – At the **Ciottuli di i Mori hut**, if you prefer, take the white/red-marked *GR 20* to the right which will bring you back in a good 2 hours to the bend in the road, »**Le Fer à Cheval**«.

Capu Tafunatu with the enormous rock window as seen from the western peak of Paglia Orba. Below: the ascent to the summit leads through deep gullies that may be coverd in snow, even in summer.

80 Tassineta valley

2.15 hrs.

Picturesque side valley of the Stranciacone

The pools at the start of the Tassineta valley are a popular and much-visited place for swimming. So it is quite strange that so few walkers venture into this pleasant valley. Unfortunately the former hiking path from the Bergerie de la Tassineta to Ondella waterfall is closed off.

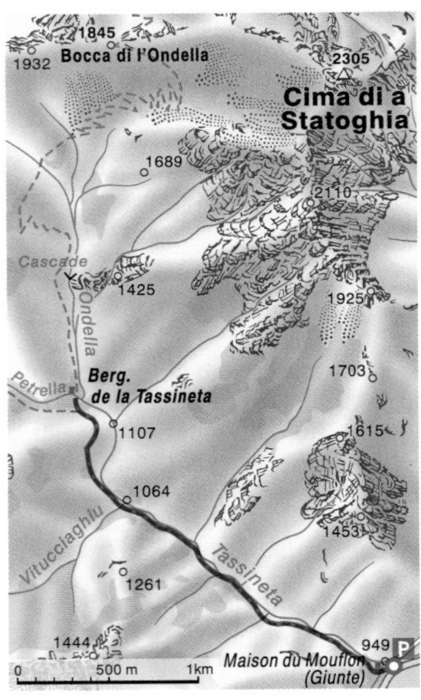

Location: Asco, 620m.
Starting point: car park where the Tassineta stream flows into the Stranciacone stream, 949m (Giunte). On the road from Asco to Haut-Asco turn right after 7km (signpost »Camping Monte Cinto 2km«).
Height difference: 200m.
Grade: the walk follows a predominantly leisurely path.
Refreshment and accommodation: restaurants and hotels in Haut-Asco and in Asco, campsites at the beginning of the Asco valley and on the road to Haut-Asco (2km from the car park).
Important tip: a protected area for mouflon has been developed in the region so the continuation of the path from the Bergerie de la Tassineta to Ondella waterfall and to the Bocca di l'Ondella is no longer open to walkers. No dogs allowed on the hiking path.
Map: ign 4250 OT (1:25,000).

From the **car park**, walk a short way upstream to the bridge and cross over to the other bank of the Stranciacone stream. At least 50m to the right and above and also to the right of the **Maison du Mouflon**, a tree with yellow and blue waymarkers indicates the beginning of your route. The footpath leads above and to the left of the **Tassineta stream**, through pleasant pine forests, at first accompanied by the fence of the mouflon protected area. You will discover many inviting

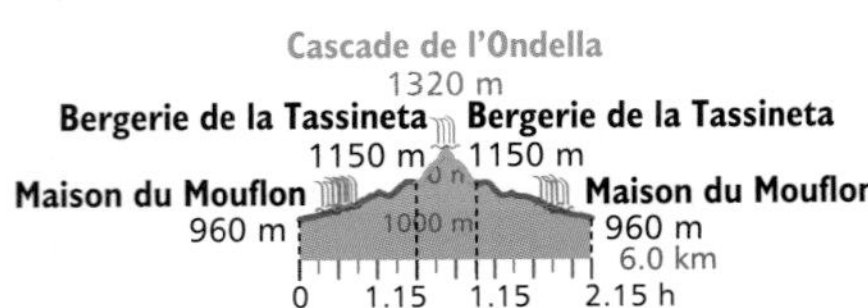

bathing pools – the most attractive ones after 15 to 30 mins. of walking. Afterwards, negotiate a tricky area of rock slabs – you can avoid this by taking the easier route which leads above. After ¾ hour, cross over a side stream. Now the footpath leads away from the Tassineta stream and continues across a hillside covered at first in ferns which then becomes wooded again (marvellous view of the Cinto massif) until reaching the stone huts and walls of the **Bergerie de la Tassineta**, 1150m (1¼ hrs.).
Directly after passing the first hut, the path forks – the left fork leads into the Petrella valley while the right-hand path leads over the Petrella stream and ascends the left bank of the Ondella stream to the Cascade de l'Ondella (¾ hr.). Unfortunately, in 2006, both paths were closed to walkers in order to protect the mouflon.

Previously you could continue from the bergerie up to Ondella waterfall.

81 Bergeries de Manica and Capu Borba, 2305m

7.10 hrs.

Trip into the kingdom of the mouflon

There's hardly another valley on Corsica that can boast such impressive mountain backdrops as the Manica valley. It extends directly along the foot of the mighty Cinto mountain chain and some beautiful cascades with correspondingly inviting pools are a great destination for less ambitious walkers – experienced, fit walkers will not want to miss out on the rest of the ascent to Capu Borba or even to Monte Cinto.

One more tip: keep your eyes open above the forest boundary and with a bit of luck you might discover a few extremely shy mouflon that like to linger in this remote mountain region.

Location: Asco, 620m.
Starting point: Pont de Manica at the mouth of the Manica stream in the Stranciacone, 995m. On the Asco – Haut-Asco road, after 8km (a good 1km before Camping Monte Cinto).
Height difference: just under 1400m.
Grade: long and strenuous mountain walk that requires sure-footedness and a good degree of fitness. The hiking path is somewhat overgrown in places.
Refreshment and accommodation: restaurants and hotels in Haut-Asco and Asco, campsites at the start of the Asco valley and 1km above on the road to Haut-Asco.
Linking tip: with Walk 82.
Map: ign 4250 OT (1:25,000).

View from the ridgeline over the Manica valley to Monte Cinto (centre) and Capu Borba (right).

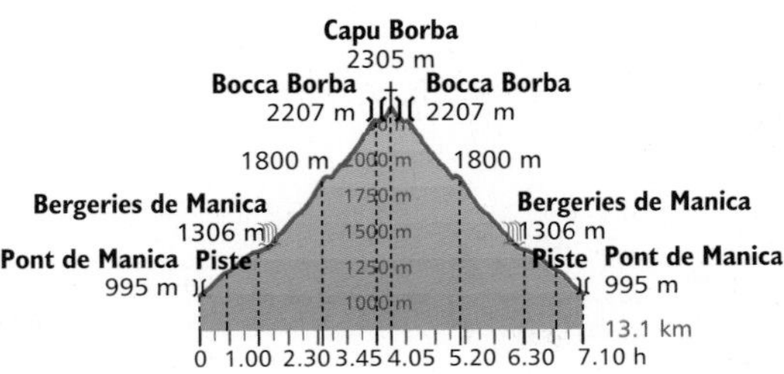

20m before the **Manica bridge** an unclear path forks off left from the road. It runs along the track of a former forest road through lovely pine forest and is heavily overgrown in many places (young pines; if you prefer to avoid this laborious section of the route, walk up along the *Piste de Manica* which begins at the hairpin bend straight after the Camping Monte Cinto). Your path keeps to the left-hand side of the valley. After just under half an hour it crosses over a largish stream with a large pipeline and a few minutes later you come to a broad forest track, the ***Piste de Manica*** (there's a bridge 100m on the right).

The track gets narrower shortly afterwards and brings you in half an hour to the (predominently derelict) buildings of the **Bergeries de Manica**, 1306m.

The forest path comes to an end here. Cross over the Manica stream at the weir and continue opposite along the initially broad path, past another stone hut. 30m afterwards a path forks off left (red dashes as waymarkers) that passes a cascade after 10 mins. and another one some minutes later. Half an hour after that – you walk across an idyllic stretch of land with *laricio* pines, alders and birch trees – eventually the end of

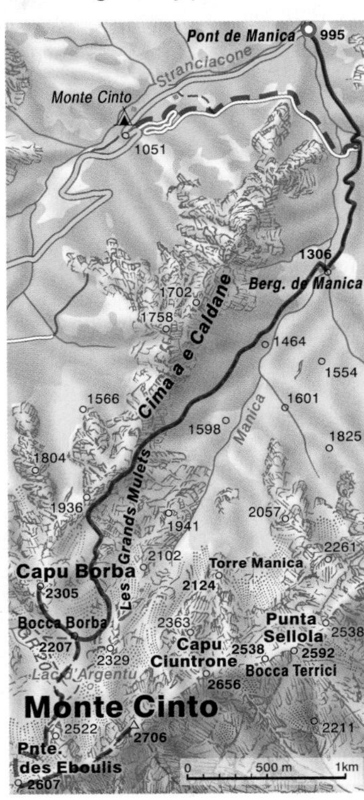

From the Bocca Borba, the ascent to the summit of Capu Borba takes only another 20 minutes.

the valley comes into view with Capu Borba. About 1¼ hours from the Bergeries de Manica you reach the forest boundary. The path then ascends some rocks and 20 minutes later reaches the **top of the ridge**, 1800m, above the valley – the view opens out here towards Haut-Asco.

The hiking path now runs for a few minutes along the ridge then turns towards the left-hand side of the ridge and steeply descends 25 vertical metres into a wide hollow full of debris with a tiny lake. After a short traverse it continues up through the scree-covered hillside crossing over a small ledge at the foot of Capu Borba. Just under an hour from the debris-filled hollow you arrive at the broad col of **Bocca Borba**, 2207m. On the left, the path joins with the ascent path onto Cinto from Haut-Asco (→Walk 82; after a short ascent, we are tempted by the little Lac d'Argentu on the left) – to the right, it's only a stone's throw away now to reach the nearby summit of **Capu Borba** (20 mins.) that affords a fabulous panoramic view of the Cinto massif and the Asco valley.

In the Manica valley, waterfalls invite walkers to take a break.

6.45 hrs.

Cirque de Trimbolacciu and Capu Borba, 2305m 82

Walking through the fascinating landscape at the foot of Monte Cinto

A fantastic natural spectacle unfolds in the natural amphitheatre of Trimbolacciu: the Tighiettu stream plunges dramatically down to the valley floor while the rocky crags and laricio pines tower imposingly to create a scene of overwhelming beauty. Make sure you walk at least as far as the wooden bridge spanning the Tighiettu stream.

Starting point: Le Chalet hotel in Haut-Asco, 1422m, at the end of the road into the Asco and Stranciacone valley.
Height difference: 950m.
Grade: easy hillside walk through the valley as far as the bridge, the ascent to Capu Borba is sometimes somewhat exposed, some stretches of easy scrambling (I, some chain protection).
Refreshment/accommodation: in Haut-Asco hotel/restaurant with bunks; restaurants, hotels, campsites in the Asco valley.
Linking tip: with Walk 81.
Map: ign 4250 OT (1:25,000).

Monte Cinto comes into view in the middle part of the ascent.

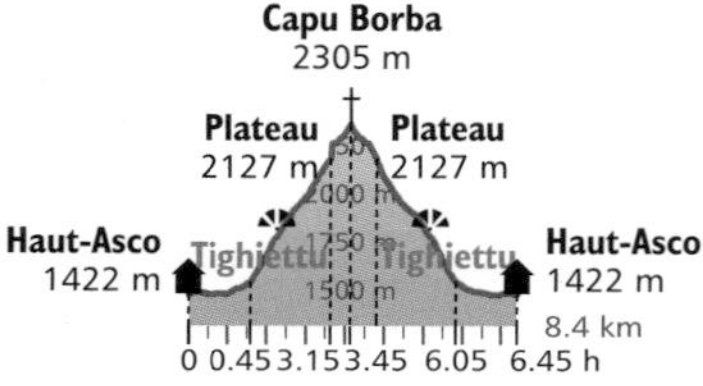

At the left-hand edge of the **car park**, a trail sign (»Monte Cinto«) points out the outset of the path. Our walking route follows the *GR 20* (white/red-marked) and traverses a slope above the road down into **Tighiettu valley**. After ¼ hr. cross over a stream (in case of flooding, a little below where it divides) and continue to the Tighiettu stream, enjoying a view of Capu Larghia at the head of the valley. Finally, pass some commemorative plaques and reach the **wooden bridge** spanning the Tighiettu stream, 1488m (¾ hr.). Physically fit and sure-footed mountain hikers cross over the bridge and ascend the path towards Monte Cinto (others are recommended to continue along the right bank of the stream to enjoy a wonderful view from the gigantic boulder in the middle of the high valley). Crossing over the bridge, follow the white / red waymarkers over rock ledges and scree to reach a small gully (I), then ascend over crevices and crags (some light scrambling; protected by chains) to a small **viewpoint** with a first view into the awe-inspiring gorge that reveals the way for your ascent to Bocca Borba (1 hr. past the bridge). Now, climb to the foot of the towering crags, then head towards the valley. After ¾ hr., the path passes through a large patch of alder scrub and a good ½ hr. later, reaches a larger plateau. Here, you have to make a choice: turning left is an ascent to **Bocca Borba**, 2207m (10 mins.) and then onwards to **Capu Borba** (20 mins.). Fit and experienced mountain walkers on the other hand will not want to miss an ascent onto Monte Cinto and so, from the plateau, ascend along the *GR 20* straight ahead over scree and snow (in early summer) to the main ridge where you veer to the left and follow the red waymarkers (gray at the outset) over the south-western ridge in strenuous up and down to reach the **summit** (2 hrs.).

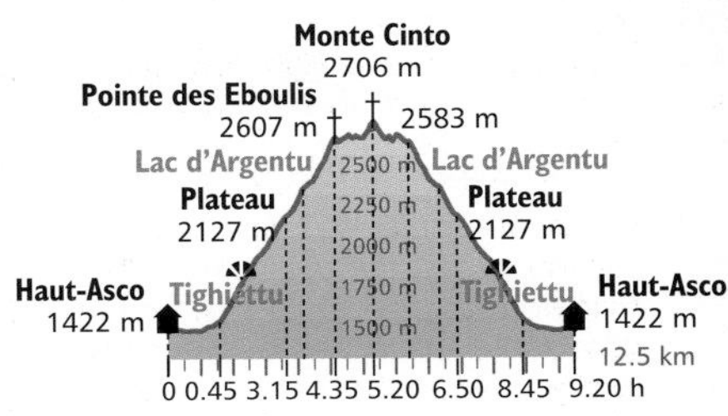

Panoramic view from Capu Borba of Monte Cinto. Right: Capu Larghia, Capu Rossu and Punta Minuta.

83 A Muvrella, 2148m

3.45 hrs.

A steep ascent with a superlative panoramic view from the summit

A Muvrella is famous for its grandiose panoramic view from the summit encompassing the peaks around Monte Cinto as well as the Gulf of Calvi. Nevertheless, this popular excursion should not be underestimated – you not only face an exceptionally steep and strenuous ascent, but also some rather unpleasant and exposed »scrambling fun«.

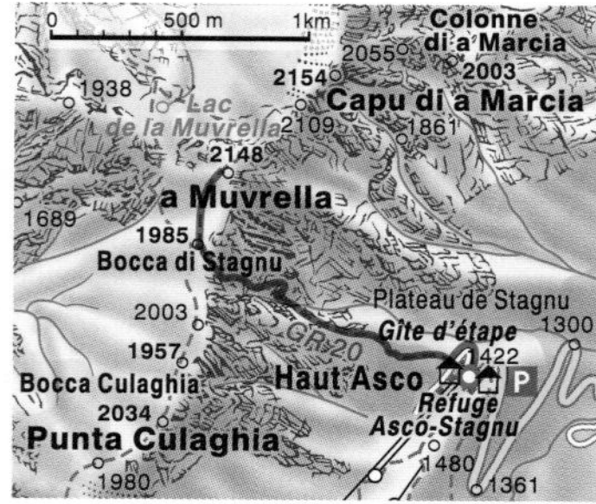

Starting point: Haut-Asco, 1422m.
Height difference: 750m.
Grade: steep climb to Bocca di Stagnu; easy, but sometimes exposed scrambling (Grade I) to the summit.
Refreshment and accommodation: in Haut-Asco a hotel with restaurant and bunks; restaurants, hotels and campsites in the Asco valley.
Linking tip: with Walks 16 and 84.
Map: ign 4250 OT (1:25,000).

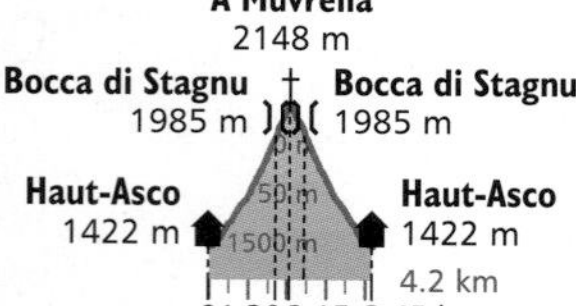

Just behind the **Le Chalet** hotel, walk in a north-westerly direction along the white/red-marked *GR 20* that, immediately next to the *refuge*, enters a pine wood. The footpath ascends through the wood in zigzags and after 25 minutes reaches a **gorge** filled with scree and boulders. This valley notch stretches up-

At the outset of the gorge – a view of the Cinto massif.

wards until ending at the Bocca di Stagnu. Continue walking at first along the left-hand side of the valley near the stream, later the footpath leads to the right over a small plateau with a boulder and continues along the steep slope to reach the **Bocca di Stagnu**, 1985m (1½ hrs.).

On the other side of the gap, and 10m further on, a cairn- and faded turquoise-marked footpath forks off to the right and leads up a gentle incline across the hillside. When you meet steep rock go round to the left and then continue relatively easily up to the summit of **A Muvrella** (only a few sections of scrambling). From the Bocca di Stagnu you can also ascend directly, more or less, up along the ridge but this requires negotiating several sections of Grade I+ scrambling.

The ascent to the summit skirts left around the jumble of boulders on the ridge.

84 Punta Culaghia, 2034m

4.45 hrs.

Impressive ridge walk high above the Plateau Stagnu

This marvellous but demanding ridge walk should only be undertaken by experienced mountain hikers. Your efforts will be rewarded with a magnificent view of the Cinto massif and of the west coast.

Starting point: Le Chalet hotel in Haut-Asco, 1422m, at the end of the road into the Asco and Stranciacone valley.
Height difference: a good 750m.
Grade: strenuous day's hike on well-marked footpaths, precipitous stretches over scree and rock combined with easy scrambling (I).
Refreshment and accommodation: in Haut-Asco hotel with restaurant and bunks; restaurants, hotels and campsites in the Asco valley.
Alternatives: from the Bocca di Stagnu ascent to the summit of A Muvrella (→Walk 83), alternatively, descent to the Auberge de la Forêt de Bonifatu (→Walk 16).
Linking tip: with Walks 16, 83 and 85.
Map: ign 4250 OT (1:25,000).

Start the walk as in →Walk 85 from **Haut-Asco** along the trail crossing over the ski slope then, before the stream, climb up the path to the left of it (you can also ascend directly on the left next to the course of the ski-lift then, after the steep incline, go left to reach the trail again). After 1¼ hrs., the path forks at a prominent red arrow; take the right fork along a sporadically white / red-waymarked alternative route of the *GR 20*. Make sure that you turn off onto the correct fork at the arrow and pay close attention to the waymarking, otherwise a muddle is inevitable!

View from the ridge with the eastern summit of Punta Stranciacone to Monte Cinto.

Soon you come to a steep gully which climbs to the **Brèche de Missoghiu**, 2048m. On the other side of the notch, the trail turns right and skirts to the left of the pinnacles of **Punta Stranciacone**. In early summer, some snowfields can make crossing dangerous here, but even later in the summer, irksome fields of scree must be negotiated and in places, somewhat precipitous rocky sections demand scrambling (I). After half an hour, pass a small peak affording a view of Lake Stagnu below. With a little luck, you could also cross paths with a mouflon or two, although this wild mountain goat has become quite rare. Now descend for a short distance to a small gap, 1980m, and then ascend to the summit of **Punta Culaghia**, 2034m.

Here, bear slightly to the left of the ridge and continue over moss-flecked broken boulders, precipitous ledges and slabs (some somewhat exposed). Little by little, a view of Calvi opens up. The next stretch descends to **Bocca Culaghia**, 1957m. After one hour reach the main route of the *GR 20* (white/red, at the end painted over in gray). Turn right to ascend to the col of the **Bocca di Stagnu**. The following steep descent through tangled scrub, boulders and a steep gully sometimes requires the use of your hands. At the end, descend through a pine wood to **Haut-Asco**.

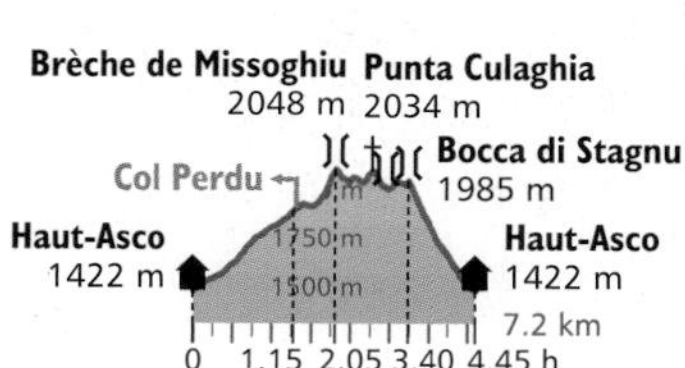

85 Col Perdu, 2183m

4.30 hrs.

Along the GR 20 to the mountain pass overlooking the Cirque de la Solitude

Col Perdu (Bocca Tumasginesca) marks the passage from the Asco valley into the Niolu and offers a marvellous view of the Cirque de la Solitude, one of the most primeval and secluded high mountain valleys on the island. Up until 2016, the GR 20 led through here, however, after a landslip occurred in the Cirque de la Solitude, the GR 20 was re-routed.

Starting point: Le Chalet hotel in Haut-Asco, 1422m.
Height difference: 800m.
Grade: easy mountain walk at first, but more demanding at the end.
Refreshment and accommodation: in Haut-Asco hotel with restaurant and bunks; additional restaurants, hotels and campsites in the Asco valley.
Alternatives: from Col Perdu, traverse into the Viru valley (→Walk 78, demanding stretches with fixed rope!).
From Altore plateau, ascent to Pic von Cube, 2247m (1½ hrs., II).
Linking tip: with Walk 84.
Map: ign 4250 OT (1:25,000).

From **Haut-Asco**, at first the trail ascends along the ski slope, but some minutes later, before the stream, forks away to the left to join a path. After half an hour's walk, ignore a path forking off to the left and, after that, cross over a field of boulders. 1¼ hours later, reach a fork marked with a red arrow (→Walk 84); continue here to the left staying on the former *GR 20* (to the right, an ascent is possible to Bocca Stranciacone, 1987m, ½ hr.). Shortly afterwards, the scree path climbs steeply on.

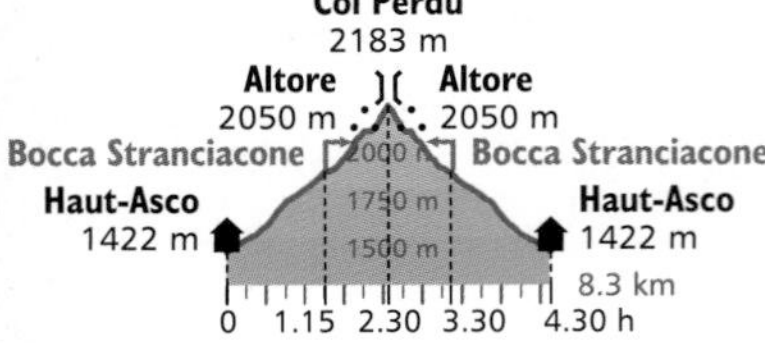

The final ascent to Col Perdu is rather strenous.
Below: view from Col Perdu into the Cirque de la Solitude with Paglia Orba.

After a good half an hour, pass a field of scree where the **Altore mountain hut**, 2020m, once stood (to the left of the path, the foundations are still visible). The path now descends a short way to a valley basin sporting two tiny tarns, then turns to follow the left flank of the valley and crosses over scree, through boulders and also, even well into the summer months, fields of snow, until ascending at last to **Col Perdu** (Bocca Tumasginesca; some sections of easy scrambling, ¾ hr. from the Altore plateau).

Index

To compliment this guide, we recommend the road and leisure map »AK 0407 Corsica« (1:150,000) from Freytag & Berndt

Cover photo:
In early summer, the head of the Stranciacone valley shows its most beautiful side. In the middle of the photo, the twin peaks of Capu Larghia.

Frontispiece (photo on page 1):
Tour de Capu di Muru overlooking the Gulf of Ajaccio.

All photographs are by Annette Miehle-Wolfsperger and Klaus Wolfsperger.

Cartography:
Walking maps to a scale of 1:25,000 / 1:50,000 / 1:75,000
© Bergverlag Rother, Munich (drawn by Gerhard Tourneau)
Overview maps to a scale of 1:650,000 © Freytag & Berndt, Vienna

Translation: Tom Krupp and Gill Round

5th edition, extended and updated, 2019

ISBN 978-3-7633-4819-0

We heartly welcome any suggestion for amendment to this walking guide!
BERGVERLAG ROTHER · Munich
D-82041 Oberhaching · Keltenring 17 · tel. +49 89 608669-0 Fax -69
Internet www.rother.de · **E-Mail** bergverlag@rother.de